Full Circle

Full Circle

A True Story of
Murder, Lies and Vindication

Gloria Killian and Sandra Kobrin

New Horizon Press
Far Hills, New Jersey

Killian, Gloria and Kobrin, Sandra
Full Circle: A True Story of Murder, Lies and Vindication

Cover design: Wendy Bass
Interior design: Susan Sanderson

Library of Congress Control Number: 2011928841

ISBN-13: 978-0-88282-376-8
New Horizon Press

Manufactured in the U.S.A.

16   15   14   13   12   1   2   3   4   5

Authors' Note

This book is based on the experiences of the authors and reflects their perceptions of the past, present and future. The personalities, events, actions and conversations portrayed within this story have been taken from interviews, research, court documents, letters, personal papers, press accounts and the memories of some participants.

In an effort to safeguard the privacy of certain people, some individuals' names and identifying characteristics have been changed. Some characters may be composites. Events involving the characters happened as described. Only minor details may have been altered.

Dedication

This book is dedicated to the victims of injustice
and to the women who suffer behind bars.

Contents

Prologue

E d Davies stepped out of his sports car and ambled toward the supermarket in the leafy Rosemont suburb of Sacramento.

"It's him!" Stephen DeSantis yelled to his partner, Gary Masse. The thirty-two-year-old first cousins had been following the coin collector and casing his house for the past month. Now they sat in the supermarket parking lot in a telephone repair truck DeSantis had stolen, drinking coffee, listening to heavy metal music and waiting for Davies to come out of the store. When he did, they put their plan into action. DeSantis changed into his "telephone repairman" attire, shoving his new .22 down the front of his pants. Masse started the truck and drove to the parking lot exit. It was time.

DeSantis was wired on caffeine. He needed the intense energy to keep him focused and moving forward. Next to him in the front seat of the stolen repair truck, his partner and cousin Gary Masse popped another tranquilizer. He was out of heroin, highly nervous and couldn't function without the pills.

Masse drove them to Davies' house, parking on the street in front of the home.

Around 2:00 P.M., in broad daylight, DeSantis walked up the couple's flower-lined walkway and knocked on the front door. Ed was in the kitchen with his wife Grace, who was fixing lunch. Grace went to the door.

"Hello, ma'am," said DeSantis, smiling broadly at the petite, grey-haired woman. "I'm from the phone company. We've gotten reports you've had trouble on the line. May I come in?"

He was smiling and earnest.

"Well, I don't know," Grace Davies said. She was hesitant to let a stranger into her house. They were not expecting a repairman.

DeSantis pressed. "We've gotten reports..."

"Oh, that's right." Mrs. Davies remembered her friend had said she had trouble getting through to Grace on the phone earlier that day. And the repairman wasn't a particularly threatening-looking individual. He was short, barely five feet four inches, and his face was calm, with sad eyes, dark hair and a drooping mustache.

"Come on in," Mrs. Davies said, opening the front door wide and leading him to the kitchen where their telephone was located.

Exactly the way DeSantis had planned it.

DeSantis' smile disappeared as he pulled his gun on the woman and her husband, who was sitting at the kitchen table. His face tightened into focused anger.

"Get down on the floor!" he barked at the couple, shoving them down. He placed them facedown, pulled handcuffs out of his pocket and grabbed a rope from his belt.

"You're hurting me!" Grace Davies cried out in pain as he tightened the knots to hog-tie her feet.

"Shut up!" DeSantis screamed. He knew he had to be a badass and scare the couple quickly. The faster he put fear into them, the quicker they would give up the whereabouts of the loot. After securing their hands and feet, he hog-tied them together and threw dishtowels over their heads so they couldn't see.

A whimpering Mrs. Davies shook off the dishtowel, lifted her head up and looked with frightened and pleading eyes at DeSantis. It only made him angrier. He didn't like being stared at. The last thing he wanted was to be identified. "I'm going to shoot you!" DeSantis yelled at her. He raced into the living room, grabbed a throw from the sofa, rushed back and tossed the heavy blanket over both Grace's and Ed's heads.

He ripped the phone out of the wall and pulled down shades and closed curtains all around the house as the couple writhed on the kitchen floor.

Outside in the truck, Masse was getting nervous. Almost half an hour had passed and DeSantis hadn't come out to get him. Masse's drug addiction had given him an enormous tolerance and even seven or eight tranquilizers didn't calm him anymore. He popped another pill and decided not to wait any longer. He put on a white hard hat, walked up to the door and rang the bell. DeSantis ran to answer the door.

"What, um, what's going on?" Masse asked.

"Everything is under control. You get rid of the truck. I'll work on them," DeSantis told him. Masse nodded, happy that things were going as planned.

Inside the house, the couple wriggled on the floor, whispering to each other for the few moments DeSantis was gone.

"Grace, are you okay?" Ed Davies asked his whimpering wife.

"My wrists hurt," his wife said. She was trying not to cry. She was concentrating on the pain in her hands, trying to think it away.

"Just give them what they want, Ed, and they'll leave," she whined.

"Try and be calm," Davies told her firmly. "I'll take care of things."

"Please," she pleaded.

DeSantis walked back into the kitchen as Masse drove the truck a few blocks away, parked it and raced back to the house. DeSantis ransacked the house, rifled through the kitchen drawers and eventually found a huge knife. Masse returned and the two criminals stood over the frightened couple. Time was of the essence. They had been there for over an hour, had scoured the house and still had no idea where the gold and silver they were told Davies had was hidden. DeSantis wielded the knife, took the blanket off the couple on the floor and circled them, barking orders at Ed Davies.

"Tell me where the gold and silver is or I'll kill you!" he yelled.

"I don't have anything here. It's all at Virgil's store," Davies replied.

DeSantis didn't have a clue who Virgil was, but Masse knew Davies was talking about Virgil Fletcher, the owner of a coin and pawn shop in downtown Sacramento. Masse liked coins and had been in the store once or twice.

"No way. We know it's here," Masse said from behind the couple. "We've been watching you."

"It's not here. It's at the coin store," Davies repeated. "I swear."

"You're lying," DeSantis said. He grabbed Grace Davies and placed the knife's blade to her throat. "I'll slit your wife's throat if you don't tell me the truth."

Ed Davies flinched when he saw the guy manhandle his wife. His eyes filled with tears.

"The garage," he cried, breaking down. "They're in the garage." Davies told Masse and DeSantis the exact location of seven safes, some hidden behind a workbench, others buried under two-by-fours in the garage floor.

DeSantis threw the woman down to the floor as her husband breathed a sigh of relief.

"Virgil Fletcher set me up," he whispered to his crying wife.

The two thieves ran into the garage and smiled as they found the small safes exactly where Davies had told them they were hidden. But getting them open looked to be a problem. They carried the extremely heavy safes into the kitchen and placed them on the floor next to the couple.

"Where are the keys?" demanded Masse as the frantic DeSantis attempted to use brute strength and a screwdriver to break into the safes. But there was no need for keys, because shortly after Masse uttered the question, an adrenaline-fueled DeSantis pried all seven of the safes open.

Every safe was filled with mostly silver and some gold. There were silver dollars, half dollars and dimes, some loose and some in collector's albums. There were silver bars as well. This was more than the career criminals had hoped for. They slapped five and hugged, excited by their score. But soon their exuberance turned to concern. How were they going to get this heavy haul home? The silver weighed a lot and they certainly weren't going to walk the safes across the front lawn back to their car at the supermarket parking lot. Masse demanded Davies tell him where he kept the family's suitcases and, with painstaking care, the two cousins filled six suitcases with over six hundred pounds of silver that they decided they would load into the Davies' sports car in the garage. This way no one would see them taking the haul and they'd use the sports car as a getaway vehicle.

They carried the hundred-pound suitcases across the house three times before the loot was finally all loaded into the car. Not satisfied with their score or perhaps just plain greedy, the two raced through the house, ripping open drawers and cabinets and taking whatever valuables they could find, including costume jewelry and gold coins. Masse found a unique gold coin that had a picture of the Golden Gate Bridge. He had seen a coin like that in a coin shop valued at seventeen thousand dollars, so he put it in his pocket. DeSantis found an antique sterling silverware set in the china cabinet in the dining room. It looked expensive and he felt his wife would like it so he filled a pillowcase with the heavy cutlery, but he left behind the antique wooden box it was stored in.

Once everything was in the car, DeSantis discovered a number of rifles Davies had hidden in the garage.

"Should we take these, too?" he asked Masse. "Maybe we can sell 'em?"

"Nah," Masse said. He was tired. "My contacts, they just want the coins. We got enough already. I think we should get out of here." They left the rifles lying on the garage floor.

Something was nagging at DeSantis. If by chance he and Masse got caught, the couple had seen his face and not Masse's. Besides, he knew if police questioned them for any reason, Masse was likely to turn on him. He had to do something to make sure the elderly couple never talked and to make Masse an accessory to a crime he couldn't snitch on.

Murder.

DeSantis had never shot anyone, but there was too much at stake here. He would lose his wife, he would lose everything if Masse opened his mouth. He had to make sure no one would talk.

With Masse close behind, DeSantis calmly walked back into the kitchen. He paused for a moment, looked at the couple, then matter-of-factly shot Ed Davies in the head. He looked back at his cousin and then shot Grace Davies in the head, too. One shot each at close range.

"What the fuck?" Masse yelled at his cousin. This was not part of the plan. "What did you do?"

"We can't have any witnesses," replied DeSantis, his hands shaking just a little.

"How could you do this? I mean, how…" Masse was confused and slurring his words. The drugs were kicking in, big time.

"It's not difficult," DeSantis replied. "It's like killing an animal."

Masse popped another pill. He was now nervous again, sweaty. The two had committed many crimes together but never murder. Masse had promised his wife there would be no violence.

"You're crazy," Masse said to his cousin as they walked toward the garage. But he didn't want to rile DeSantis. He had never seen his cousin look as blank as he did then. He felt afraid of him.

"Look, Gary, now you're in this as deep as I am so you better not say anything. Understand?" DeSantis replied. "Partners in crime can't snitch on each other. If we get caught, you'll get the needle just like me."

As they fled the scene, Gary Masse hoped no one had heard the gunshots. He was pissed at his cousin for the killings, freaked out and afraid. He knew they were in much bigger trouble than he had planned. No one was supposed to die! The police would make this case a priority, but cops might be the least of his problems. His contacts would be sure to ask about the murders and they might turn on him.

Inside the Davies' car, Stephen DeSantis was hyperactive and fidgeting as they drove to his brother's house. He wondered how fast he could get rid of some of the silver, hoping to skip town in a matter of days. He was also worried about Gary opening his big mouth to his motormouth wife.

"Don't tell Joanne nothing, neither," he hissed at his cousin. "She can't keep her mouth shut and nobody needs to know, understand?"

But Masse was more worried about turning the lights on in the getaway car. Dusk was falling and he didn't know where the light switch was on the foreign car.

In a panic Masse drove down the street fiddling with what he could find on the dashboard, turning on the windshield wipers, the windshield washer fluid, then the hazard lights. As he zigzagged down the street in a drug-fueled blur, he finally found the switch that controlled the lights and a beam of light bathed the street. They drove quickly south, out of

Rosemont, and in twenty minutes were back to the squalor of Del Paso Heights and at the house of DeSantis' brother.

Soon Masse, DeSantis and DeSantis' brother were loading the heavy suitcases into DeSantis' red van in the garage, preparing the shovels they needed to bury the loot at a prearranged spot near land the family owned in the country. As the three men's wives gathered to watch them load the loot, DeSantis showed his wife Gaila the expensive silverware set. She looked pleased. She fingered the ornate set with the antique pattern.

"Where's the box?" she asked her husband as she looked for a place to store the cutlery. "Didn't it come with some sort of case?"

"Yeah," DeSantis said and, not wanting to disappoint his wife, he added, "I'll get it."

Masse froze. Go back? DeSantis couldn't possibly be serious.

But he was.

"We need to go back, Gary," he yelled at his cousin. "I can't let the cops find them tied up like that."

The police knew DeSantis had a pattern of securing victims by handcuffing and hog-tying them and the cops would look in his direction if they found the bloodied bodies tied up like that. He planned to take the handcuffs off the Davies' wrists, cut the ropes and then pick up the silverware box for his wife.

With DeSantis following him in his car, Masse drove the Davies' car to a nearby shopping center, parked it and left it there. He threw his gloves in a dumpster behind the supermarket and climbed into the van with DeSantis. As they sped away from the stolen car, Masse tossed the car keys on a nearby lawn and the two raced back to the scene of the crime.

The December night darkness had settled and stilled by the time they got back to the Davies' home. DeSantis parked in front.

"You go. I'll wait here," Masse told his cousin. He was spooked, nervous, high, didn't like being back at the house and didn't want to go inside.

"Don't do anything until I come out, you hear me?" DeSantis said and he strode up the driveway and stealthily reentered the house.

The interior of the house was pitch black, the kitchen floor covered with blood. He grabbed the heavy wooden silverware box from the dining room then walked over to the couple.

Mrs. Davies, lying in a pool of blood, had been floating in and out of consciousness. When she heard DeSantis return, she lay on the floor, immobile, silent, in pain. She felt DeSantis remove the cuffs and cut the hog-tie ropes, leaving her ankles bound. Out of the corner of her eye she saw her husband's leg twitching uncontrollably as DeSantis removed his restraints.

Then she heard Ed moan. Unfortunately so did DeSantis.

"Shit," he said and quickly fired another shot into Mr. Davies' head.

Ignoring the immobile Grace Davies, whom he assumed was dead, DeSantis gathered up the ropes, the handcuffs and the antique silverware box and left the house again.

"What happened?" Masse asked DeSantis as he got into the waiting car.

"The guy didn't die," said DeSantis.

The two drove away in silence. DeSantis had nothing to say to his cousin and Masse was afraid of DeSantis' anger. Each of them thought about how much they might get for the six hundreds pound of silver. Both felt sure there were no witnesses, but they didn't trust each other. They returned to DeSantis' brother's house and finished dividing the property. DeSantis reiterated that Masse had better not say anything to anyone about what they'd just done. Masse agreed, took his cut and went home to his wife.

At the Davies' house, Grace Davies was not dead. She had blacked out for hours after DeSantis' second visit but regained consciousness. Remembering there was a knife in the drawer above her head, she pulled herself up. Then she got the knife and cut the bonds on her ankles. Crawling over to the telephone, she realized it was dead, then crawled into the living room, pulled herself up onto the couch and laid on it, drifting in and out of consciousness until the early dawn hours. Grace waited until she saw light outside, pulled a cushion off the couch and put her bloody head against it. Then she crawled, slowly and painfully, through her pillaged home, out her front door and across the lawn to the sidewalk.

A neighbor out for a morning walk found her lying unconscious on the sidewalk. Grace Davies was battered, bloody and had a bullet lodged in her head, but she was still alive.

The news of the Davies robbery and murder made the front pages of the newspapers and was the lead story on every television news program. Everyone in the city was only six degrees separated from the Davies family, from Rosemont, from coin shops, from something related to the robbery-murder. The heinous crime was the talk of the town.

A town that proved far too small for the two cousins. Within hours the buzz in criminal circles became that Masse and DeSantis were involved in the crime. Two days later an anonymous tip to the police named the two men as the perpetrators of the Ed Davies murder. The anonymous tip line at the *Sacramento Bee* also received a phone call from a female who said that the mastermind, the brains behind the robbery plan, was a woman studying to be a lawyer at a nearby college.

| 1 |

Death in Sacramento

The chill of December nights in Northern California seeps into the very bones of those who live on the open plains of Sacramento. The wind whips around the two rivers that circle the city and the cold air can be felt all the way to the coast. It was one of those chilly evenings, December 10, and Gloria Killian poured two cups of hot chamomile tea for herself and her roommate, Virgil Fletcher, and settled in beside him on the floral couch to watch the evening news. They had shared Fletcher's South Sacramento ranch house for the past four months, but she never felt precisely comfortable; this was, after all, Virgil's home, not hers and she didn't like his young girlfriend, who was in and out of the house all the time. At fifty-five, he was thirty years his girlfriend's senior and Virgil liked to brag about how much the thin, sallow girl loved him, though Gloria knew it was more likely the fancy car he drove that the girl loved. She thought Virgil was like many older men who choose young girls: too egocentric to realize his girlfriend was using him.

But living with Virgil seemed the prudent thing to do at this point in her life. Gloria had recently been through some tough times: a breakup with a boyfriend and a burglary that robbed her of all her valuable possessions, both of which forced her to take a leave of absence from her final semester at McGeorge School of Law.

Four months earlier, a mutual friend had introduced her to Brian Byers. Brian was exactly what Gloria was looking for: quiet, kind and unassuming. That first night he asked her to meet him at a nearby bar after work.

Normally Gloria never frequented such down-and-out places— she didn't like bars. She preferred the kind of establishments that served drinks with umbrellas and where strobe lights lit the dance floor. Still, she walked in determined to ignore the unfamiliar working-class surroundings and approached the trim, attractive man.

"So, you like cars," she said, smiling. Brian turned to look up at her and smiled back.

"Sure do," he said. "You?"

She nodded. "So, what can you teach me?" she asked seductively as she sat down next to him. She listened as the usually quiet man rambled on about the racing engines he loved. It was easy for Gloria to listen. She loved cars and the genial banter was a respite from the intense, intellectual jousts she and her ex had shared.

Gloria and Brian were an odd match. She was well-read, erudite and talkative, a law student who liked verbal fencing. Brian was a quiet, laconic business owner. They found a common bond in their broken hearts.

Brian was a longtime drinker, ever since he divorced and lost custody of his children to his ex-wife. It had taken an enormous toll. He spent most of his time at a bar or in his shop. He and Gloria, a beautiful and equally broken woman, fell into each other's arms. They went to bed together that night and within the week they were sleeping together every night in the back apartment over his shop.

Brian had a friend, a man named Virgil Fletcher, who once ran a bar across the street from where Brian used to work. After Gloria's home was robbed, Virgil offered Gloria a room in his house in exchange for some cooking, cleaning and a small amount of money. The solution seemed as good as Gloria could expect. It was an opportunity to get herself back together, save some money, make plans to return to school, finish her last semester and take the bar exam. She would, she decided, stay there until she got her bearings. *At least,* she thought, *it will be safe.*

A few days earlier Brian had gotten a DUI and he had been placed on a work furlough; that is, he was permitted to go to work, but he had to spend his nights at the Work Furlough Facility. So Gloria had been stuck at home alone with Virgil all week.

As Gloria and Virgil settled in to watch the news, Gloria placed her cat, Miss Kitty, on the couch between them. She sipped her tea and watched as the finely groomed newscaster announced a story that seemed to pique Virgil's interest. A noted coin collector who lived in the suburban Rosemont area had been brutally gunned down and his wife had been shot in the head and left for dead.

"Oh my God," Gloria gasped. "How horrible."

"Sure is," Virgil said. "I knew him."

"From the shop?" Gloria asked. Virgil owned a coin and pawn shop downtown and Gloria was aware that Virgil knew almost all the coin collectors in town—not to mention some of the less savory folks who frequented the shop.

"Yes," Virgil nodded.

Disturbed by the newscast, Gloria shook her head. "Awful," she reiterated. She couldn't imagine how Virgil must have felt. She tried to imagine what it would be like to know the victims of such a heinous crime and she shivered—not just from the nighttime chill. Lately there had been a rash of crimes in Sacramento. The city was beginning to feel unsafe.

The home of Sutter's Mill and the famous California Gold Rush, Sacramento has always been viewed by the big cities to its north and south as the ugly stepchild of the Golden State. California's state capital is a place brimming with politicians, transients and hustlers.

Those with money or who play in politics live downtown in statuesque Victorian homes and they're often found having cocktails or dinner in the city's upscale and trendy restaurants. Numerous pieces of legislation are conceived over plates of steak kew and memos written on napkins often find their way to the Senate floor. More than 25 percent of the locals work in government, which leads to a unique population upheaval every four or six years.

For all its political business, Sacramento still feels like a small town, a "cow town" to those who live in the Bay area, Los Angeles or San Diego. The Capitol building, old and stately with a marble rotunda and a gold dome, sits in the middle of downtown in the center of a large park. For years a peanut vendor sold peanuts to anyone wanting to feed the squirrels that inhabit the park. In the late 1970s the peanut vendor died. The squirrels almost starved to death until the legislature passed a special appropriation to buy food for them. So much for big-time politics!

A less transient segment of Sacramento society revolves around the other big business in town: the state prisons. California boasts the largest state prison population in the United States and with a budget of eight billion dollars, the California Department of Corrections holds more prisoners in its jails than the entire prison population of China. Folsom, San Quentin, California State, Sacramento, Mule Creek and Vacaville penitentiaries are all a short drive from the city and home to some of the most notorious prisoners in the world: Charles Manson, Sirhan Sirhan, Erik Menendez, Juan Corona and Scott Peterson are just some of the area's high-profile residents. Keeping those prisons filled is necessary for keeping much of the city employed. Many long-term residents of the Central Valley are police, county sheriffs and prison guards and most know the local criminals by sight. The lines between the two groups are often blurred by their similar backgrounds and upbringing, out of which personal vendettas naturally arise.

Take the former Sacramento County Sheriff, John "Big John" Misterly. Misterly ran the department for over three terms in the 1960s and 1970s until he was finally voted out under a cloud of corruption. Misterly controlled the town with an iron hand and had a particular dislike for the Hells Angels. Vowing to keep the motorcycle gang out of the city, Misterly regularly stationed one of his men on the border. Whenever Hells Angels' founder Sonny Barger crossed the city line on the Tower bridge, one of Misterly's men grabbed him, turned him right back around and threw him out of town.

At this time, Sacramento was desperately trying to change its image as corrupt, provincial and inept. But success was not easily attained. Out of the fifty murders that had occurred recently in the county, zero had been solved. The Sacramento police and sheriff's departments were unable to corral any suspects, leaving the district attorney's office sitting around with nothing to do. Newspapers like the *Sacramento Bee* and the *Sacramento Union* spread the word. By autumn, local law enforcement officials were very frustrated. They had to catch criminals. Make some high profile arrests. More than that, they needed to solve some murders. Fast.

| 2 |

Planning the Crime

Reeking of fire, metal and sweat, the vocational school welding shop was reminiscent of the juvenile halls and prisons where Stephen DeSantis had spent most of his thirty-two years. The alarm clanged, marking the end of welding class, and the short Italian student struggled to switch off his leaden welding torch. He glanced around the workshop feeling dwarfed in the one-size-fits-all bright green trainee jacket and the large metal helmet and jealous of the community college students who filled the lab. The bulk of these young, hopeful guys starting out in a new vocation towered over his five-foot-three-inch frame, not to mention that they were at least ten years his junior.

In one more semester he'd be certified as a welder and ready for placement at a local steel mill or shipyard. However, he wondered why the hell anyone would hire him, a felon, instead of these fresh-faced college students. But what else could he do? He had to find a market-able trade that would take him away from a life of crime, the only life he knew. Going back to prison wasn't an option. He was in love, newly married. He'd already lost one wife due to years spent at Folsom Prison. He wasn't going to lose Gaila, his present one.

DeSantis had met the leggy blonde at a bar less than a year ago. He was eighteen months out of prison, flush with cash and shocked when the five-foot-eight-inch statuesque beauty started up a conversation with him. She was funny, smart and shapely, with a steady job at the Air Force Base. He bought her drinks and made her laugh. She didn't mind that he was short, like some other girls he talked to. Gaila found him handsome with his olive skin and twinkling hazel eyes and she rather liked their difference in height. She also liked that he was generous. He bought her nice things, like expensive clothes and jewelry. And she loved the fact that he was totally smitten with her.

Stephen packed away his helmet, washed his hands, hung up the protective jacket and walked out of the technology building toward his red van parked in the lot. If he could just stay clean and if the friggin' cops would leave him alone, everything would be okay. He'd get a job, play it straight. It was old news that the cops didn't like him or the rest of the DeSantis clan. His family had been thorns in the side of local law enforcement ever since his father Columbino DeSantis emigrated from Italy to the farmlands of California's Central Valley.

Columbino DeSantis felt at home in a place where violent crime rates were twice as high as the rest of the state and 30 percent of the population lived below the poverty line. While many in the Central Valley worked on local farmland, DeSantis disdained the farmer's life and taught his nine children how to steal.

Stephen DeSantis turned his red van onto Suisun Valley Road. He saw red lights flicker on behind him, followed by a blaring siren.

"Shit," he angrily exclaimed. The blinkers were working, the lights were on and the tags were current. "Not again."

He pulled over and parked. He waited for the cops and rubbed his wrists, hoping they weren't going to clamp those damn cuffs on him again. From the rearview mirror he watched the cops swagger toward his car, hands hovering over their guns. *Typical officers,* he probably thought, *white, buff and arrogant.*

The two police officers sauntered up to DeSantis' van. They raised their sunglasses and smiled at the intense, swarthy Italian. To them, he was bad news. His years of criminal behavior stuck to him and in their minds there was no way he could change. He was scum and always would be. Fingering their guns, the cops peered at DeSantis.

"I thought we told you we didn't want you around here," said the taller cop leaning into the open window.

"Fuck you. I go to school here," DeSantis spat back. "I ain't doing nothin' wrong."

"Don't care," the cop said. "We don't need people like you around these kids. Get out of town or we'll put you back inside."

"Yeah, we got our eye on you," his stocky partner added. "Don't let us catch you around here again."

"I'm only going to school. Why are you fucking with me now?" DeSantis protested.

"'Cause we can," the cop said. "You heard us: Get the fuck out of town."

They laughed as they watched DeSantis drive away angry and scared. This was the second time in a week the cops had stopped him for no reason. Just a few days earlier he was stopped on Franklin Boulevard. He was lucky his sister was on her way home and saw him handcuffed behind his car, facedown on the trunk and surrounded by two cops. She stopped and pulled up to the officers as DeSantis watched in silence.

"I'm his sister. What's going on?"

"None of your business," sneered one cop and walked back to the squad car.

But the other cop pulled the sister aside, away from his partner.

"If I were you I'd tell your brother to get out of town, because Sacramento isn't healthy for him," he said. She nodded as the cop uncuffed her sullen brother.

That evening his sister called him and told him he wasn't safe in Sacramento. But he already knew that.

DeSantis drove around for what seemed like hours trying to figure out his next steps. He wasn't safe in town, he wasn't safe at school, he couldn't catch a break. Why the hell should he even try to go straight? He vowed that the cops were not going to screw his new marriage up for him. If he stayed in town it was only a matter of time before the police arrested him for something and he wound up back behind bars. He needed to do something to get Gaila and himself out of town and fast, legal or not.

He drove across town to North Sacramento, where his cousin Gary Masse lived with his wife Joanne and their children. He pulled his red van into the cluttered driveway of his cousin's bungalow and waited. As the din of the Del Paso Heights slum echoed around him, DeSantis sat inside his van debating whether or not to go inside. He rolled down the windows and breathed the crisp cool air, nonplussed by the chained dogs yelping in the front yard of the house next door. Nor could the loud whizzing of the power saws and metal grinders screeching out of the front lawn repair shop break his concentration. Not usually one for introspection, he was struggling to make a decision. Even though it had never worked out well in the past, he was considering getting involved with Gary Masse yet again.

DeSantis knew his first cousin was always involved in some crime, some scheme, some shady way to get quick cash. Once, he and Gary had been best friends and partners weaned on a life of crime. Masse's rap sheet was even longer than his. While Masse sometimes worked odd jobs, his primary income came from criminal activity like robbing houses and stealing cars. A thirty-three-year-old father of four, he had serious financial responsibilities and found himself always in debt, always broke. But it wasn't the children who used up whatever money he brought in. It was drugs. Masse's wife, Joanne, was addicted to drugs and Masse was a longtime heroin addict. A history of mental illness had haunted Masse since childhood and he was always on some mixture of pills or powders, some prescribed and some bought on the street. Drugs not only kept the family teetering on the financial edge, but also kept Masse in constant contact with most of the unsavory people in Sacramento County. He was deeply hooked into the criminal element around town and had a reputation as a guy who could get a job done.

Ironically, Masse had often aided the police to cover his own ass, including snitching on DeSantis a few years earlier, which sent DeSantis to Folsom Prison, a fact DeSantis was loath to forget.

DeSantis took a deep breath, stepped out of his van and opened the unlocked door of his cousin's home. This time he hoped he could trust his cousin to have some caper going on and to have his back.

Masse was sitting in the messy living room with the television set blaring but so spaced out he didn't seem to be watching. His youngest two children, a son, twelve and a daughter, eight, were lying across the floor. DeSantis took a seat on the tattered couch next to his cousin. They hugged and smiled.

"Got anything going on?" DeSantis yelled over the blare of the TV. Masse slowly stood up and pulled DeSantis into the dining room, away from the noise. At five feet, eight inches, Masse towered over the other DeSantis family members. He was also darker than his cousins, with thick black hair and a bushy beard. Though larger and more physically imposing, his affect was slower and dizzier due to years of drug abuse. His speech was often muddled and unclear. It was not unusual for Gary to contradict himself within the same sentence.

"Yeah, I got this job from my contacts, robbing some guy they say has a lot of gold and silver," he said, taking a seat at the table. Drugs made him tired.

"At his house?" DeSantis asked. It was important to have Masse parse out all the details.

"No, um, yeah. I think, um, yeah, they say he don't believe in banks and keeps the stuff buried in the backyard or in secret safes at home, something like that," Masse told his anxious cousin. "But don't worry, it's gonna be easy. He's an easy mark. If you want in, it's your job to figure out how to get us inside."

"How much does he have?"

"A couple of hundred grand, which we gotta split fifty-fifty with my contacts. But they say they got another job for a million if I do this one right."

"What kind of job?"

"Didn't say, but we gotta do this one first."

"What kind of people?" DeSantis asked. He needed to know as much as he could about the job. Knowledge was power. And it was dangerous to get involved with strangers.

"People I know. Just people," Masse said evasively. He wasn't sure he wanted DeSantis in on the promised million-dollar job and he didn't want DeSantis to have the contact in case he decided to cut Masse out. Blood went only so far.

DeSantis slowly shook his head. This wasn't a lot of information, but he knew better than to press Gary. That would make him nervous.

"Let me think about it," DeSantis said.

Joanne Masse walked out of the kitchen into the dining room where the two cousins sat. Her dark, curly, uncombed hair partially covered her thin, dark face. She was as wired as Gary was slow. An addiction to crank, the powerful methamphetamine, made Joanne's eyes flicker and even when she moved slowly, the rail-thin, five-foot tall Armenian seemed tense.

"Want some coffee, Steve?" she asked. But DeSantis only wanted to go home and think about his next move.

"No thanks, Joanne. I gotta get home. Gaila's waiting."

DeSantis hurried outside and drove home, pondering his options. A hundred grand would get him out of town and another quarter of a million would set them up in style. Coming up with a plan would be easy. He figured he would do what he'd done for a home robbery once before: disguise himself as a repairman and weasel his way inside the house. DeSantis' size and pleasant demeanor were to his benefit in this situation. People never felt nervous or threatened when he came knocking on their doors.

He stopped to pick up flowers for Gaila on his way home and thought about how he'd tell his new wife he was going to do a job that would net them some real money to take them out of town.

She smiled when saw him at the door, let him in, took the flowers and put them in a vase.

"Sit down, honey," DeSantis said and then he told her of his plan and pending partnership with Masse. But Gaila wasn't so sure this was the way to go.

"I don't know, Steve," she said standing up and pacing their small apartment. "I don't trust Gary and I won't be able to take it if you go to jail. I'll leave you if you get caught." The tall beauty had no intention of spending the rest of her life visiting her husband behind bars.

DeSantis didn't deliberate for long about whether to get involved again with his shady cousin. Thinking wasn't his strong suit, action was. He was back at Masse's house the next day.

"I'm in," he told his cousin, who was still wearing the same dirty shirt and jeans from the night before and looked like he hadn't left the couch. Gary had been rotating his drug use from painkillers to heroin, neither of which gave him much energy to do anything but doze.

"When do I meet the contact?" DeSantis asked.

"I'll take care of them," Masse answered, committed to keeping his contact and DeSantis apart.

The night before, Joanne and Gary had had a long talk about DeSantis and his possible involvement in the job. Masse asked her to do the job with them, but Joanne didn't want to be involved. She urged Gary to keep the contact away from DeSantis, because "Blood or not, I don't trust him," she said. "Steve's gonna go straight to the contact and cut you out. Don't tell him nothing."

Masse followed directions, as he did most of the time when Joanne issued an order. She made the bulk of the family's decisions.

Trust was never the basis of the cousins' relationship, but, as in many partnerships, both men had a need. Masse didn't have the expertise to do the job alone. He needed DeSantis to get the wife to open the door. DeSantis was reluctant to let Masse be their only tie to the contact, but he was desperate for fast cash and didn't want to wait for a better time.

"Okay," DeSantis said reluctantly and they set his plan in motion. "Let's see what we need."

The two drove in Gary's souped-up car from their tract houses in Del Paso Heights to Rosemont. An upper-middle-class suburb of the city but still in Sacramento county, Rosemont was where the "easy mark," Ed Davies, lived. One of the sprawling developments built in the late 1950s and 1960s when the Central Valley was beginning to boom, Rosemont's homes were nice. There were no cars parked on front lawns or barking dogs on chains.

As if it was their full-time job, every day for two weeks the two grabbed cups of coffee at the local convenience store, cranked up some heavy metal tunes and drove past the Davies' ranch home, monitoring the movements of the retired coin collector and his wife, Grace. Later they stopped for a sandwich at a market a few blocks away, only to return and watch the couple some more. Most days and nights Grace stayed home and watched television. Mr. Davies did some local shopping and occasional errands. They were a typical retired couple who spent almost all of their time relaxing together in their home.

It only took a few days for DeSantis to steal the necessary equipment to pull off the scam to get into the Davies' home. He grabbed a white hard hat off an unguarded telephone company truck, also stealing a tool belt with a phone attached, an orange plastic jacket and finally a telephone repair truck. But something nagged at him. Once inside, where would they find the gold and silver? Days before the robbery, during one of their daily casings, DeSantis voiced his concerns.

"Your contacts, they know where the stuff is buried, right?" DeSantis asked his cousin as they sipped coffee down the block from the Davies' house.

"I told you," Masse replied, "it's, like, buried in the backyard and stuff. I ain't worried. My guy said if you threaten the wife, the old man will give up everything. It'll be easy. I guarantee it."

DeSantis was not so sure. They were thieves, not killers and they were used to breaking into places when people weren't home. But just in case the plan didn't go as easily as Masse promised, DeSantis bought a pistol and a silencer. He had never shot anyone during any of the crimes he committed.

In the days following Thanksgiving, DeSantis called Masse numerous times pressing for a date. Each day in town made him more and more nervous. He saw police everywhere. He didn't want to lose his wife or his freedom.

On December 9, DeSantis phoned his cousin at the break of dawn and told him he believed today should be the day. Finally Masse agreed. The time was now.

On that sunny, fifty-degree December day, as the criminals drove into the parking lot at the supermarket to pick up the stolen truck, they saw Ed Davies walk into the store.

"It's him!" DeSantis yelled excitedly.

That was when the two criminals followed Davies home and put their robbery plan into action. A plan that spiraled into murder.

That evening DeSantis said nothing to Gaila or his brother about the shootings. He went home to his wife and bluffed his way through the evening as they talked excitedly about where they would go to begin their new, happy, prosperous future.

That night no amount of tranquilizers could help Masse close his eyes. He kept seeing the Davies couple lying on the floor, the blood pouring from their heads. He kept seeing the look on his cousin's face as he shot the couple. Before dawn Masse had confessed everything to Joanne.

| 3 |

Investigating Murder

The small farming community of Elk Grove was only fifteen miles south of Sacramento, but farms still covered the rural municipality that was founded in 1850 as a stagecoach stop and a home base for gold miners. While Sacramento experienced growth and development, Elk Grove remained a small, close-knit rural western community where men wore cowboy hats, boots and guns. They worked in the dairy with cattle or grew row crops and were still wary of the citified Sacramento lawmen. It was a great place to hide if you had to.

Joanne Masse knew that. She paced her parents' small ranch house, smoking. She and Gary were there alone. She had left her children at their house with her fourteen-year-old daughter. Taking care of the younger children often fell on the girl's shoulders. Joanne knew her eldest child was capable of watching over the other three and making sure they went to school while she and Gary hid out at her parents' home. It was December 12, two days since her husband confessed that the Davies robbery had gone wrong and turned into a murder scene. The police repeatedly called their home looking for Gary and she knew it was only a matter of time before they showed up at their house. They wouldn't know to look for them at her parents' home. And their neighbors in the close-knit community wouldn't think of telling anyone from the sheriff's office anyone's business either. She and Masse needed to hide out and think. They were in trouble, big trouble.

Joanne knew Steve DeSantis was also in a panic. The day before, he had called Gary asking for a meeting. He told him they needed to talk. He needed to get rid of some of the loot and wanted to get out of town as soon as possible. Joanne and Gary agreed to meet DeSantis in a public place: the parking lot of the market in Sacramento. She and Gary were afraid to be alone with him.

Joanne pulled Masse's car up to where DeSantis' van waited. He was sitting in the van listening to hard-driving heavy metal. She thought he looked as wired as the night of the crime, adrenaline still pumping through his veins. Everyone was nervous.

Masse lumbered out of the car, jammed his hands into his pockets, leaned against the car door and told Joanne to wait inside. DeSantis moved like a compact package of coursing energy as he got out and stood next to his cousin. Masse looked tired and drugged. Neither man had slept, much, if at all.

"You know, you, really, um, like, messed this job up," Masse said to his cousin. "You really made a mess outta it."

"Yeah, well they saw us. Nothing else I could do," DeSantis said. "I'm getting out of town. We got to wait to move the stuff 'til the heat is off."

Masse nodded. He was in bad shape, very stoned and out of it, unable to deal with running from the police. The constant police phone calls made him nervous and what scared him even more were his contacts, the masterminds of the robbery, who were calling him anxious to get their share of the loot. Masse knew those people could be dangerous. He was also afraid to tell DeSantis that those same contacts had asked about DeSantis too. DeSantis was a little crazy now, wound a little too tight. Who knew what he might do? Masse thought he and his family might be in jeopardy if they talked too much to anyone.

The cousins looked each other in the eye, silent for a moment. They knew they were in this together, but neither really trusted the other. DeSantis knew Masse's staying in town might mean he'd get snitched on again but he hoped the murder would keep his partner quiet. Either way, he wasn't waiting to find out. He was leaving town.

Joanne peered out the car window, trying to listen in on the cousins' conversation. She hoped that DeSantis would say where he was going as she rolled down the window and stuck her head out, a better position to eavesdrop on the two men. She was thinking of calling the cops and the more information she had, the better.

But she heard nothing useful and watched as, after just a few minutes, Masse grabbed DeSantis and patted him on the back, all warm and brotherly. DeSantis nodded toward Joanne, still quiet in the car, and walked back to his van. Masse got back in the car, slowly shook his head and looked at his wife, filled with dread.

"Boy, that crazy sucker told me he shoulda offed me in the house along with them."

"I don't trust Steve," Joanne told him, putting the car in gear.

"I ain't gonna give him up," Masse said. But as she drove them back home, Joanne had other ideas. If Steve thought heat was coming down on him, it was only a matter of time before it caught up with them as well. If DeSantis was leaving town, they'd hide, too.

From the moment Grace Davies was found on the sidewalk in front of her home and her husband's body was found inside shot to death, Sergeant Harry Machen and Detective Joseph Dean immersed themselves in the search for the killer. Both men were veteran investigators at the Sacramento Sheriff's Department. They were good cops and had worked together numerous times before. They'd been assigned the high profile Davies murder, because they could handle the intense pressure. It had been over a year since the department had solved a murder and home invasions and robberies were rampant. When the case of the coin collector hit the news, the homicide staff was told to work the case nonstop. It was the second home invasion and murder in one month. Just a few weeks earlier, thieves had entered a home and shot a woman in the head right before her husband's eyes. Those criminals were still at large and people in Sacramento were becoming increasingly nervous with this latest murder. The police had to solve this case fast to avoid chaos.

Machen and Dean vowed to each other to solve the crime, whatever it took. From their years of homicide experience both detectives had vast lists of informants, snitches and contacts within the local criminal population. The two men interviewed suspects and informants day and night.

Good police work involves talking to anyone even remotely involved with the perpetrators and the victims. Equally as essential to the investigation is to see who shows up on their own and whom the police have to bring in. Some are genuine "helpers," others look to clear their names and some have completely selfish agendas.

The first person to call the homicide department after the Davies murder was Charlie Duncan. Duncan was a local coin dealer who had known and dealt with Ed Davies, the murder victim, for many years. The fifty-year-old had been, until recently, the partner of Virgil Fletcher in his coin and pawn shop. But the two had dissolved the partnership under acrimonious terms and were still hostile toward each other.

Duncan called the Sacramento Sheriff's Department hotline, nervous and upset by the Davies murder. He was transferred to Sergeant Hash, a tall detective with an imposing manner.

"I'm a friend of Ed Davies," Duncan said, his voice cracking on the line. "I've got some information regarding the business dealings of Ed Davies that I believe would be of some significance in the investigation."

Hash said he couldn't talk to Duncan right then. "We're short on men and I don't have an investigator to contact you at this time." Hash advised Duncan to come into the Sheriff's Department homicide bureau to be interviewed and to make a statement.

Duncan thought that was odd. Here he was offering help and they were too busy? But he was also the kind of man who was never comfortable in a police station. Most of the time when he was in a police station, he didn't walk in on his own.

The next day, Calvin Duffy, a middle-aged man who recently moved to Sacramento and his young, attractive girlfriend came in to the homicide bureau. Duffy was shaking and close to tears.

"I just read the paper this morning and found out about Ed," Duffy wailed at the cop at the reception desk in his thick Teutonic accent.

The officer directed Duffy and his girlfriend to Detective Machen. They walked over to the six-foot-tall cop with bright green eyes and a thick mustache sitting at his desk drinking coffee. After leading them to a nondescript interview room, Machen brought them cups of coffee, too.

"So, what can you tell me?" Machen asked smiling, doing his best to put the nervous immigrant at ease.

"We'd been friendly for about a year when Ed and I met about some property he owned that I was thinking about buying," Duffy said, his voice breaking, barely able to hold back tears. "I really liked the guy and I think he really liked me."

He added that he had completed some work for Ed on his house four or five months ago. But what Duffy really wanted to talk about was the relationship between Ed Davies and Virgil Fletcher. Discussing Fletcher, Duffy became very distressed, talking too fast, which made him hard to understand with his thick accent. Several times Machen asked him to speak more slowly and carefully. Duffy told him that Fletcher and Davies knew each other quite well and had more of a hostile relationship than a friendship.

"Ed told me he got involved with Charlie Duncan at the coin shop. He helped fund Charlie for his business and later Charlie took on a partner named Virgil Fletcher. Ed didn't like Fletcher and I don't like him either," Duffy said.

"Why not?" Machen asked. This was the first time he had heard about Virgil Fletcher.

"I would say Duncan is an up-front, honest individual and a coin man at heart. I've known Duncan for many, many years. But Fletcher is another story. He is a man I think is deceitful and I feel is not always honest."

"How do you know this?" Machen asked and sipped his coffee.

"He tried to play me against Ed for a while," Duffy continued. "At one time Fletcher told me that Ed was going to Mexico and running guns and dope. I thought this was rather odd, knowing Ed the way I do, so I went and asked Ed. Ed said, 'Well, who are you going to believe?' I believe that Fletcher was just trying to cause problems."

"Why would he want to do that?"

Duffy shrugged. "He's not a nice guy. I've done work for Fletcher and heard comments from several people. I found that he has a lot of very unsavory and scroungy looking people around him frequently. And he told me that Ed kept money buried in his backyard in a can."

Machen wondered how Duncan, Duffy and Virgil Fletcher were connected with Masse and DeSantis, the men the cops were tipped off to for perpetrating the crime. He understood that Fletcher and Duncan were coin shop owners who knew Davies. But how did they all connect?

The next morning as Machen walked into work, he got a call from fellow detective Dave Koupel. As part of the intense investigation for this high-profile murder, Koupel and the entire detective staff were canvassing every confidential informant (CI) they knew. CIs were sometimes straight people who had connections to the criminal world, but more often than not they were career criminals, pimps and addicts who helped the cops. Masse had worked as a CI more than once.

"Besides Masse and DeSantis, we need to look for a female named Gloria who is living with or has gone with an ex-owner of a coin shop somewhere near Stockton Boulevard and Fruitridge," Koupel relayed the information from his CIs. "They said this Gloria is an intern going to law school in town and that she also knows Ed Davies."

Machen knew right away that the coin shop the CIs mentioned was the shop owned by Charlie Duncan and Virgil Fletcher. Did this Gloria live with Fletcher? Were they a couple? It must be the same Gloria they got off the tip line from the newspaper.

Later that day Machen got a call from Detective Joe Hegseth, who had additional information from his CI. Hegseth's informant put Davies in Virgil's coin shop. "Not only that," Hegseth went on, "my guy said he heard that Virgil told a female he's living with—named Gloria— that someone should do Davies. The CI said Fletcher knew that Davies didn't believe in banks and had three hundred to four hundred thousand dollars worth of gold and silver, some buried in his backyard."

This was the same thing Machen had heard from Calvin Duffy. He believed the case was starting to come together.

Machen knew sometimes CIs were right and sometimes they were wrong, but after hearing similar information from several, he knew he needed to talk to Virgil Fletcher and his roommate Gloria.

Virgil's kitchen was redolent with the smell of garlic sizzling in olive oil as Gloria stood by the stove chopping green beans on the evening of December 14. Virgil strode into the room and peered over her shoulder to see what she was preparing for them that evening. Gloria, a dedicated gourmet cook, fumbled with his very basic knives which she considered a bachelor's cooking utensils. She hated the lack of spatulas, knives, whisks, spoons and measuring cups, but she wasn't willing to get her own items out of storage, so she made do with what was available. *Men just don't know how to outfit a kitchen appropriately*, she thought as she chopped the beans. Virgil smiled at her, hoping she was making some kind of potatoes to go with the vegetables and meat. He'd whined numerous times that he wanted to lose weight, but he was not willing to deprive himself of the things he liked and meat and potatoes were things he liked.

Virgil also liked having the smart law student around. She was educated, witty, informed and stylish. Gloria always knew what was happening politically and socially, loved to talk and had a great sense of humor. He liked that she knew a lot about antiques, jewelry, porcelain and other collectibles and enjoyed talking about that field. He did as well. He thought himself a connoisseur of jewelry and fine things and they had fun talking about the fascinating world of antiques.

Since his divorce a few years ago he also missed the home cooking he was used to and deep down he was lonely, even though he would never admit it. He liked to talk, but it wasn't much fun with no one to listen. Gloria gave him the audience he craved and she was an enjoyable companion during their few evenings at home together. He could talk to her about his business problems and get good advice. She was one very smart law student and he thought she would make a hell of a lawyer. Most of the time as a roommate she was fine.

What he complained about on occasion was Gloria's cat. While at times he seemed happy to have Miss Kitty move in, because his cat had died a couple of months previously, he was an extremely neat man and he hated it when Gloria's large calico spat up hairballs all over the house.

"By the way, Miss Kitty threw up again in the living room," he said, interrupting Gloria's chopping as if he wanted her to drop what she was doing and dash into the living room to clean.

"Do you need me to get it?" Gloria asked, wiping her hands on her jeans. She wanted to keep their relationship cordial and friendly and didn't want the cat making any waves. After all she had been through the past few months, all she wanted was a quiet place to keep her stuff where she could feel safe and secure until she got her life back in order. She knew that she needed time to recreate her entire life and saving money and staying with the older man seemed like a simple, safe way to do so. She could see where her relationship with Brian would take her as well, while maintaining a secure home base.

"I took care of it, but you have to take better care and clean up more," Virgil said, opening and closing the pots on the stove, savoring the scent of the cooking food.

Gloria refrained from calling him a neat freak or making some sarcastic comment and guided the conversation to something more pleasant for her roommate. She knew he was upset about the Davies murder. He didn't want to talk about it so she wasn't going to pry. If he had done anything sinister, it never occurred to her.

"Where's your girlfriend tonight?" she asked him instead. Virgil loved to talk about his pretty young girlfriend who was not one to make him home-cooked meals.

"She wanted to see me, but I was a little tired tonight," he said. "She just can't get enough of me." He added, "You know I saved her life. I got her off heroin."

Gloria knew. She also knew Virgil would now probably launch into another story in which he was yet again the hero. If she got him going he'd talk about the people he loaned money to, interest free, so they could get back on their feet. He'd talk about the cops who loved to hang out with him when he owned his bar. He'd talk about his ex-wife whom he'd pulled a fast one on. Or he'd talk about Charlie Duncan, whom he'd lace into any time he was given a chance. He'd call Charlie a crook, a thief, a cheat, but he never mentioned his own record to Gloria or anyone else.

People who saw Virgil with his smiling, calm resemblance to Santa Claus and his good ol' Texas boy demeanor never suspected there was nothing saintly, jolly or soft about the coin shop owner. Virgil Fletcher had been arrested many, many times. As a teen, he'd been accused of child stealing and rape. Later he was arrested for rape again as well as twice for battery and disturbing the peace. Fifteen years later he was arrested for assault and battery and served time in the county jail. And just two years before the Davies murder, Fletcher was arrested and convicted in March for drunk driving, possession of a loaded firearm in a public place and receiving stolen property. In September of the same year he was arrested for another possession of a concealed gun.

Under his affable demeanor was a man who was no stranger to violence or crime. He always had a gun hidden in the door pocket of his blue luxury sedan.

The next day, Machen and Dean decided to pay a visit to Virgil Fletcher and his roommate Gloria. They drove to Fletcher's small house at 3 P.M. and found a woman conversing in the front yard with a heavy-set older man.

"Looks like we hit the jackpot," Machen said to Dean and parked the unmarked car across the street. "Must be Fletcher and Gloria." But they were dismayed to see the woman get into her car.

"Let's trail her," Dean said, pulling the car out. They followed the white sedan a couple of blocks before he turned on the siren and pulled the driver over to the side of the road.

"Wha...what did I do?" asked the woman, fidgeting in her seat.

"Let me see your license and registration," Dean said, watching the woman search her purse.

"The car isn't mine. It belongs to Neva," the woman replied. Hands shaking, she handed her driver's license to Dean.

He looked at the name: Lila Hines. He looked at Machen sitting in the car and shook his head. It wasn't Gloria.

"Are you Lila Hines?"

She nodded, fearful, close to tears.

"What were you doing at Virgil Fletcher's house?"

"Gloria told me to come pick her up there."

"What's Gloria's last name?"

"I...I d–don't know," she stammered. "We're friends and she called me to pick her up. She wanted to go shopping."

"You're her friend and you don't know her last name?"

"She's more a friend of Neva's. I met her at Neva's."

Dean fingered the registration of the car. "The Neva Snyder who owns this car?"

"Yes. She called me at Neva's and asked me to pick her up to go shopping, but when I got there fifteen minutes later she wasn't there."

"Do you know where she is?"

"I have no idea," Lila said.

Dean handed Lila her documents and told her she was free to go. He joined Machen back at the squad car.

"Let's get Fletcher."

After reparking the car across the street, Machen and Dean walked up the cement steps to Fletcher's front door. The front yard was straggly and in need of pruning. Circling the trees, the overgrown chrysanthemums drooped, waiting to be cut or tied. Machen knocked once, then twice. They heard Fletcher's heavy step amble toward the door. He opened it as if he already knew who was there.

"Can I help you guys?" Fletcher asked in his genial, affable way.

"I'm Sergeant Machen and this is Detective Dean. We'd like you to come downtown to talk to you about the Davies case."

"Of course," Fletcher said. "May I take my car?"

"No," Machen replied. "Come with us; we'll bring you back when we're done."

Fletcher nodded and grabbed his coat. He had expected this and was well prepared. He had known Ed Davies and didn't like him. They once had been more cordial, even friends. A couple of months prior, before his partnership with Charlie dissolved, he'd bought Ed a bottle of bourbon, even though he himself liked to drink higher grade scotches. He knew Ed was a little strange. Ed once asked him if he could arrange a hit on then Senator Alan Cranston, offering him ten thousand dollars and saying he wanted the meddlesome senator gone. Fletcher knew he wasn't going to tell the cops about that.

Virgil Fletcher sat in the interrogation room with the two detectives, completely at ease. They brought him water to drink and started by asking not about him but about Gloria.

"Yes, she lives with me," Fletcher said. "I met her through my friend Brian Byers. She's a graduate student at McGeorge School of Law and is planning on taking the bar exam in February."

"What's your relationship with her?" Dean asked.

"She's my friend's girlfriend. That's all," Fletcher answered testily.

"What do you guys talk about?"

"We don't have a whole lot to talk about," Virgil answered. "She fixes dinner and I'm always on her about her cat and cleaning up after it."

"What else do you know about her?" Machen pressed.

"Well, her mother is in the hospital somewhere in Sacramento. Gloria went to see her recently," Fletcher said and paused to think more. "She's got my garage filled with some of her law books."

"She have a car?"

"No," Virgil said. "Brian or Lila drive her everywhere. Lila drives a white car; Brian drives a souped-up rice burner."

"She ever talk to you about the coin business?" Dean asked.

"We talked about my business partnership breaking up."

"The one with Charlie Duncan?"

Virgil nodded. "And we talked about accounts receivable and some of the bad debts a few times. She came into the coin shop once with a girlfriend while I was still in the business."

"Did you see Gloria last week?"

"Yes," Virgil said. "Gloria was at the house all of last week. She has been sick. Sunday night she went to Brian's and hasn't been home since. She rarely stays around the house a lot. Once in a while Lila will pick her up. I won't allow her to have others at my house."

"Did you have any problems with Duncan?

"I think Charlie is jealous of me, because some people would rather deal with me than him."

Virgil failed to mention that he knew all of Charlie's dealings, because he watched through a peephole he created in the wall of the coin shop's private back room specifically to spy on whatever was going on in the shop. Sitting in a small chair hidden from view, Virgil watched Charlie deal with his clients, saw what they brought in and easily heard whatever was said.

The detectives were satisfied when Virgil said Ed dealt more with Charlie and that Ed acted strangely toward Virgil when the partnership ended. They never asked if he knew Masse or DeSantis or about his relationship with Duffy. The detectives also did not inquire if Fletcher knew about buried silver, gun running or any of the issues that Duffy had talked about.

At the same time that Machen and Dean were talking with Virgil Fletcher, in another interrogation room at the Sheriff's Department a second group of police officers were conducting an interview.

That afternoon Joanne Masse had arrived at the Sheriff's Department ready to talk. She was handed off to Lieutenant Ray Biondi and Detective Stan Reed. They were determined to find out what happened and to press her to bring her husband in.

Joanne stared nervously at the wall of the small interrogation room, picking at her hands, pulling at her long dark hair. She hated the cops almost as much as her husband did, but she knew the rule: whoever talks first wins. She knew about the murder, but she didn't want Gary to be the one to get the death penalty.

Lieutenant Biondi played the good cop, opening up their talk by offering her refreshments and making sure she was comfortable. She was by far the best witness they had and now that he had her there and talking on tape, he was going to make sure she told him all she knew.

He knew the best way to get to a woman, to relax her, was to let her tell the story of how she met her husband then ask about her children. Never start out with the crime; ease into it. Joanne spoke for a couple of minutes about her family. Once Biondi got her smiling, he asked her about the case.

Joanne replied that she was afraid of the killers and the people who set Masse up for the job.

Biondi pressed her for more information.

"Steve steals a telephone truck," Joanne said, "and he acts like he was from the phone company and says something was wrong with the phone. The broad that set this up, she said that the old man and the woman would talk and there was no reason to hurt them, but Steve, you know, he wasn't disguised enough. The wife seen him and she could identify him, so that's it. He just shot 'em. What can I say?"

"And the stuff?" Biondi needed to find the stolen goods. That was solid evidence and there would be fingerprints.

"You know we've been trying to find out. Gary didn't get nothin'. Steve, he's got everything."

"And what's Steve's last name?"

"DeSantis."

Joanne went on to describe to Biondi her version of the crime, the guns and the entire scenario at the Davies' house as if she was there. She talked about a man named Bob who gave them the guns and where they dropped off Masse's and Gary's cars. The police had not yet put together that Bob was Bob Hord, Neva Snyder's son.

"And what happened after it was all done?" Biondi asked.

"First Steve calls and asks me and Gary to meet him. And then the girl calls."

"You mean Gloria?"

"Yeah. She says she's shocked and all. Something like that."

"How did you meet Gloria?"

"I just, uh, when, uh, Gary, uh, he went to talk to her. I was with him."

"You were with Gary?" Detective Reed was surprised. "And where did you meet her at? A house? An apartment?"

"A parking lot. I don't know where she lives or her last name. Gary don't know either. She told us there were these two people, a couple out in the Rosemont area and they have a lotta gold and silver and valuable things. Silver crystal, china, you know, stuff worth a lotta money. She said he was a gunrunner, maybe into drugs. She didn't know but said he ran to Mexico once or twice a year. That the Mafia was after him and the IRS, too. And there was some businessmen that wanted him hit. She wanted him hit for some reason."

"What was she supposed to get out of this?" Reed asked. He knew that with thieves there was usually a problem dividing the loot.

"Half of everything that came outta that house."

Reed established that Joanne had met Gloria around two months before the robbery.

"How many times did you meet with her?"

"Anywhere from six to maybe ten times. She was pressin' him to do it. Right after the first time we met her at the parking lot and she told us she wanted the job done real bad."

Joanne told them that Gloria went to the Davies' house about four times. "She went there pretending like she needed the phone and she said they came to the door. At one time she went in and checked the house out. She was asking for different people. I think they only let her in once. And then we met her after the job was done. 'Cause she called us and said, 'Did you see the news?'"

Biondi and Reed interviewed Joanne for hours during which she reiterated that Masse had no loot from the robbery, DeSantis murdered Ed Davies and Gloria masterminded the entire thing.

The next day the entire Sheriff's Department had a meeting and agreed it was time to bring in Gloria Killian. With Joanne's testimony they had enough to arrest her and, given enough time, they would get her to talk. They figured a woman without a record of arrests wouldn't be able to withstand their interrogation. She'd crack and the case could be closed.

Machen and Dean sent Sergeant Hash and three plainclothes officers to pick Gloria up at Brian's shop, while they followed one more lead and paid a visit to Neva Snyder.

| 4 |

The First Arrest

Gloria walked Brian's Rottweiler past the old Victorian homes downtown and back to Brian's shop on the morning of December 16. A smile crossed her lips as she thought about the plan she had put together for that afternoon. She'd cancelled any appointments they had midday so she could lock the shop and they could make love. It had been over a week and she felt terrible that he had to spend each night in jail.

It was early, so Gloria sat at the small desk in the front of the shop to work on Brian's accounting. He wasn't great with billing or keeping any other kinds of records and Gloria had promised him her work on his books would save him thousands in the long run. A short while later she phoned her mother, because she still felt it was her duty to check in, especially since her grandmother Mina had died five years earlier and Gloria's mother lived alone.

By late morning, Gloria had other things on her mind. She wanted to make Brian feel special and to thank him for all his support. As the clock struck twelve, she bolted the front door, leaned seductively across the office couch and flashed her intense blue eyes at Brian. "Forget lunch," she smiled, toying with the buttons on her expensive sweater. She had been quite relieved when her clothes weren't stolen during the robbery at her apartment. Dressed nicely, she could still feel put together even though parts of her life had spiraled out of control.

Brian stood up, walked toward Gloria, took her in his arms and began to undress her. Suddenly there was a knock at the door.

"Let's not answer it," Brian said. "It's just a customer. Let's just wait and they'll leave."

But Gloria hesitated. "We can't," she said, quickly pulling on her jeans. "What if it's your probation officer?" Gloria hastily pulled on her sweater and finger-brushed her long dark hair, doing her best to cover up their afternoon plans.

Brian ambled to the door and opened it to find three grim-faced men staring solemnly back at him.

"We're looking for Gloria Killian," said the largest of the three, his eyes resting on Gloria who stood behind the counter.

"I'm right here," she said, fingering the buttons on her sweater to make sure she hadn't missed one.

Brian stepped aside as the three men strode inside and began to look around, carefully scanning the room. Gloria smiled her nicest smile, though she felt a sick sense of foreboding in the pit of her stomach. She couldn't help wondering why these men were so grim.

"I'm Sergeant Hash," the largest cop stepped right up to her, using his height and mass to intimidate the petite brunette. "Do you know Virgil Fletcher?" he asked.

"Of course," Gloria said. "He's my roommate."

"When did you last see him?" Hash asked.

"Last night," she said. "And I know he talked to detectives."

Virgil had stopped by Brian's shop the evening before to let her know he had been questioned by the homicide bureau about the murder of the man in Rosemont. Even though he had expected to be interrogated because he owned a coin shop and the victim was a coin collector, he'd told Gloria the questioning had upset him and he asked her to stay home with him that night. He had a heart condition and wanted her there just in case.

Now Hash was staring at her. "Would you please come downtown and answer a few questions?"

"Sure," she said, trying to mask her anxiety. She quickly gathered her purse from under the counter and once again touched her buttons to make sure she was put together. She smiled at Brian. He smiled back, took her hand for a moment and let go as she walked toward the silent cops. Gloria was sure she could clear up any questions the police might have about Virgil. She knew the coin and pawn business was a little shady, but she felt could she could answer any of their questions and clarify anything they were having trouble understanding.

Gloria was worried the officers might realize she and Brian had locked the door to have sex and that embarrassed her. She decided to try to joke her way out of this one.

"You know," she said, smiling hard to cover up her discomfort as they walked outside toward an unmarked police car, "you have the worst timing. I always get caught." But the cops didn't smile back. Instead, they fell into the formation used when walking with a criminal: one on each side of her and one behind. They were making sure she couldn't run.

Hash and his men placed Gloria into the backseat while two of them climbed into the front. The third got into another unmarked car parked directly behind them where a fourth cop sat waiting.

The strangeness of the situation began to unnerve Gloria. She asked herself why it was necessary for four cops to collect her just to ask her questions about Virgil and the shop. Her instincts were screaming danger and once inside the car she lit a cigarette. Like many smokers, she lit up whenever she was nervous. "What can I use for an ashtray?" she asked.

"Just roll down the window," Hash answered.

"I didn't want you to think I was going to crawl out," she said flippantly, hoping to inspire the hint of a smile.

But the men remained stone-faced and Gloria's stomach clenched. *Why didn't they laugh?* She had a quick, smart sense of humor and most people responded positively to her wisecracks.

For the next ten minutes, as they drove to the Sheriff's Department in downtown Sacramento, Gloria looked out the window in silence. The Sheriff's Department was one more dreary government office building surrounded by other dull government buildings incongruously set amongst the beautiful old Victorian homes. Gloria followed the men toward the elevator and they rode in silence to the third floor. There they walked her through a room that looked more like an insurance office than a homicide squad room and into a small, windowless inter-rogation room that, to Gloria, felt a little more like the kinds of rooms she had seen on television programs, the places where TV cops put the suspects they were ready to browbeat.

"Sit down," Hash said coldly. As she did, the detectives walked out and closed the door behind them.

Gloria looked around the dull grey room with nothing in it except for a long metal table and a few uncomfortable metal chairs. It was completely silent and she could hear nothing of what was going on outside in the station, nothing of the outside world at all. There was nothing to read, nothing to watch, nothing to do but stare at the walls and wait. And think.

She knew from her law school training that it was a typical police ploy to leave a suspect alone to wonder what would happen next. It was a maneuver designed to make people nervous, to make them sweat. But why would they do this to her? She was just there to answer questions about Virgil.

As she waited for what seemed like hours, her thoughts wandered, pausing on the day she'd spent with her mother last year, right before her breakup with her boyfriend. She thought about law school and why she was in this bleak interrogation room. *And where the hell are those cops?*

Their ploy was working. She was feeling increasingly uncomfortable, growing more and more nervous as the minutes ticked away.

Detectives Machen and Dean sat in the Snyders' crowded living room. Neva Snyder and her husband Ellis lived in a home that seemed part museum and part auto repair shop. It was filled with wall-to-wall china cabinets packed two and three rows deep with valuable porcelain, pottery, glass and antiques. Neva owned entire sets of rare English bone china, gold plates, antique jewelry and art. On the walls hung expensive artwork, including original Maxfield Parrish prints that Neva had collected and shelves stocked with high-end pieces of porcelain or glass.

It was also jam-packed with tools, broken appliances and car parts. Ellis, tall, rangy and always in overalls, lived primarily in the backyard where he spent hours each day fixing old cars, but his tools and parts found their way inside the house. Neva was a collector, Ellis a fixer. Often Ellis was covered in grease and dirt while petite Neva was always put together well in one of her many blonde wigs, whether a short-haired strawberry blonde or long ashen tresses. She draped herself in expensive clothes and jewelry with flashy rings on every finger.

Neva was very soft-spoken and conveyed a sense of caring and compassion in her gentle manner. Ellis, whom everyone called Snyder, was more laconic but still affable and friendly. Their home was an open door, a revolving door for family and friends, many of whom spent time in prisons and jails.

Ellis and Neva were key people in the investigation, because Joanne told the detectives that her husband met Gloria through Neva and the duo met regularly in Neva's house. Neva considered Gloria a friend. Perhaps she was looking for the daughter she never had and perhaps Gloria was looking for a warmer, more caring mother. For the past year, the women spent hours each week talking jewelry, art, pottery and porcelain and going to swap meets.

The detectives interviewed the couple both together and separately. Neva and Ellis admitted they knew Masse, because Ellis fixed his green car, but neither mentioned that Masse bought speed for Joanne from Neva. They said they were friends with Gloria as well but never introduced the two of them.

The cops spent another few minutes asking more innocuous questions, then thanked the couple for the information. As they left they noticed the couple owned a portable scanner for police radio transmissions. It was turned on and they paused as an officer reported that Gloria Killian was at the station. Machen and Dean left in a hurry.

After what was actually only forty-five minutes of waiting, two strangers walked into the interrogation room and Gloria wondered what had happened to the other officers. She was too nervous by that time to ask.

Machen and Dean, just back from Neva Snyder's house, were distinctly unfriendly as they stared at Gloria for several silent minutes.

Finally Dean spoke. "I'm Joe Dean and this is Harry Machen. We're investigating the death of Ed Davies," he said as he at last took the seat next to Gloria. Machen stayed silent, his penetrating green eyes never leaving her face. Both men possessed an intensity and focus that radiated from the core of their beings.

Dean went on to initiate some small talk about cigarettes, December weather and the flu going around town, but soon the polite conversation ended. "I'm going to advise you of your Miranda rights so that we're covering all the bases. And since you've studied for the bar, you're aware—"

"Am I under arrest?" Gloria interrupted, her stomach dropping to the floor. This was not the way things were supposed to proceed.

"No, not right now," Dean answered.

"Thanks a lot," she quipped, but knew quite well what the reading of her rights meant. Only suspects were Mirandized. *But how could I be a suspect?* She inhaled deeply. She had nothing to fear and nothing to hide and she hoped to be out of there fast. She decided to waive her rights to counsel and agree to speak with the police. After all, they only wanted to know about Fletcher and she could easily answer their questions on that topic; she'd known him only a couple of months and she thought he couldn't have been involved with the Davies robbery.

The detective pulled a Miranda waiver form from a briefcase and slid it across the table for her to sign. They explained her rights; she signed the agreement.

Then the real questioning began.

"Are you willing to talk to us about anything you may know about Ed Davies?" Dean asked.

"Yes," she said.

"Okay," Dean responded. "What can you tell us about Ed?"

"Nothing. I saw the report on TV and I know what Virgil told me last night about being questioned."

"I believe you have more information on Ed Davies' death than you are letting on," Dean said.

"But I don't," Gloria insisted. "I don't know anything about the man."

"How many times have you been to his house?"

"To whose house?"

"To Ed Davies' house."

"I've never been there."

"Never?"

"No," Gloria repeated and lit a cigarette, taking a huge inhale. *This is getting really weird*, she thought.

"You talk to his wife?" Dean continued.

"I've never been to his house," Gloria reiterated.

"Have you talked to his wife?" he repeated.

"I don't even know what she looks like. If I met her somewhere it's possible, but I can't think of where I would have met her."

"How about at her front door?"

"At her front door? I told you I've never been to the house. I don't know where it is."

Gloria's nerves were beginning to fray. The detectives kept asking her questions she'd already answered, pressing her to say something different from the answer she'd given—from the truth. She began to feel as if they were trying to break her, trip her up or force her to say something untrue. Their faces, body language and the tone of their voices were hostile.

Machen and Dean were convinced Gloria was involved with this crime. They knew she hadn't pulled the trigger, but they believed it was Gloria who had put Masse and DeSantis up to the job.

"Tell me what you know about a scheme to obtain some of Davies' money. Some of his metals," Dean continued, staring intently at her.

"A scheme to obtain his what? His metals? What do you mean by that?" Gloria asked confused.

"Precious metals. Gold. Silver coins."

"I don't know anything about it."

"Cash. Nothing?"

"Well, I know that obviously someone robbed him," Gloria replied sarcastically.

"How do you know that?" Dean pressed, leaning in.

"Because it said so in the paper," Gloria said matter-of-factly.

The questioning was going nowhere and Dean was frustrated. He decided to get more personal. "We've talked to a lot of people and your name comes up as an organizer," he said.

"An organizer of what?"

"Of the robbery."

"You're kidding," Gloria said disbelievingly, peering directly into the eyes of the stone-faced detectives. What she read in those eyes shocked her. She leaned back in her chair. "You're not, are you?" she asked, incredulous. "In the first place, that's hardly the sort of thing that's recommended if you're getting ready to take the bar exam. In the second place, I don't do robberies. It's that simple. I've never committed any crime except getting a parking ticket."

"Do you know Gary Masse or Stephen DeSantis?" Machen pressed on, showing her mug shots of both men whom she didn't recognize.

"I know a few Garys," she said, "but that last name doesn't sound familiar. And I can't think of anybody I know named Steve."

"You aren't being honest."

Gloria was flabbergasted, frightened and annoyed all at the same time. "I can't think of anyone named Steve and you tell me I'm not being honest?"

"I'm referring to our entire conversation and your knowledge of the situation regarding Ed Davies," Dean said coldly.

"The entire conversation seems to be circular," Gloria said. "You ask me a question. I give you an answer and then you say I'm not being honest. I can't tell you what I don't know."

"Then tell me what you do know."

"I am!" she exclaimed, exasperated. "Why don't you tell me what you're thinking so I can help?"

"That's not the way it works." Dean shook his head.

Besides the anonymous tip detectives had received—the tip telling them that a student at McGeorge named Gloria was the mastermind of the robbery—Joanne Masse had also told detectives that Gloria was in contact with her husband. Now Gloria's flip attitude and nervous manner were helping to convince Machen of her guilt. He later wrote in his report, "Her hands started to shake and she began to squirm in her chair a little bit during questioning."

For hours Machen and Dean continued to accuse her of planning the Davies robbery, asking the same questions over and over. Dean's eyes bored into her as he struggled to force what he was sure would be a confession.

Gloria desperately fought to keep her cool. "Look, officer," she said, "I know I'm going to lose this staring contest, but I haven't done anything wrong."

Finally, after three hours of fruitless questioning, both men stood. Out of Gloria's earshot, Machen said to Dean, "She ain't coppin' to shit."

They turned back and faced Gloria. "You are under arrest for the murder of Ed Davies," Dean announced. "We've recovered a lot of evidence and you're gonna be booked."

Gloria was stunned. "Uh," was all she could manage to utter.

"There's gonna be no bail," Dean continued, "and you're gonna be booked for murder." He waited for a response, staring down at her. "You telling us the truth?" he asked.

"Uh huh," a terrified Gloria replied.

"Are you willing to take a polygraph examination to prove what you talked about here?"

Now Gloria understood she was in serious trouble and that the time for talking was over. "If you're going to book me I want to talk to a lawyer. I won't answer any more questions if I'm being arrested," she declared.

The detectives pushed harder, but Gloria refused to answer any more questions. She invoked her right to remain silent and that infuriated Machen and Dean. Machen grabbed her purse off the table and promptly left the room and Gloria knew he was confiscating it to prepare a property report.

Dean reached down and pulled her up by the arm. When she stood, she felt as if she left her body. As Dean walked her down the hall to fingerprinting, she felt as if she were watching herself move, almost in slow motion.

"You know you did this," Dean said, staring at her with a sly smirk. "You're going to a place that a nice, little, white middle class girl like you don't even know exists. You're going to crack into a million pieces."

Silenced now, barely present, Gloria stood at the fingerprinting desk. The room was empty and Dean grabbed each of her fingers to press them to the ink and roll her fingers onto the book. She heard nothing in her head but silence. She stared at the prints and noticed the odd scars that eliminated whorls on her left thumb. A year earlier she had gotten a splinter on her thumb and it had never quite healed; she constantly picked at it, leaving the digit with a peculiar look. Her knees shook and she leaned against the wall for support. A single thought ran through her mind in a loop: *How can this be happening?*

Meanwhile, Machen was leafing through a small datebook he'd found in her purse. Gloria always carried the notebook, in which she logged addresses, wrote shopping lists and made notes about whatever came to mind. She'd developed the habit when she worked as a process server for an investigation business delivering summonses to people all over the city. She'd learned to dress up in wigs, glasses and costumes to pretend she was anything but a process server. Now Machen copied pages of the book in which she'd logged everything—including addresses of places and people she'd served. He marked three pages "of interest." On one she had written the address of a home a few houses down from the Davies' home. On a page marked "Trip Diary," Gloria had written: "Screen door latched," "brought anybody home WER," "where garage," "she always waiting in window," "don't approach at coin shop." Another page included Gloria's handwritten note: "grey hair," "tinted glasses," "height," "clothes," "gloves," "tape," "rope," "scanner." He logged the pages as evidence but never asked Gloria about their meaning or why she carried such addresses and descriptions in her purse.

Four hours had passed since Gloria had seen the outdoors and it was time to move her to the county jail. Dean and Machen cuffed her hands behind her, walked her to the back door of the homicide bureau and led her to a door. Dean's manner suddenly shifted from accusatory to friendly.

"You might want to cover up your face," he said as he reached to open the door. Gloria meekly nodded okay and Dean placed her sweater over her head.

Gloria stepped outside to cameras, lights and reporters. Bulbs flashed and she heard the crowd screaming her name, "Gloria! Gloria!"

Every television channel, radio station and newspaper in the state capital had been tipped off to the transfer of the alleged mastermind behind the Davies robbery-murder. Just a few nights after she had sat with her cat watching the news of the murder, Gloria Killian was the number one story on the same show.

| 5 |

Gloria

The cherubic four year-old sat in her toddler seat bolted to the metal table, her hands folded across her tiny chest. Her lips were pressed tightly together.

"Eat the rutabaga. You need to eat dinner," Mrs. Erby said, pushing a fork toward Gloria Goodwin's tightly clenched mouth.

"No, I don't," Gloria said, staring into the eyes of her foster mother, her tiny hand clutching the stuffed lamb her mother had bought her and that she carried everywhere since it smelled of her mom's favorite perfume. "You can't make me eat it."

"The rest of the children are eating it and you will too," Stan Erby said, peering over the black frames of his thick glasses, glancing sidelong at his three other children who were cowering at the far end of the table. But Gloria wasn't afraid. She'd been in and out of different foster homes, passed around like an unwanted, broken doll, since her single mother, Helen Goodwin, was accepted to a master's program in Minnesota and placed her tiny daughter in foster care in Sacramento so she could pursue her schooling. Seeing her mother only during summers and placed with strange new families each fall, by age four Gloria had developed into a strong, defiant girl. She disliked being with anyone who wasn't her mother. She hated living with these families she knew didn't really want her and though she longed for her pretty mother, Gloria wondered if her mother wanted her either.

She sat staring at Mr. and Mrs. Erby, her hands folded, quiet, unbending, unyielding, just like her mother had taught her to behave. If you sat there silently and said nothing, no one could do anything to you.

"You're not getting up from the table until the food is gone," Mr. Erby said while his wife cleared the table of the rest of the family's plates. Gloria sat silently in her chair for hours, refusing to eat. She thought mostly about her mother, Helen, about how much she missed her and how she wished Helen would come get her. Gloria often was sick, sniffling, allergic to everything it seemed. She thought her mom, in a nursing program, might have the medicine that would cure her. Helen could be cold and disapproving, but she was better than the foster care moms and Gloria adored her.

Gloria's thoughts turned to her father, James Horace Goodwin, who had died before she was born and whose framed picture she kept as one of her few prized possessions. She imagined her handsome father laughing and dancing with her mother. Gloria daydreamed at the table until almost 11 P.M. when Mr. Erby walked into the kitchen and found her asleep, head on the table, rutabagas untouched. He picked her up and carried her to bed, amazed by her obstinacy and her ability to sit silently, internalize and withstand whatever came her way.

Most summers, Helen sent Gloria to stay in Washington on the fruit farm run by her brother Edgar and his wife, Louella. Edgar, like Helen and the rest of the stoic family, was stiff and quiet, but Louella was fun. She enjoyed her clubs and activities and she even loved little, talkative Gloria. Gloria adored sitting on Louella's bed and watching her dress in matching suits and hats. This, she was certain, was when she developed her passion for fashion.

Edgar, in his quiet way, cared for the lonely child. Every morning Gloria gripped Edgar's large hand and followed him as he did his daily rounds of the farm, letting her "help" him with the chores. When he laid irrigation pipe, Gloria carried the sprinkler heads and placed them wherever Edgar pointed. When he drove the tractor he let her stand on the hitch and ride behind him. When it came time to pick peaches, she picked from the bottom branches. Edgar even bought her a pair of rubber waders so she could follow him through the fields. At the end of each summer Edgar "paid" Gloria for her work, taking her shopping for clothes and school supplies before she went back to Sacramento and another foster home. Even with Edgar and Louella's affection, Gloria was lonely, for her only playmates on the farm were the dogs.

By the time Gloria turned six, her mother had finished her master's degree and returned to Sacramento for good. This time she brought her own mother, Mina, who was seeking to escape an unhappy marriage, to Sacramento to help take care of Gloria.

Helen wasn't fond of her mother, but with her new job as a nurse anesthetist at the hospital she was making enough money to afford two adjoining apartments in a small Victorian house in the nice part of downtown Sacramento. Gloria ran from apartment to apartment through the connecting door that was always open and mother and grandmother, with their separate spaces, could keep their distance. Gloria, with no bedroom of her own, slept on her mother's living room couch.

Helen loved her work at the hospital. She was smart and pretty and men were attracted to her. Before long the thirty-year-old Helen had a steady boyfriend: an Italian man with a warm smile named Lou Cima. Lou, only slightly taller than Helen, who was five feet six inches, was olive-skinned with a Roman nose and cropped salt and pepper hair. He was sweet-natured, gregarious and always had a smile on his face. Gloria adored him. Lou worked weekends as a card dealer at a card club and sometimes took Gloria there with him while Helen was at work.

"C'mon, Junie, let's go play some cards," Lou often said and picked up little Gloria and carried her over to his car parked out in front of their apartment. He called her Junie, because he said she was bright and sunny like the month of June.

"You bet," she always answered, her smiling face pressed against his scratchy wool shirt, breathing in the scent of his ever-present cigar. They drove to the club where most days he sat her on a stack of magazines beside him at his table. While he dealt cards, she read comics and storybooks he'd brought from the cigar shop he worked in downtown. Sometimes he let her come to the cigar shop with him, too.

"You wanna work the register today, Junie?" he called out from the living room and Gloria ran to the door, excited to help him. He taught the bright young girl to work the cash register and to deal with the public and because Gloria was always small for her age, he bought her an extra tall stool that he put beside the register so she could watch the transactions and make change for the customers. By the time she was ten, Gloria was running the front counter all by herself.

Lou bought her gifts and toys. Gloria's mom and grandmother rarely bought her anything but necessities. When she was seven years old, he bought her a large stuffed panda that was bigger than she was.

"If you want it you can have it, but you're carrying it home," Lou told her. Gloria picked up the bear and walked the ten blocks home, refusing all assistance from family or people passing by staring at the little girl and the huge bear.

Unfortunately, Grandmother Mina hated Lou, so he refused to come around when Mina was there, which was most of the time. Helen and Lou spent most of their time together out of the house, their dates often in local motels. Sometimes they took Gloria along and she spent hours swimming in the pool or reading books.

Gloria was sixteen when Helen and Lou finally married. That night Helen insisted Lou was moving into their house, but Mina forbade it.

Uncharacteristically, the two women began to scream at each other and as the fight escalated, Lou picked up his coat, yelled that he couldn't take it and stormed out.

Gloria was terrified; no one in their house ever raised a voice and now she sensed danger. "Gloria, let's go." Helen pulled her frightened daughter out of the house to Lou, who was waiting downstairs. Gloria had never seen him so agitated and red-faced and the uproar terrified her.

For the next few hours the three of them walked around the block in silence, the quiet punctuated by only occasional whispers between Helen and Lou. It was after midnight when Helen and Gloria returned upstairs, but Lou never came back.

He simply vanished from their lives and Gloria was too afraid to ask Helen what had happened. Gloria knew that, even if she had asked, it wouldn't have mattered. Helen told Gloria only what she wanted her to know, nothing else. Gloria mourned for the father she almost had.

Almost a year later Helen took Gloria to the mall. Gloria believed it was going to be a normal shopping day, but as they parked the car, Helen looked at her daughter and solemnly, "We're here to say goodbye to Lou."

Gloria didn't know what to say. *Say goodbye? Where has Lou been? What is going on?* But she didn't dare ask these questions aloud and so she followed her mother into the food court where Lou sat alone at a table, ignoring the din of the yapping, hungry shoppers swirling around him.

He stood as they approached; he kissed Helen's cheek. He looked thin and forlorn, his broad smile gone.

Gloria hugged him and they sat down. Gloria looked around, inhaling the smell of greasy hot dogs and fresh popcorn, confused by the strangeness of this scene.

"How are you?" she asked.

"I'm okay. Are you?" Lou asked. She nodded yes and they sat in silence, the air thick with unspoken words and feelings. After a while they chatted about nothing in particular and thirty minutes later Helen and Gloria stood up and left. Gloria never saw Lou again and Helen never again mentioned his name.

Gloria moved out of the sad, solemn house as soon as she graduated high school. She was so different from her mother; even in that quiet, stifled atmosphere, she had grown up to be talkative and gregarious. "As friendly as a dog in a meat house," Helen often said, making fun of what she saw as Gloria's desperate need for attention and affection.

Gloria decided to go far away to a place filled with adventure and men: Alaska.

It was exotic and different and the attractive girl with the big blue eyes, long dark hair and curvaceous figure found herself attracting the admiration and attention she so desperately craved. Men were a whole new adventure and, for Gloria, lots of fun.

For two years she played the field in Sitka and Juneau working odd jobs: a dispatcher for a cab company in Sitka, a waitress in a Filipino restaurant in Juneau. She explored nature and nightlife with equal passion, with frequent visits to the Mendenhall Glacier and local clubs. It was at a restaurant in Juneau where she met her new boyfriend. He was a well-traveled, educated and charming man who wore silk suits and a set of solid gold rings that he had bought in Hong Kong. To Gloria he seemed exotic and sophisticated. He entertained Gloria with fantastic tales of his childhood and with stories of his travels around the world. One night while they were having dinner, her boyfriend removed his solid gold pinky ring, leaned across the table and put it on Gloria's finger.

"A beautiful woman should wear beautiful jewelry," he said.

"This is too much," Gloria said, handing him back the ring. His smile disappeared.

"It belongs on your hand," he said, refusing to take the ring back. "And I want you to have it."

But it proved to be more of a gesture of control than one of love. His tales of travel, romance and love morphed into stories of women he had hurt or killed and he sent Gloria greeting cards designed for people who were in the hospital or recovering from accidents. He told her he thought they were funny, but Gloria understood: These were threats.

One night Gloria made dinner for a male friend and in the middle of dinner, her boyfriend and his brother showed up at her apartment dressed like movie gangsters in trench coats and fedoras.

"Get out or I'll kill you," Gloria's boyfriend told her male friend. When he left, Gloria's boyfriend told her a tale of a woman he knew in the Philippines whose husband threw acid in her face when she tried to leave him. Gloria felt this was an even more aggressive threat than the earlier ones, but she didn't know what to do. Weeks later, he showed up at her apartment unannounced wielding a tiny brown bottle.

"You know what this is," he said with a sinister smile. "Acid."

That was it. Gloria quit her job, found a new apartment and became a dispatcher for the Alaska State Troopers. She hoped that working for the police would scare her former boyfriend, but he continued to harass her at her new job, calling her and telling her she was being watched, accurately describing the clothes she was wearing even when he was nowhere in sight. She reported his behavior to the troopers, but the troopers told her they could do nothing until there was an incident and she was hurt. The whole thing seemed terribly unfair and unjust. She thought about getting a lawyer but couldn't afford one. She even considered becoming a lawyer herself and laughed at the thought. She had no money and had never even gone to college.

Afraid for her life, she left Alaska and returned to Sacramento and the crossed arms of her mother.

Gloria sat at the bar on the ground floor of the *Sacramento Union* newspaper building, a glass in hand and surrounded by men. Since she'd returned to Sacramento, she'd been having lots of fun dating, working and playing the field. It was a time of freedom and Gloria was enjoying her life as a single girl.

But when Gerry Killian walked in one day to find his usual group of friends circling a talkative, petite blue-eyed charmer at the bar, he seemed enchanted.

Gloria was everything the blond-haired, blue-eyed electrician wasn't. She was good looking and full of life and he knew right away he wanted her. He pursued her, taking her out to fancy restaurants, buying her the expensive clothes she loved and offering her the kind of security she felt she had never had.

Gerry was well-built, solid and assured, with the large family that Gloria had always fantasized about. He radiated stability and was close to his seven siblings and parents.

Initially she wasn't attracted to him. And she didn't seem interested in an exclusive relationship. After all, he was eight years older and a divorced father of four and Gloria liked to play the field. But he was very charming, persistent and a wonderful lover. He overcame her reservations by convincing her that she would always be safe with him and she would never be abandoned again. When he asked Gloria to marry him ten months after they met, she agreed.

Gloria knew Gerry had children but they didn't live with him and he saw them only for visitation. But one week after the wedding, his ten-year-old son came to stay with his father and his new bride. Gloria was twenty-six years old, with no resources for mothering a child. Gerry asked Gloria to quit her job to take care of the boy and, like the obedient young woman she'd been raised to be, she did. Gloria tried very hard to play the mother role for five long years, but for her, those years were lonely and difficult. By the time Gloria was thirty and Gerry's son had reached high school, she pushed Gerry to let her return to work and to her amazement, it was he who suggested she take this opportunity to fulfill her dream to go to law school.

She had no idea how to go about getting into law school, but she was determined. At the library she researched local law schools and their admissions criteria. She discovered it was possible to challenge any course or degree in the California University system by passing a test to earn credit for the course and learned she could be admitted to McGeorge Law School without a college degree. Gloria studied day and night, took a myriad of college level tests besides the Law School Admission Test (LSAT), scored remarkably high and was admitted to the four-year evening program at the prestigious University of the Pacific, McGeorge School of Law.

When she received the acceptance letter, she was thrilled and scared at the same time. She knew all her fellow students would have college degrees and this left her feeling insecure. Aware of possible issues, the dean started her in summer school to give her a chance to acclimate to the intense pressure of law school. McGeorge was known for its unusually high State Bar passage rate, which was achieved by weeding out half of every first-year class. It was enough to scare most people, but not Gloria. She completed summer school with high marks and merged with the incoming class in the fall.

Professor Sheldon Grossfeld's family law class was fascinating for a number of reasons. Gloria loved to listen to the erudite professor who was exceedingly well-dressed and well-spoken. Sometimes she imagined being his law partner or clerking for him. There weren't many students in the family law class and it was taught in a small classroom as opposed to the larger lecture rooms.

One of her classmates, Kent Finch, was a married man around her age. The smart, seductive, fast-talking law student was exactly the kind of man Gloria was drawn to. He was handsome, very well-dressed and exceedingly charming, with enough of the bad boy patina to pique Gloria's interest. He asked her to join his study group and introduced her to his friends. While at first Gloria found herself attracted to Kent, she wasn't looking for a fling. She was married and had a family. But after their shared classes and during breaks Kent was always around, joking with her and debating the fine points of law. He had a great sense of humor, which Gloria liked.

One day in class the professor questioned them at least a dozen times, "Is it *a* bale of hay? Or *the* bale of hay?" Gloria and Kent spent that night studying in the law library trying to grasp the contract law concept of the particular versus the general. As Gloria stared across the table at Kent's intense eyes which were riveted on her, she felt as if her head was spinning and she couldn't tear her gaze away from him. They were the last people in the law library and they continued to stare at each until the librarian finally blinked the lights to get their attention that the library was closing.

Before long the affair became far more powerful than any Gloria ever had. She'd never before fallen in love—not even with her husband—and had always believed she wasn't capable of the intense passionate love she saw in movies or read about in books. With Kent things were different and she felt madly in love with him. They made each other laugh and their sex was intensely satisfying. She began to feel jealous of his wife and in turn Kent disliked her husband.

For two years, even as she studied hard, they carried on a torrid affair, pushing each other to get divorced. Finally Gloria divorced Gerry and soon afterwards Kent left his wife. Once clear of the marriage hurdle, the tumultuous relationship began to crumble. Within a year of Gloria's divorce, she and Kent broke up and Gloria collapsed emotionally. She had given up everything for Kent and loved him desperately. Now she was alone and shattered, unable to think clearly, work or perform at school. Her depression was so deep, she sometimes didn't venture out of her apartment for days.

She asked her mother for help. She hoped her mother could recommend a psychiatrist from her hospital connections. But Helen refused, saying that was not how they handled things. Helen told Gloria she simply needed to get past this and to move on as Helen had.

No matter what was going on in Gloria's life she still felt obligated to take her mother out every week. In the back of her mind Gloria always hoped, *Maybe if I do everything she wants she'll find a way to love me.* One day when they were driving to the store, Helen made a shocking announcement.

"There's something I need to tell you," Helen said flatly. "James Horace Goodwin is not your real father."

The shock was so palpable, Gloria almost drove the car into a wall. The handsome pilot in that black and white photo—the one she waved to and blew kisses to when her mother wasn't looking—wasn't her father? How could her mother have kept a secret so enormous for thirty-five years?

"Well then, who is?" Gloria asked.

Helen fidgeted slightly in her seat, still refusing to look at her daughter. She didn't like being questioned. She gave out information as she saw fit and when she saw fit. No more and no less.

"A country western singer," Helen said begrudgingly.

Gloria stared at her mother. *A singer? How interesting*, she thought. She had a beautiful singing voice while the rest of the family did not. She wondered if he was a friendly type, gregarious like her. She waited a moment for Helen to continue, but her mother just sat there.

"Anyone in particular?" Gloria asked, trying to smile, to ease her mother's obvious burden. She knew how hard this must be for her.

Helen never talked about her ex-husband or even about Grandma. To her, if something or someone was gone, it was gone.

"I don't want to talk about it anymore," Helen said abruptly and turned away.

"Well, at least tell me his name," Gloria pleaded, knowing quite well once her mom refused to talk, she'd get nothing from her.

"You'll find out after I'm gone," Helen said. "Don't ask again."

While enlisted as a nurse at the Fort Bliss Army Hospital in El Paso, Helen and her boyfriend, a country singer whose career was on the rise, went on vacation to Hollywood.

Her time in Hollywood was a blur of fun, celebrity, music and laughter. She came home from the club that first night with a beautiful, hand-painted black and white portrait, just like the famous one of Rita Hayworth. Her boyfriend had it framed and when she returned to the base, she placed it prominently on her night table, a constant reminder of her wonderful week in glamorous Hollywood.

But she'd also brought along another reminder of that week; she was pregnant. She learned quickly that her Texas troubadour, though fun and exciting, wasn't looking for commitment or children. Within weeks he was gone and back on the road. Helen was left on the base alone, in a quandary about what to do about the pregnancy. She knew about abortions since she was a nurse. But abortions were illegal and a stern Lutheran voice inside her left her with too much guilt even to consider that course. Having the child unwed was not an option either. She couldn't possibly tell her mother or her family her tale of love, abandonment and a bastard child.

So Helen concocted a plan she hoped would solve all of her problems. She asked a pilot friend from the base, James Horace Goodwin, a tall, lanky, local Texas boy, to marry her, give her child a name and to travel with her to Washington to act out a charade for her family. He agreed to put on a good front for her parents, to give the baby a legitimate name and then to be on his way, with no further responsibility for the child.

Jim Goodwin was an easygoing sort and he had a great time in Washington. He fished, ate steak, potatoes and a special Norwegian treat of lefsa with her parents and spent the weekend acting out the ruse. Helen counted the days until she could return to El Paso, far from her family's judgmental eyes. She missed the independent life she had created for herself.

After a week Jim and Helen returned to the base and their separate lives. A few weeks before the baby was due, Helen concocted one more lie. She told her parents Jim had died on a flight mission in Europe and then Helen gave birth to a beautiful, bright-eyed daughter she named Gloria Marie. She wrote James Goodwin's name as the father on Gloria's birth certificate.

In July, with just one semester left before graduation and unable to get past her breakup with Kent and the news about her father, Gloria decided she had to take a leave of absence from law school. She felt she couldn't move on. Instead, she locked herself in her apartment and medicated herself with alcohol and diet pills—the pills that Helen had introduced her to when she was only twelve, the pills that helped her combat her tendency to put on weight. She was so depressed that some days she couldn't move and her mind ran in obsessive circles.

It was in that frame of mind that she grudgingly gave in to a friend's request to go to dinner and a club. At dinner she was introduced to Darlene Larsen, who had come along with one of the women Gloria didn't know. Darlene also seemed depressed and she looked like if she too had been dragged out for a night of fun.

Darlene had a boyfriend, a handsome biker named Dale Herbst whom she loved madly but who seemed to be giving her the blues.

Gloria and Darlene bonded instantly over their mutual heartbreak, feeling each other's pain and agony. For a short while they were inseparable. Darlene introduced Gloria to a group of disreputable friends including Dale and a good friend of his, Neva Snyder. Neva seemed the perfect new pal for Gloria; they both liked jewelry and antiques. But Darlene was nervous about having Dale too close to Gloria. While they were similar in size and shape, Gloria was much prettier than Darlene and Darlene knew her boyfriend had a weakness for a pretty face.

Gloria didn't see these people for who they really were. She was reeling from the breakup with Kent and took up with whoever was nice to her, no matter who they were or what they did. Most of the time she walked around dazed, an emotional wreck.

Lonely and devastated, looking to replace the loss rather than heal, Gloria took up with a new boyfriend, Brian Byers.

One night when Gloria was at Brian's, Gloria's apartment was broken into and everything of value she owned—her jewelry, her stereo, her art objects and her television—were stolen. When she walked in and found the mess, she immediately called the police and told them she felt that Darlene, with whom she had recently had a falling out, was responsible.

The police took the call but no arrest followed. It was just another of the spate of robberies that were plaguing Sacramento during that year. In the past few months the police had gotten reports of numerous home invasions and Gloria's was just one more. But Gloria began to feel afraid to stay alone in the apartment. She asked Brian to help her find another place—somewhere she could leave her cat, Miss Kitty, her law books and the few things the burglar hadn't taken.

Regrettably, Brian introduced her to Virgil Fletcher.

| 6 |

Pressure Mounts

Bringing Gary Masse in was easier than Lieutenant Biondi imagined. The detectives had help from Joanne, who seemed almost anxious to get rid of her drug-addicted husband. After she went to see the thick-mustached, dark-eyed Italian lead detective, she put strong pressure on her husband to turn himself in.

For two days Joanne paced her parents' living room, badgering her scared, pathetic husband. Masse hadn't stopped popping pills for days and he was out of it, sluggish, stupid and stoned.

"The cops know, Gary. You need to turn yourself in," Joanne said, prodding his rank, bloated body that barely left the couch. Masse's hands shook. He wasn't eating or sleeping. His haunted black eyes were red-rimmed. His hair and beard were matted. He smelled of sweat and fear.

"I'm not going to jail again. I ain't gonna admit to anything," he told his wife. "I'd rather blow my brains out than do more time in prison. You know that."

"You've got to talk to the police. What if Steve goes in first?"

"Steve ain't going anywhere. He left town."

"You've got to turn yourself in," Joanne persisted. "It'll look better. They know you're here."

"But I ain't admitting anything. If I go back to prison, they'll kill me in there." Masse knew his years as an informant wouldn't help his reputation in prison.

Joanne picked up the phone. "You need to talk to Biondi. He'll help us. He'll make sure you'll be safe."

Joanne dialed. "Lieutenant Ray Biondi, please. It's Joanne Masse."

Biondi picked up the phone, adrenaline pumping. He knew Joanne was trying to help bring her husband in.

"Hi, Joanne," he answered. "Look, I need to speak to Gary."

"Okay. I'll get him."

Biondi waited, excited. They almost had him. He turned to Machen, sitting at an adjoining desk.

"Harry, get a tape recorder on this phone quick. We're getting Masse on the line."

"Hello," Gary's slurred, slow voice came on the line.

"Gary, this is Lieutenant Biondi. You need to come in and give yourself up."

"I don't know what to do," Masse whined. "I can't. Those guys are out to kill me and if they catch up with me they will kill me."

"What guys?" Biondi asked. "No one's going to hurt you here."

"Bullshit. All you guys want to do is put me in jail and I can't be in jail. I got, like, a…a nervous condition. "

"We'll take care of you."

"Bullshit," Masse exclaimed again. "I don't know what to do. I might as well blow my brains out rather than do time in jail. I can't go to prison. If I go to prison they will kill me. I'm really in a bad spot."

"Look," Biondi said, "we're going to be right there for you, but you understand, we are going to arrest you for the murder of Mr. Davies and the attempted murder of Mrs. Davies. But listen, Gary, what we're really interested in is the person who actually pulled the trigger and if, at some point, we can prove that you didn't pull the trigger, we can work out some kind of deal, understand?"

"But they're going to try and kill me."

"We'll protect you," Biondi pressed. "But first you have to come down and turn yourself in and talk to us."

Masse started to sweat. He was so heavily into the drugs he knew he couldn't go cold turkey in the sheriff's office. He was too addicted. Too high.

"I can't come in without my…my, uh, special medication from my doctor. I've been on some heavy shit since I got shot a couple years back." Masse had been shot through the scrotum in an attempted robbery and was in constant pain. "I can't talk without my medication. I need to see my doctor before I come in."

Biondi asked for the doctor's name and number, which Masse gave him. Machen called the doctor to find out what medications Masse was taking while Biondi stayed on the line with Masse.

"We have your doctor on the line, Gary. Come on in. You'll be okay," Biondi reassured him.

"No," Masse said. "I need to talk to my doctor myself. And I won't be okay. Only reason you want me to come in is to fuckin' clear this case. You don't give a shit about me. All you care about is clearing this case."

"Of course we want to clear this case and find the killers. That's why we want you to cooperate."

"You guys set this whole thing up," Masse said, breaking into tears.

"I don't understand," Biondi said. "You mean the Sheriff's Department?"

"You guys set the whole thing up so you can make a case against him."

"Listen, Gary, whoever set anything up is going to be arrested. Tell me who set it up and if your information is good, we'll arrest him."

"I didn't know there was going to be any violence. The guy is crazy," Gary cried.

"What guy?"

"I'd rather not say."

"Look, Masse, you're in a tough spot. DeSantis is looking to kill you, Gloria is after the loot and the cops are after you for the homicide charge. You either have to come in or run. You got the resources to run?"

"Whaddya mean, resources?"

"Money, a car, a place to stay to hide from the cops."

"I don't have shit. Look, I gotta go," Masse said and quickly hung up the phone.

Biondi called the Masse house in Del Paso Heights looking for Gary, but again got only the eldest daughter saying neither parent was home. When Biondi tried to play back the tape that Machen made of the phone call, nothing was on the tape. The recorder had apparently malfunctioned. Biondi transcribed the contents of the call from his memory.

The day after Gloria Killian was arrested, Joanne turned her husband in. Gary Masse was quiet, sullen and stoned when Biondi and Hash met them at the back of the Sheriff's headquarters at 3:30 that afternoon. Immediately they Mirandized Masse, who told them he wanted to talk to an attorney. They booked him and put him into a cell.

Joanne, however, asked for no such privileges, wanting to talk some more about DeSantis. She knew a wife could not be forced to testify against her husband, but she could say whatever she needed about DeSantis.

The cops placed Joanne in a small interview room with Sergeant Hash, where she told him she heard that after shooting the victims once each in the head, DeSantis left with Masse. DeSantis went back four times to clean out the house and that was probably when he shot Ed Davies in the head a second time, when Masse wasn't there. She also heard DeSantis sold $2500 worth of silver to the son of the owner of an auto wrecker.

Afterwards she asked to see her husband. They said goodbye and she went free, never to see the inside of a jail cell herself. Masse would never leave one.

| 7 |

First Night in "The Dungeon"

At the time, the Sacramento jail was housed in an ancient building considered a nightmare by all those who knew it. Built in the 1840s, it had served as the state capitol in the 1850s.

In criminal circles, the jail had earned the nickname "The Dungeon" for good reason: The walls were always damp, the bars were solid metal and the jailers walked around carrying huge rounds of skeleton keys. The entire building smelled of dust, mold, sweat and human excrement.

Gloria, who had never been arrested, was thrown into a place she couldn't have imagined in her wildest nightmares.

The women housed in the female division of the Sacramento County jail were a mix of hustlers, whores and drug addicts. As in many jails, there were those who treated the penal system as a revolving door: a couple of months in, a few months out and back in again. The cops knew the girls, the girls knew one another and everyone knew the rules and how to get along. Everyone, that is, except Gloria.

Not only was she new, she was booked for murder. Female murderers are a rarity, particularly in crimes that don't involve domestic violence. When women kill, it's usually a husband, a partner or someone they know. A woman who kills a stranger for money is an anomaly and someone many officers and prisoners consider should be shunned. Female cops particularly dislike female killers and when they get one, the catch is like landing a big fish: a capture meant to be enjoyed and savored.

Dean walked Gloria into the female section of the jail and handed her to three policewomen who once again fingerprinted her. Afterward, Gloria stood silently, picking at the black ink which had rendered her hands and nails filthy. She had always taken excellent care of her hands and nails and seeing them this way made her uncomfortable. She focused on her hands to avoid her terror.

"Come with me," one of the cops said and walked her into a small grey room with a bench. The other cops followed and the last one in closed the door.

"Can I wash my hands first?" Gloria asked. The cops ignored her.

"Undress," the first cop ordered. The policewomen watched as Gloria stripped down to her underwear, folding her pants and shirt into a neat pile.

She stood there almost naked, embarrassed and cold.

The three women began to laugh and one pointed at her under-clothes. "Take those off, honey," she said.

Gloria stared at the officer and then slowly took off her panties and bra, carefully folding these on top of her pile of clothing. She began to shiver with cold and fear.

"Open your mouth," the policewoman said. She picked up a small flashlight and looked into Gloria's open mouth and ears.

"Pop your hands on your head," the cop continued and when Gloria obeyed, the woman checked her underarms. "Lift those up," she added, nodding toward Gloria's breasts. Gloria did as told as the women looked under her breasts to make sure she had hidden no weapons or drugs. When Gloria reached to pick up her blouse, the women began to laugh again. "We're not done."

The third cop put on a pair of rubber gloves and Gloria stared, mortified.

"Squat and cough," the cop said. As Gloria squatted the officer held a mirror between Gloria's legs to look into her vagina. "Now bend over, spread 'em and cough," she ordered and Gloria felt eyes on her anus. She felt sick and violated. As one officer took away her jeans and blouse, logging in what she owned, the others doused her with white powder then handed her an orange jumpsuit.

The powder burned her throat and eyes. "What's this?" Gloria managed to ask between hacking coughs.

"Lice powder, honey. You'll need it. Now get dressed."

"Please, may I have my phone call now?" Gloria begged.

The officers didn't respond but one marched her to a holding cell and shoved a red pay telephone on wheels in behind her. Gloria was shaking so hard, she could barely hold the receiver. She stared at the phone, trying to figure out how to make a call without a dime. Utterly at a loss, she glanced around the room, focusing on the bail bonds company advertisements plastered on the walls of the cell. Finally, Gloria realized she would need to call collect. She picked up the phone with shaking fingers, unable to remember anyone's number. She took a deep breath, sat down and when her breathing was somewhere near normal, she remembered. She dialed Brian's number.

"Hi, baby," he said. His voice brought on the deluge of tears she'd been fighting back all afternoon.

"Honey, I've been arrested," she choked out between sobs. "Please tell my mom. I don't want her to find out some other way."

"I'm so sorry, babe," Brian said. "But she knows. Everyone knows. It was all over the news."

"What is happening to me?" Gloria wept. "Call Neva. I want Ken Jaffe."

Gloria's newest best friend for the last year couldn't be more different from the law students she had befriended in her first three years at law school. Not only was Neva Snyder old enough to be her mother, but also she was a small-time crank dealer and user of crystal meth. She had her defense lawyer Ken Jaffe on speed dial.

For the past fifteen years Jaffe had been butting heads with the Sacramento prosecutor's office. He had one of the highest success rates in the state and in criminal circles he was known as the kind of lawyer you needed if it was going to be a rough case. What Gloria knew was that he was a great lawyer and from her perspective at that moment, that was all that mattered.

She glanced up through her tears at the female cops who sneered at her. In an effort to regain her sense of dignity, she straightened her spine, dried her eyes and vowed that no matter what, she wouldn't let these cops see any weakness. She was, after all, Helen's daughter. She said goodbye to Brian.

"I am finished with the phone," she said tersely to the officers. "Thank you."

They led her out of the holding cell to an eight-woman tank. One cop pulled out a key ring, unlocked the door and motioned to Gloria to go inside. Two steps in she heard the bars slam behind her and the lock click shut.

The cell smelled of urine and sweat but mostly of lice spray. The lights were dim and the air was damp and cold. There were six other women in the cell. Gloria's gaze landed on a young woman slouched on a bench in the back. Her hair was strange, almost moving. She stared at the girl for a few moments and slowly realized that it wasn't her hair that was moving; it was the lice that crawled through her hair. Gloria moved to a corner as far from the woman as she could and sat alone on a dirty wooden bench. As she stared at the other women, she tried to imagine what she could possibly have in common with them. Most were younger than she was; many were of color; each wore a tough, been-there-done-that expression. One or two had the nodded-out look of drug addicts. All of them scared her.

Within minutes a young man in a suit rushed up to the bars and called her name.

"Gloria! Gloria Killian! I'm from the public defender's office and we won't be representing you," he said. "I am here to warn you: Whatever you do, don't say a word and don't talk to anyone." With that he vanished.

She shook her head, still more puzzled. *Talk about what? With whom?* She had already told the police everything she knew.

A few minutes later, a young woman with highly styled blonde hair and wearing an orange jumpsuit was marched down the hall. The cell door opened and the woman was pushed inside. She took a seat beside Gloria.

Gloria was overjoyed. This woman seemed to be from an upscale background. Here, at last, was someone she might be able to talk to.

"Hi. Let's hope we're not here long," the woman said, smiling at Gloria.

"You don't wanna be talking to her," a pretty, dark-haired woman from the opposite corner of the cell said before Gloria could respond. "She's a cop."

"Oh, thanks," Gloria said. She stood and walked over to the woman. They sat down beside each other on another bench. "My name's Delores," the woman said. "You hungry?"

Gloria nodded yes and tears formed in her eyes. This was the first kindness anyone had shown her in hours and the gesture was balm. Delores stood again, walked to the far corner of the cell and returned with a small box of cereal. She handed it to Gloria and Gloria ate in grateful silence, but they said little to each other the rest of the day.

That night she sat trembling and staring at the filthy walls, stunned, unable to sleep or even close her eyes.

The next morning, the cops returned. Due to a federal lawsuit settlement, prisoners were to be held in the downtown Sacramento jail only for one day or for court appearances. They were not permitted to sleep there for more than twenty-four hours.

Exhausted and hungry, Gloria was taken to another holding cell where she was handcuffed, belly chained and her feet shackled. In the prison world, belly chains and shackles mean you are dangerous, someone to be feared. A murderer. Her humiliation was complete. She shuffled to a waiting van as the others stared at her. Gloria wasn't "on the chain" like the rest of the prisoners being transferred, who were merely handcuffed and chained to one another. Rather, she was heavily secured and kept away from the others.

The van drove forty minutes to the Rio Cosumnes Correctional Center (RCCC) in Elk Grove. "The Branch," as it was called by those who inhabited it, was a fairly new facility, fewer than ten years old and clean. When Gloria arrived, the request from the homicide bureau was honored and she was booked as a dangerous person. They placed her in a special cell, one called the iron tomb, normally used to house women who were dangerous either to themselves or to others or for psychotics who required close observation. It was also the cell the cops employed in an effort to make people break down and confess. It had no windows and the door was solid metal. Lights were controlled from the outside and were always dim. An intercom speaker in the corner of the ceiling emitted a steady low drone and was on constantly so guards could listen to anything happening inside.

A sheriff's officer unchained Gloria and gave her a yellow T-shirt and blue pants with RCCC printed in white block letters down the leg. The officer walked Gloria to her new cell, placed her inside and closed the door.

Gloria's first response when she noticed the speaker was to laugh. *Do they think I am going to write out a confession and read it aloud to them?*

Do they expect me to yell out that I did it? She sat down on the bed and stared into the dimness. Her mind was moving quickly, replaying recent events and trying to figure out what she needed to do to get herself out of there. She was terrified, but she would not give in to the fear.

Once again she did not sleep.

For the next two days, Gloria saw no one except police officers—no friends, no family, no lawyer. Every few hours the police moved her, transporting her back and forth from The Branch to county jail numerous times, which made scheduling a meeting with Jaffe or a visit with Brian impossible. But she remained silent.

On her third day, Brian and Gloria's mother finally coordinated a visit with her. Helen rarely went out and lived off disability payments and a veteran's pension. Now, visiting the daughter she so seldom saw, she remained her silent, stoic self. She had never liked her daughter's gregarious nature. "You're as friendly as a dog in a meat house," she had always said. "It's only going to get you in trouble." Now she felt she had been proven right.

When Gloria saw the two of them through the glass partition, she fought back tears. Then she picked up the phone receiver to speak to them.

"Mom, you know I didn't—" but before she could say another word, her mother interrupted. "Of course you didn't. Don't say another thing about it."

Gloria stared at Brian for a moment, who then picked up his receiver.

"I need money for Ken Jaffe fast," she said. "Sell whatever jewelry I have and sell the oosik. We should get a couple of thousand for that."

While living in Alaska, an elderly Inuit she had befriended had given her a rare oosik, a carved petrified walrus penis, as a gift. It was an unusual talisman, supposed to be very lucky and worth a lot of money. The thought of giving it up hurt Gloria's heart, but she knew she had no choice. After that the three of them talked about the weather, the food and the cat—anything but the case. Helen and Brian promised they would return as soon as they got the money to Jaffe.

Within hours of their visit, Helen and Brian had gathered up everything of value Gloria owned and had emptied their own bank accounts as well. Everything totaled came to twenty thousand dollars. This they gave to Jaffe as a retainer.

Later that day, police walked Gloria to the small grey attorney's room where Ken Jaffe was already waiting. He was tall, slim, good-looking and, at close to forty years old, already had a thriving law practice. He stood as they brought Gloria in. She noticed his expensive suit and kindly expression. She was impressed with both. She took a seat at the table and offered her hand.

Jaffe spoke first. "Say very little—I suspect the attorney room is bugged."

"I'm not surprised," Gloria said and shook her head. She looked into Jaffe's eyes and saw something there that made her trust him and listen to him.

"You know you're being charged with murder, attempted murder, robbery, burglary and grand theft auto," he said.

Gloria started to laugh. "Grand theft auto? How's that?"

"A car and a telephone truck were stolen."

"Jeez, what's next?" she asked.

"You'll be arraigned tomorrow, but don't worry, they have no real evidence against you."

"What should I do?"

"Sit tight. I'll see you then."

He stood to leave, then turned and smiled at her. "By the way, I put some money on your books."

"Thanks," Gloria said, though she didn't have a clue what he meant. She didn't know jail slang beyond what she had learned her first day— a "fish kit" was the basic toiletry kit that contained the bare necessities: toothbrush, toothpaste, comb. She figured she would ask Judy Bracamonte, the trustee whom she had "met" through the flap what "on the books" meant. Each cell door had a flap for passing meals through and on Gloria's second day Judy had opened the flap, leaned down and asked Gloria if she needed anything like soap or tampons.

"No," Gloria said, unnerved at the strange feeling of talking to a disembodied voice outside a door flap. "Who are you?"

"I'm a friend," Gloria heard Judy say. She listened harder and heard her take a seat outside in the long hallway lined with cells. Then Judy passed Gloria a couple of cigarettes and a bar of chocolate through the flap.

"Thanks," Gloria said.

"So what was it like?" Judy asked bluntly.

"What was what like?"

"You know, the crime," Judy whispered conspiratorially. Judy, Gloria learned later, was a drug addict, a known police snitch and a trustee of the women's jail. "Did you tell anyone? Did you call anyone?"

Gloria remembered the public defender's words about talking to people in jail and she did not talk about the murder. Still, she was glad to accept the candy and cigarettes and she sat on her floor wondering how stupid these people thought she was. Between the speakers and the trustees, it seemed they thought she was bursting to confess something she hadn't done.

When she asked Judy what "on the books" meant, the trustee explained this was money in her jail account, money she could use to purchase things from the jail canteen. Gloria then learned that in jail, like everywhere else, you needed money to get along. Through Judy she quickly learned that the State provided nothing for inmates but

$1.50 worth of very bad food per day. Anything else one might need or want—snack food, paper, tampons, deodorant—needed to be bought at a jail commissary. Jaffe's putting twenty dollars on the books meant Gloria could buy some essentials.

She asked Judy to buy some paper and colored pencils for her, fig-uring she would draw to keep herself busy and her mind from obsessing over the situation. She had been in the iron tomb for three days and her arraignment, where she would be formally charged and have the oppor-tunity to enter a plea, would be the next day. Maybe she would get out. Get bail. Go home.

In the back of Gloria's mind she knew that nobody charged with a capital case was given bail, but she ignored her educated inner voice and focused on going home. Whatever was going to happen, for the time being she would occupy herself drawing cats and flowers. If she drew, the time would pass. If she drew, she wouldn't cry.

After three days without a shower, Gloria did her best to comb her hair and look presentable for the arraignment. After shackling her, police led her into the holding tank behind the courtroom where she sat with other criminals waiting to see their judges. The labyrinth of corridors and holding rooms filled with bailiffs, clerks, lawyers, cops, marshals and criminals surprised her—she had never thought about the back of the courthouse, the world the public and law students never saw. It was there she waited until finally, still in chains, she was escorted by cops into the courtroom and placed next to a stranger, whom she soon learned was Gary Masse and her codefendant and who, Jaffe told her, had given himself up to the police. Jaffe walked over to stand beside Gloria and she noticed someone else she didn't know—another lawyer standing beside her codefendant.

Out of the corner of her eye, she peered at Masse. He was clean-shaven and looked different from the pictures she saw of him during her interview with Machen and Dean. He was around her age, but he looked weathered and tired. She stared at him. The stocky man looked weak and scared. Had she seen him before? She didn't think so, but she couldn't say for sure. Jaffe told her that Masse's wife, Joanne, had told cops that she and Gary had met Gloria at Neva's. She didn't remember ever seeing him, but she couldn't swear to it since she had been spending a lot of time at Neva's place and there often were other people around.

She and Masse said nothing to each other as they waited for the judge to appear. She kept shaking her head, trying to make sense of this surreal scene—charged for murder with a partner she was nearly certain she'd never even met.

Within minutes John O'Mara strode in. The young, handsome assistant district attorney, with his thick brown hair and brawny build, charged over to the prosecutorial side of the court, barely glancing at Gloria and Masse. He was eager, ready to begin.

Once the judge entered and was seated, O'Mara approached the bench.

"Your honor, this is the worst crime Sacramento has seen in years," O'Mara said to the judge. "This woman is a cold-blooded killer!"

Gloria looked at Jaffe, who motioned to her to say nothing. She knew from law school that this was what prosecutors did at arraignments. She knew they tried to tell the judge that the defendant was a horrible criminal and, if given the chance, would kill again. But this was her they were talking about; she swallowed hard, uneasy saying nothing but knowing she had to remain quiet.

O'Mara finished his rant and read the charges against Masse and Gloria. "Murder, attempted murder, robbery, burglary and grand theft auto," he said definitively. "This is a capital crime and we will be seeking the death penalty."

At the sound of those words, Gloria felt weak, as if someone had hit her with a mallet, and visions of herself approaching an execution chamber ran through her mind. Still, she stood tall, stoic, trying her best to fight her fear and put this madness into perspective. No one could convict an innocent woman; such travesties of justice, she believed, just didn't happen.

The judge spoke first to Masse. "How do you plead?" he asked.

"Not guilty," Masse replied, never once making eye contact with Gloria.

The judge turned to Gloria. "How do you plead?"

"Not guilty, Your Honor," she replied, her legs twitching in her shackles. "Not guilty."

The judge set the preliminary hearing for forty-five days hence— that would make the date in early February. At the hearing, both sides would have the opportunity to present abbreviated versions of their cases and the judge would decide whether there was sufficient evidence to bring either Masse or Gloria to trial.

Then came worse news, which she had anticipated but hadn't wanted to believe: There would be no bail. Both she and Masse would have to wait in jail for the hearing. She hoped since Jaffe had said they had nothing on her, everything would soon be cleared up and she could go home. *Mistakes like this don't happen. Just forty-five days*, she thought. If she could make it through forty-five days, everything would be okay. She wouldn't allow herself to think about the death penalty or anything else. She would stay quiet, strong. She wouldn't allow herself to cry.

| 8 |

Ten Percenters

Bob Hord walked into his mother Neva's kitchen and grabbed a beer out of the refrigerator. Ever since his mother had remarried, the house was always stocked with food, because his stepfather liked to go to the supermarket. Neva was more interested in shopping for jewelry, art or wigs. She had very little motivation to shop for food even when her four children were small.

What one could always find in the Snyder home were drugs. Bob, her youngest son, had been in and out of prisons almost all his adult life, mostly on narcotics charges. Pot, speed, valium, crack, crank, meth— Hord had been though nearly everything in his thirty-two years.

Hord had just come home to Sacramento a few months before the Davies robbery. He had been paroled from San Quentin in December and released a few months later. He gave his legal address as his mother's home, but he didn't really live there or anywhere else full time. Most of the time, the long-haired, heavy-browed ex-con parked at friends' homes, dumpy motels or at a trailer park not too far from his mother's house.

But he was in and out of Neva's home a lot. His stepfather, Ellis, was ill and Hord was doing what he thought was right by spending as much time as possible with the sickly man before the inevitable time when Hord would be sent back to prison. But his stepfather didn't care for Hord all that much. He didn't trust him. From Ellis's viewpoint, Hord used prison as a revolving door and had a rap sheet as long as the rivers he grew up next to.

Since his parole he hadn't been clean either. There was drug use and sales, but the bulk of the money he made came from being a "ten percenter," a guy who sets up robberies and takes 10 percent of whatever is stolen. Hord came out of the penitentiary ready to contact all his prison cronies and set up robberies all over town. He knew snitches who worked in pawnshops, jewelry shops and other places people go to buy or sell valuables. Sometimes Hord set up robberies on his own and sometimes with a partner. His latest partner was a friend of the family, a Hells Angel he met at Neva's, Dale Herbst.

Herbst had performed the role of a ten percenter for Masse and DeSantis numerous times over the last year. Since his breakup with his girlfriend a few months back, Herbst had been living in the small guesthouse behind Neva's home. Herbst was a mechanic, ostensibly there to work with Ellis, and though he said he owned an ice cream business, there was never any evidence of an ice cream truck. He was handsome and charming, slim, with chin-length, straight brown hair, brown eyes and a brown mustache—the quintessential sexy biker. To Hord, Dale seemed like the ideal partner at first, well connected without a recent police record. But what Hord didn't know was the reason Herbst was rarely arrested: It was not because he was such an adept criminal. For the past two years he had been a confidential informant for the Sacramento Sheriff's Department.

In the few months before Hord arrived at Neva's, Herbst had set up Masse and DeSantis a number of times. Earlier in the year, he sent the cousins to rob the manager of an apartment complex near a maintenance shop at the executive airport. DeSantis and Masse put stockings over their faces, went into the manager's office and robbed the place. Next Herbst sent the duo to rob an elderly man. Herbst also told the cousins about numerous other people they could rob. They held up a drug dealer in North Sacramento and Gary and Joanne tried to rob a woman in South Land Park who owned lots of jewelry, all on the information given by Herbst.

Hord was upset when he found out his good buddy Gary Masse had been arrested for the Davies robbery-murder. Hord had known Masse since they were both seventeen years old and met in juvenile hall. Masse was a regular visitor at Neva's and for years he hung out with Bob off and on, during the times when both of them weren't in prison. Most recently, since Hord had come home from prison, Masse seemed to be there a lot, working on his green car.

But Hord was even more upset Masse had been nabbed by the cops, because big-mouthed Masse knew a lot about Hord's role as a ten percenter. Hord had solicited Masse for more than one home invasion over the past few months. He knew, as did most of their friends, that once the cops got Gary it was easy for them to get him to sing and Hord was hoping Masse wouldn't prove to be a snitch again. Hord considered Masse "a junkie with a big monkey on his back." He knew drug addicts could be easily bought and Hord sat quiet and laid low after Masse's arrest. He hung around Neva's and sat tight. Let the cops come for him.

For Joanne, however, Masse's arrest wasn't so easy. She left Elk Grove and went back home to be with her children.

In late December Joanne walked through the mall looking in the store windows filled with wreaths, trees, tinsel and Santas. It was terribly sad in the house. Gary had been arrested and she wanted to cheer the children up by buying them Christmas presents. But she had no cash and she needed money badly. She was desperate and she thought maybe she could trust Hord.

Joanne walked into Neva's house one cold December evening, exhausted and depressed. She saw Bob sitting on the couch watching a

TV show and hoped Neva was in her office where she usually was. She didn't like selling things to Neva, whom she felt was shrewd.

"Hey, Bob," she said, glancing around the house. "Neva home?"

"No," Bob said and looked Joanne over. She looked awful, thin and pasty with white, dry, cracked lips. She carried a brown bag that clanged noisily whenever she moved. Hord sized her up and felt he knew what she was after. "What's up?"

Joanne stood over him and handed him the heavy bag. "Bob, I need you to buy this tea set from me. I need money for a lawyer for Gary."

Bob took the bag from her hands. He would have asked her to sit, but he knew she wouldn't, because he could tell she was high. *Money for Gary?* He knew there was no way the Masses could afford a lawyer. He knew how expensive they were.

Bob opened the bag to find a seven-piece tea set. He grabbed a large silver tray with small legs, placed it on the floor then pulled out an ornate teapot, a creamer, a sugar bowl, salt and pepper shakers, a napkin holder and a small warmer for the tea pot to sit on. He looked at the shiny, ornate set. It was it in good condition and well taken care of. He figured it was worth at least $3500.

"How much you want?" he asked Joanne who was pulling at her hair, looking around the house, twitchy and nervous.

"I want two thousand," she said.

"Where did you get it?'

Joanne hemmed and hawed. She said it was from a relative, an aunt, but Hord tried to narrow her down.

"Joanne, did Gary get this from the Davies robbery?"

"No, um, not this," she said.

Hord nodded. He felt sure she was lying about the tea set, but he didn't care.

"I'll give you five hundred for the set. I got a couple of dollars now and I can give you some crank, too," Hord said, knowing quite well the crank would seal the deal at any price.

Joanne nodded. That was fine for her. This whole deal was less about the money for a lawyer for Gary and more about her. She knew they would never be able to afford a lawyer. She knew he did it, he'd get a court-appointed lawyer and he'd be sent away for a long time. All she was worried about was covering her own ass, keeping herself high with drugs and getting something for the children.

"I can give you about two hundred now," he said, handing her the cash and a folded paper filled with crank. "Come back and I'll give you more later."

"Just two hundred?" But she opened the paper, saw the crank and smiled. A done deal.

Joanne returned within days. This time she brought a gold watch that she said came from the Davies robbery. Hord looked at the watch and knew better. He thought it looked like junk, something he saw in a catalog for $29.95 and he told her he wasn't interested.

He gave her another twenty dollars, another bag of crank he owed her for the tea set and told her they were even.

Joanne reiterated that she had more stuff to sell.

But Hord balked. She made him nervous. "I don't know, Joanne. I ain't buying right now."

After she returned several times over the next few weeks, Hord began avoiding her. He told friends he was "shining her on, staying away from her." She had told him so many lies and changed so many stories he didn't trust her anymore. He was trying to distance himself from the Masses.

| 9 |

Locked In

Gloria had been at RCCC over a week and it was close to Christmas. The days in the tomb were bad, but the hour or two she spent in the dayroom with the other prisoners was often worse. The dayroom was filthy and depressing, with sickly green walls, repulsive beige furniture and a large television set mounted dangerously on the wall. Gloria hoped at first that the huge wooden bookcases at the back of the room would provide some solace from this hellish nightmare, but there was little to read but Bibles.

Most of her time out of the cell Gloria sat in the dayroom, which felt far more jail-like then her cell. All the women looked the same: yellow blouses, elastic waist pants with RCCC down the legs and the dead eyes of hopelessness. Many of them had been at RCCC before, knew each other and the cops who guarded them. The inmates turned and looked at her with "who the hell are you" expressions while she sat quiet and scared, weakly trying to smile.

One night, her picture came on the TV screen during the ten o'clock news as the alleged mastermind of a brutal murder. Inmates turned, stared, then smiled, nodding their heads in respect. Without doing anything, Gloria had achieved enough street cred so the predators would leave her alone. Ironically, *she* scared *them*.

The cops were different. They had never seen a woman quite like Gloria, a highly educated law student, in jail for such a heinous crime. She was an anomaly in every way, not only in her look and attitude, but also in what she read and the things she cared about.

She read fashion magazines, current best sellers and historical memoirs about the Empress Josephine, Catherine the Great and Elizabeth the First that Helen brought her. The cops sometimes thumbed through her fashion magazines before they gave them to her, but they couldn't fathom her taste in literature.

On Christmas Eve, during her second week at RCCC, a stern-faced deputy opened her iron door, stood there and stared at her.

"What's happening now?" Gloria asked, petrified. She knew she didn't have a hearing; it was almost Christmas and it wasn't her time out. *Has something happened to my mother? To Brian?*

"I've been watching you," the fearsome black-haired guard said. At five feet ten inches, she was one of the largest and most imposing officers on the wing. Suddenly a smile lit the corners of her deep blue eyes.

"It's Christmas; I'm going to move you to a glass door."

Gloria's eyes filled with tears for the first time since she'd arrived at the Branch. She was touched by the officer's kindness and thrilled to be moving out of her iron tomb. It didn't matter that she was just going to another cell down the hall. She was no longer being treated as a feared murderer, kept like an animal in a box. She was being treated like everyone else in Ramona Hall, the maximum security wing at the Branch. Now she was going to be behind a bulletproof glass door where she could see people walking by and look out the barred windows at the top of the wall in the hallway. If she stood on her tiptoes she could see a little bit of blue sky.

Within days of moving into a regular cell, the guards realized they had an ideal prisoner on their hands, one they could use, so they made Gloria a trustee. No longer locked in a cell, now with freedom to walk the halls, Gloria delivered tampons and pads to women in need, gave out cleaning supplies for inmates to wash their toilets and delivered the traveling telephone to women when they needed to make phone calls. She listened to the women if they needed to talk and helped them, particularly with legal issues. She wrote a number of modification letters that assisted her fellow inmates in getting their sentences reduced. She also filed various motions and helped numerous women understand the legal proceedings they were facing, thrilled that she could put her law school knowledge to use. It helped her keep her mind off the nightmare she was living and increased her popularity with the inmates and with the guards.

Most days she stood in the hall, tampons, pads or matches in her pocket and thought that her ward on RCCC looked more like a hallway in a cheap motel than a prison. She was baffled by what a strange world jail was.

The cops found her so trustworthy that, after less than a month, the jail commander offered to move her out of a cell and into a dorm with other women, but Gloria made the decision to stay in her cell, which intrigued her captors more. She started writing poetry, limericks and satirical revisions of various works to amuse her cell block. When the staff had a retirement party for one of the lieutenants, Gloria wrote a parody for him called "The Lieutenant's Lament," which she read at the party. She was the only prisoner invited to the party and the lament was a huge hit.

But never once did she forget where she was, why and what was hanging over her head. One afternoon, Jaffe arrived at their meeting in the attorney's room, eyes aflame with anger.

"Who the hell is Wade Medina?" he snarled, pacing like a caged lion.

"I have no idea." Gloria said. She had never seen Jaffe like this and stared at him wondering what was wrong. *What is he talking about? Why is he so angry?*

"You need to tell me the truth or I'm not going to help you."

"I am telling you the truth," Gloria protested. "I have no idea who he is."

"Then what's this?" Jaffe threw a stack of white papers on the desk that fluttered like seagulls on the beach. "He says he met with you and Masse to plan this job. He says you met in a parking lot a couple of days before the job." Jaffe peered down at her, staring, inches from her face. "You need to tell me the truth. I have to know what I'm dealing with."

Gloria was stunned. *Who are these people making up stories about me?*

"I swear I have no idea. Where did he come from?"

Finally Jaffe's whole body relaxed and he took the seat opposite her at the desk.

"Jail. Where else? Broke his leg inside then told the cops he had information about this case. Said he met you and Masse a couple of times together. Then he said he saw you the day of the robbery sitting outside Davies' home in a white car."

"What?" Gloria asked, confused.

"I know. Even Joanne Masse doesn't put you at the scene. I knew it wasn't true. I just needed to be sure."

Gloria took a deep breath and let it out. Then she laughed. "You could have just asked me."

"We're going in for preliminary hearing. They will bind you over for trial, but they have nothing. Remember the standard of proof is so low, the Easter Bunny would be bound over for trial. Don't worry."

"That's easy for you to say." She watched him gather up the papers and finally smile at her.

Both she and Jaffe understood that the State had a weak case. One of the major problems of the State's case against her was that 95 percent of the evidence the police had—the guns, the IDs, etc.—had nothing to do with Gloria. She knew that Jaffe wasn't the type of lawyer to handhold her through the proceedings, so they had little to discuss. She trusted that he could fix this error of justice.

She believed she just had to wait until her case got to Superior Court, where the real evidence would be laid out and the judge would see the State had no evidence against her.

But it wasn't easy. Every day she tried to make herself busy by cleaning, reading and trying her best to not think about what happened and why.

Finally, after four months, it was time for her re-arraignment in Superior Court. She was led into the courtroom in her jail garb, shackled, handcuffed and belly chained. She looked up at the bench to find Judge Sheldon Grossfeld, her Agency and Family Law professor at McGeorge, staring at her.

She silently prayed that he wouldn't recognize her from the lecture class she took with him less than a year ago. She thought about the bet she made back then with a fellow classmate that during lectures he would glance her way every time she crossed her legs. She remembered she occasionally daydreamed about becoming his law partner.

He peered at her from the bench. She couldn't tell if he remembered her name or her face and, although he gave no sign that he did, she felt mortified. She couldn't believe where she was a short year ago compared to where she was now. She felt like Alice in Wonderland falling down the rabbit hole, having no control over her life or her reality. *How did I get to a place where people could handcuff me and drag me around? Is everything I learned in law school just crap? Don't they need evidence? Proof?* She felt she couldn't possibly be convicted of something she didn't do, yet five minutes later she was envisioning her execution. In moments John O'Mara stood up, glanced at Gloria and Jaffe then stared straight at Judge Grossfeld.

"We're almost ready for trial, Your Honor. We're just waiting to present a surprise witness who will prove beyond doubt that Gloria Killian is the mastermind of this heinous crime. If the judge would please give the people another three weeks, they will be ready to proceed in the trial of Killian," the prosecutor said.

"What is he talking about?" Gloria whispered to Ken.

"I have no idea." Ken shrugged. "He can't say he has nothing."

"What about Masse?"

"They're going to try Masse. He's pleading innocent."

"What do we do?" Gloria asked anxiously.

"We wait."

And they did. Three weeks later Gloria appeared in front of Judge Grossfeld a second time for another hearing. She looked at Jaffe. He was calm. She felt petrified, yet hopeful. The judge had been pretty firm last time: O'Mara better be prepared.

"They don't have their mystery witness. I don't think this witness ever existed," Jaffe whispered to her as the judge took the bench. "I don't think they have their case together."

Gloria looked at him and nodded.

Judge Grossfeld took the bench and then looked sternly at the prosecutor.

"Are you ready, Mr. O'Mara? Because if you're not ready, I'll dismiss."

"Judge, we need…" O'Mara stammered, hoping to ask for another postponement.

Grossfeld raised his gavel and looked at Gloria.

"I'm dismissing this case today. The defendant is free to go." His gavel hit the pad with a loud thwack.

Jaffe looked at Gloria, who was stunned and silent. He hugged her stiffened body.

"I'll talk to you later," he said packing up his briefcase. "I'm sorry I'm not allowed to give you any money or anything. Legally you're still in custody until you're processed out."

Money? For what? Gloria thought as a tall, thin bailiff led her out of the courtroom. *What does this mean? What next? Where are we going?* she wondered but was too nervous to talk to her stern escort. The bailiff walked her through a back stairway in the Sacramento County Courthouse. She'd never seen these dark, dingy stairs before, which to her felt like a walk to an execution. He brought her into a small empty room, removed her shackles and handed her a white plastic bag containing the same clothes she wore last December when she was booked: black crew neck, heavy sweater coat, pants, underwear and shoes.

"Get dressed," he said and walked out, leaving her alone in the strange, cold room.

Mechanically she took off the shirt and pants she'd worn every day for almost five months, folded them neatly and laid them on the bench. Slowly she put on her clothes, which felt odd. *Where are they taking me now?*

After a few minutes, a court officer walked into the small room. He asked her to sign for her clothes and for her release then he opened a metal door. The intense light and warmth of the April day flooded the room, making Gloria blink and step back. Flecks of cottonwood from the trees by the river danced in the air. It was warm. It was now spring.

"You're free to go," the court officer said, flat and unemotional, nodding toward the light outside the door.

"Where's my purse? I need my money. My ID."

"Sorry, it's been booked into evidence. You'll need to petition to get it back."

"But I have no money. No ID."

The officer shrugged. He didn't care.

"Can I at least make a phone call?"

"No. You need to leave." With that he pushed the door open wide and motioned for her to walk through it. Gloria had no idea what awaited her though those doors and even though she and Jaffe had talked of dismissal she had no idea it would happen like this. It was all so strange.

She walked outside and found herself alone at the back of the courthouse building. She breathed in the fresh air. She was really free. Very afraid but free. Cautiously she walked around the corner of the street where she found a public phone. Hands shaking, she picked up the receiver and turned the dial to get the operator.

"I'd like to make a collect call," she said, her voice quivering. She waited a few moments, then heard Brian's soft "Hello?"

It seemed to take forever for the operator to finish asking him if he would accept the charges and before he could say a thing Gloria blurted out, "Brian, can you come get me? They let me go." And finally she started to cry.

| 10 |

Cops and Robbers

Late that fall, with Masse in custody and Gloria back on the street, the cops refocused on finding DeSantis. The Sacramento cops enlisted the FBI to help locate him, focusing the search in Texas, Oklahoma and Louisiana. He'd escaped from California prisons twice before and those were the places where he'd previously run.

Stephen DeSantis grew up on the outskirts of Sacramento as the fifth of nine children of a petty thief and prostitute. When he was only two years old he was sent to foster care, because his parents' home was declared unfit. He lived in numerous foster homes for the next five years until the state put him back with his parents, Rose and Columbino "Bill" DeSantis.

The DeSantis children grew up always hungry, in a home where a lock was kept on the refrigerator and no one was allowed to eat unless the parents were home. Rose DeSantis, a local Mexican girl who dropped out of high school and spent two years in a girl's juvenile facility before she got pregnant, taught her children to steal food from markets, pick pockets and pilfer local crops from the farms that surrounded them. When they didn't obey or steal enough for the family's dinners, they were severely beaten.

As early as elementary school, the DeSantis boys were caught stealing pots and pans from the school cafeteria. When the police arrived at their home, they found Rose DeSantis cooking dinner using pots and pans branded as property from the Sacramento Board of Education. According to his sister, six years his senior, Steve and his brothers regularly stole lunches from other children. Steve and his elder brother were treated with particular cruelty by their parents, suffering torture similar to waterboarding, during which one of the parents tied the child's hands behind his back, filled the sink with water and held the child's head under water for the slightest infraction.

As a young teen, DeSantis complained to the California Youth Authority that he witnessed his mother prostituting herself and she beat him if he did not steal enough. But at the youth authority and throughout all of social services, the DeSantis family had been branded bad and incorrigible, not without reason.

When Stephen was fourteen, a deputy probation officer summed up in a report what he believed was the ethos of the DeSantis family and the likely outcome of Stephen's future. It was grim.

The probation officer wasn't wrong. All of the DeSantis boys served time at the California Youth Authority for robbery, burglary and petty theft. Within a year, DeSantis was kicked out of high school, taken from his parents yet again and made a ward of the court for the second time.

The court recommended that DeSantis go to Fouts Springs Youth Facility, a juvenile jail where the county sent court wards who had serious delinquent histories, posed a public safety risk or had not been amenable to prior treatment efforts. An order to Fouts Springs was generally made as a sanction for ongoing offensive behavior and a failure to respond to less restrictive therapeutic efforts.

But what followed at Fouts Springs proved not to be therapeutic for Steve. Once released, DeSantis continued in a life of crime that began with more juvenile arrests for burglary, petty theft, curfew violations, vehicle code violations and loitering. One arrest report cited him as a "compulsive liar and a sophisticated thief who has no compunction about his criminal activity." The assessing officer in those thefts felt DeSantis was "San Quentin material and due to his extensive involvement in criminal activity in the community and his apparent lack of respect for any form of authority, the structured environment of a prison is necessary."

When he was twenty-five, Steve was sent to San Quentin State Prison together with his cousin, Gary Masse. He, Masse and fourteen others were charged with participating in multiple burglaries and armed robbery. DeSantis was locked up on a multi-year sentence, but within the year he escaped, the first of many breakouts. He was captured locally in California and transferred to Folsom State Prison, where he again escaped. This time he managed to get to Oklahoma.

But DeSantis wasn't out of custody for long. He quickly resorted to the only thing he knew, a life of crime, and he was arrested in Oklahoma and sent back to California. Forced to spend years behind bars, DeSantis decided he needed to learn how to do something other than steal when he was released. He enrolled in the prison welding program. Once released he married Gaila, the sister of his brother Robert's wife, and enrolled in a welding program at a local community college. He said he was tired of living in prison.

A year after the Davies' murder and Gloria's arrest, DeSantis was hiding in Texas under an assumed name. But the FBI had been tipped off and they were on to him. The day before Christmas, the bureau initiated a multi-state manhunt and found DeSantis in Port Arkansas, Texas, where he had been living a quiet life with his wife for the past year. Officers captured him and brought him back to Sacramento in chains. They didn't want another escape.

The trial of his partner in crime, Gary Masse, was set to begin in February, just six weeks away. The State expected Masse's conviction to be a snap. They assigned the case to a new prosecutor, a young, hand-some, upcoming go-getter who was tough on crime. Christopher "Kit" Cleland was now the assistant district attorney prosecuting Masse and he felt sure it would go easy. They had a lot of evidence against Masse. They had a confession.

Hollywood couldn't find a better fit for the role of prosecutor than Kit Cleland. Six feet tall and broad-shouldered with dark blond hair he wore swept back, Cleland made a striking presence. His nickname among local defense lawyers and those who had to go up against him in court was "The Nazi," given to him for his Aryan countenance and unquestionable zeal for justice. Cleland commanded a courtroom, often in the guise of an avenging angel.

Cleland began his career in the Sacramento district attorney's office right after he graduated Loyola Law School as a young man of twenty-six. He went straight to the homicide department and had been there a little over ten years when he received the Davies murder case.

As Gary Delsohn notes in his 2001 book *The Prosecutors*, in which he spent a year at the Sacramento District Attorney's office studying the attorneys there, including Cleland, "There are prosecutors who behave as rigid, fire-breathing ideologues, firm in the belief they're doing the Lord's work keeping the capital city safe from depraved killers." Cleland was that type of prosecutor. Unlike his supervisor, John O'Mara, who had released Gloria the year before and who saw shades of grey, Cleland's world was black and white: the good guys, the bad guys; the black hats, the white. He never used profanity and he had the reputation of being like a Boy Scout, a man who was squeaky-clean.

Cleland was not one of the attorneys who participated in the weekly office ritual known as the Four O'Clock Follies, when, according to Delsohn, "attorneys return from court and sit around on the couch and chairs outside O'Mara's office riffing back and forth about what happened in trial that day, what some fool defense attorney tried to pull off, how a witness tanked, or what a judge ruled." Cleland didn't have gallows humor like some of the other attorneys in the office had. He was straight-laced. He was serious.

Cleland was also not the type of prosecutor given to self-doubt. Once he had his mind made up about a case, he pursued the defendant relentlessly, with a ruthlessness that could border on obsession.

Cleland was convinced Gloria Killian was guilty.

Cleland was assigned to the high-profile case in a city that was quickly becoming known as the murder capital of California, home to a veritable plethora of mass murderers. In the 1970s and 1980s, Sacramento hosted 15 percent of the country's serial killers, a very high rate for the twentieth largest metropolitan area, easily earning its name as the "Valley of Death."

According to Michael Newton's book, *The Encyclopedia of Serial Killers*, sixty-five serial killers were captured in the United States between 1971 and 1992, seven from Sacramento.

In the early 1970s, Juan Corona was caught and convicted for the murder of twenty-five Sacramento farm workers. During the late 1970s, more than fifty women in the Sacramento area were assaulted by the East Area Rapist, who later also terrorized Contra Costa County and also has been linked through DNA to ten serial killings in Southern California. In 1979, Richard Chase, the Vampire Killer, a bizarre murderer who drank the blood of his victims, was jailed for the murder of six people, including one child.

And the most infamous pair of local killers was Gerald Gallego and his wife Charlene Williams. Their search for a sex slave led to the murder of nine women and one man. They were captured in early 1982 after they abducted a young couple from the Arden Fair Mall. Charlene Williams and Gloria were hall-mates at the Branch.

"We've had more than our share of serial killers," Lieutenant Ray Biondi told one newspaper. "Sacramento is a crossroads," he explained. "It's where I-5 and I-80 intersect. It's also a melting pot and still growing."

Soon, a tough-on-crime, seriousness-about-murder attitude permeated the city's justice system.

Only a couple of weeks before the Masse trial, Cleland was pleased with the way things were progressing. They had Masse's phone confession to Lieutenant Biondi and a slew of evidence. Cleland knew that Masse had perpetrated the robbery that turned to murder and that California gives the same first-degree murder charge, which comes with a sentence of life without parole, even if the suspect didn't pull the trigger. Cleland wanted to make sure Masse would never get out of prison.

He looked forward to trying the DeSantis case as well. Now that they had caught the criminal who ran, Cleland wanted to go after him with a vengeance. Masse and DeSantis were "some of the worst ilk of people that you could ever hope to run into," Cleland later opined in court. In those same closing arguments he described DeSantis as a "cold-blooded murderer" and Cleland hoped DeSantis would be the one facing a death sentence.

Cleland vehemently believed Gloria Killian was the mastermind behind the robbery Masse and DeSantis committed. Even though he had no solid evidence against Gloria and couldn't re-arrest her after O'Mara let her go the year before, he was convinced, as he later stated in court, that "Ed Davies' blood is on her hands, and she is trying to wash it off."

But sometimes evidence appeared that didn't fit with Cleland's vision of how the crime was committed.

In early February, right before the start of Masse's trial, Cleland heard from an FBI special agent regarding a criminal named Gary Lee Smith who claimed he had information on the Davies case.

The tall, blond, buff thirty-two-year-old Smith was looking for "consideration" on his pending cases in return for the information he could provide on the Davies case and had called the FBI rather than the Sacramento police, because he said he trusted the FBI more than the local law. Smith told the FBI he was being prosecuted in Sacramento County on six charges: two drug charges, two check charges, one credit card charge and one ex-con with a gun charge. Smith said he wanted to exchange the information he had on the Masse case for help with those new charges. A judge had given him five years. He didn't want to go to prison just yet; his wife was dying of cancer.

The FBI told Smith that they would put him in touch with the local district attorney's office. They could do nothing for him.

Within days, Pat McCarthy, Smith's attorney, called Kit Cleland. He told Cleland his client had been approached by Bob Hord in the fall to rob Mr. Davies and had been asked to make a silencer for a .25 caliber automatic. Smith had also heard that Masse was solicited for the crime, but Hord told him Masse was initially reluctant to become involved because of the potential for violence. Cleland listened to McCarthy. He asked if Smith knew Killian or DeSantis. The answer was no.

This was far from the information Cleland sought. Smith implicated Hord as the mastermind who had orchestrated this plan.

Cleland wrote in a memorandum that he told McCarthy he was "unable to make any representations concerning possible leniency for Mr. Smith. If he wants to talk to the sheriff's investigators, they will be glad to listen. However, no promises are being made in advance of such discussions." Six days later, McCarthy brought Smith to talk with Detectives Stan Reed and Harry Machen. Knowing that there might be no deal, Smith still wanted to tell what he knew.

The energy in the investigation room was tense. Smith was nervous, the detectives wary. They too had a lot to lose if Smith was telling the truth. They had been doing their best to get any evidence they could to prove Killian was behind the crime.

"We're not going to do any deals up front," Machen told Smith. "We want all your information, which will then be evaluated, and it will be up to Mr. Cleland of the DA's office to decide if any consideration will be given to you and your present charges."

Smith agreed and told the cops a detailed story, one that didn't quite gel with the theory the cops had of how the Davies murder had happened.

Smith told the detectives that two months before the Davies robbery, his wife was approached in their home by Robert Hord, who asked her if she wanted to be involved with the Davies robbery. Hord told Smith and his wife he knew of two people who had a lot of gold and silver coins. He wanted Smith's wife to go to the door and pretend that her car was broken down. Then they would come in, guns blazing, behind her. Hord told them Davies' loot was buried in the backyard or in the walls of the house. He said they would hold a gun on the lady and make the man talk. If the husband didn't talk they would kill him.

Smith said he and his wife weren't interested in the job. But, two or three weeks before the Davies robbery, Hord visited the Smith's home again and asked Smith to drive to the Davies' home and see if a green car, the same car Gary Masse drove, was parked anywhere near the place. Hord told Smith he was afraid the people he got for the job might be doing the job without him.

Smith cased the area, did not see the car, called Hord and told him so. Smith saw Hord soon after the robbery and asked if it went down, which Hord confirmed. At Smith's house, Hord showed him a gold pocket watch with a hunting scene on it and a chain. Hord told Smith he had proceeds from the robbery and complained that some of the proof sets that were stolen were broken up and taken out of the plastic holders.

Machen and Dean looked Smith over. This was not good news. It certainly didn't help their cases against either Stephen DeSantis or Gloria Killian. Smith didn't even have any real proof to help them put away Gary Masse. The only thing the information really did was throw suspicion off Killian and onto Hord.

"What about Killian and DeSantis?" Machen asked hopeful.

But they got the same answer. Smith knew about Hord and he knew about Masse but nothing about Killian or DeSantis.

Frustrated, Dean asked about the silencer. Smith admitted that he helped Hord with the gun.

They let him go and cut him no deals. This testimony, detailed as it was, did not fit with Cleland's view of the case casting Gloria Killian as the mastermind. In fact, it could hurt his case enormously and give a jury reasonable doubt that Killian was the mastermind.

The Sacramento sheriff did not act on Smith's information. While Smith admitted to police that his silencer was involved with the crime, he was not arrested. And amazingly, neither was Hord. Police didn't even bring Hord in for questioning on this matter. They knew he knew Masse and that his mother would protect him at all costs. It seemed that Cleland and the police wanted Gloria.

Gary Masse's trial went quickly. It was an open-and-shut case. They had his confession when he turned himself in.

"I told him if he was not the triggerman to turn himself in," Biondi told the court. "Masse told me he was only there to do the robbery. He didn't know DeSantis was going to kill the couple."

The Sacramento jury took less than a day to find Masse guilty of first degree murder, attempted murder-robbery, burglary and grand theft auto. Cleland had not asked for the death penalty in Masse's trial, but due to special circumstances, Masse most assuredly faced life without parole. Judge Joseph A. DeCristoforo asked the jurors to return two days later for the penalty phase of the trial.

Masse knew he faced life without the possibility of parole. *What will happen to my kids if I never get out?* he wondered. *My marriage?* He knew he had to do something, but wasn't sure what, so he decided to wait and see what the court would do. He wouldn't make a move until he was sentenced.

In mid-May, almost three months after Masse's trial began, Judge DeCristoforo called Masse back to court and sentenced him to life without the possibility of parole. But Masse devised a plan. No way was he going to rot his whole life away in prison. He called his family and his friends.

"Get in touch with the cops," he told them, "I want to talk." Days after his sentencing, while awaiting transfer from the Sacramento jail to a state prison, Masse received a visit from Machen in the county jail. Masse told the detective he wanted to come clean about the Davies crime.

Machen and Reed brought Masse across the street to the sheriff's department and into an interrogation room where Lieutenant Biondi was waiting. The three cops sat with Masse, ready to hear him confess. This time they made sure the tape recorder was working.

Masse's first concern was that he didn't want to appear like a snitch. He had been a snitch before and he didn't want to be beaten, tortured or killed in prison.

"We have arranged, if you decide that you are going to make a statement in this case that will assist us, to change your name and put you in another county jail temporarily," Biondi told him.

Then they talked about his sentence.

"If you assist us in this case, we're certainly going to talk to the DA about consideration on your sentence. And do whatever we can," Biondi said.

"I got nothing to gain," Masse said.

"If you get some consideration on your sentence, isn't that something to gain?"

"Yeah, but, ain't no, you know. It's like you guys can't guarantee nothin'."

"I think we can guarantee that," Biondi replied.

"I just don't like the whole damn way the case went down anyway. You know, chargin' me a murderer, you know."

"That's what happens when you do one crime and something happens in the middle of that crime. That's the way the law reads; that's a murder. You go in and do a burglary, somebody gets killed, that's a murder. Let me explain it to you, Gary," Biondi went on. "You give us a statement and for your protection we're going to put you in another county jail, change your name and nobody's gonna know you're there unless you want to tell them. That's up to you. And if you give us information that's useful information and we need you to testify and you do that, then the plan is we will get you in the federal penitentiary system, out of the California prison system. And some consideration on your sentence. We don't know what that would be, but we would make any effort, all effort, to see that there's some consideration on your sentence."

"But I've already been sentenced. That's the part I don't understand," Masse said.

"That's not a problem, yet," Reed interjected. "We still have time to work on that."

"When we say we're gonna do everything we can with that DA, we're gonna do it," Biondi said.

Masse agreed to talk. This time he told the police Neva Snyder introduced him to Gloria Killian, who became the instigator and mastermind of the whole robbery.

"How many times do you think you went to Neva's house to meet Gloria?" Reed asked.

"I musta seen her over there at least a couple a dozen times."

"Anybody present besides yourself and Gloria?"

Masse nodded. "Yeah, she discussed it in front of DeSantis, too."

"So it's not like you went to Steve and said, 'Let's do this job.' He was aware of it, because he was present during some of these conversations."

"Yeah, with us," Masse said.

He went on to say that Neva was present during these conversations, though she did not participate. Masse added that Gloria went with him to the door one time to try to rob the Davies, but they didn't let her in. Then he described how he and Steve robbed the couple and how DeSantis committed the murder.

He told the police he spoke with Killian the day after the robbery and "she was really mad she didn't get her half of the loot."

In early June, Inspector Tom Brown and Machen met with Masse. This time they wanted to know about the planning of the Davies robbery and Machen suggested Masse use the dates of other robberies he committed to help him construct a timeline to the Davies murder.

"We're aware you're a suspect in some safe burglaries, but we're not going to advise you of your rights and charge you with any crimes like burglary," Machen said. They gave him amnesty on any other crimes in which he was involved. They wanted more on Gloria.

Masse smiled. He agreed to talk more. He told the cops the year of the Davies murder was a big crime year for him. He had wanted to go straight but couldn't, because "Joanne started using a lot of drugs and I got back into the same situation."

He told police most of his crimes were committed with DeSantis and almost all of them were set up by Dale Herbst.

The duo committed robberies all over town and as far away as Salt Lake City. Masse talked of robberies where he had worked with Joanne, Bob Hord, DeSantis and Herbst. He told them of robbery after robbery, burglary after burglary, listing a slew of cases that had not yet been solved by the Sacramento police. It was the same names over and over. Not once, however, in any of those crimes did the name Gloria Killian come up.

"We'll work to run these cases down and get reports on them," Machen said, "but what we really want is information on how you were approached to do the Davies job and events that led up to the job itself."

Masse had already told them much of what they wanted to know about DeSantis. He drove them on the route and told them where the loot had been buried. Now they pushed for information on Gloria. Masse was happy to give them what they wanted. It was part of the deal.

He told them again how in October he was approached by Neva, who said her friend Gloria wanted to talk with him about a job. He said he'd seen Gloria over there before when he went to buy speed for Joanne. Gloria drove him to the Davies' house and told him they had a lot of gold and silver in their home, because they didn't believe in banks.

"I know some of this information had to come out of a coin shop. I know a guy there by the name of Virgil, but I don't know his last name," Masse explained. "I have seen him in the coin shop before. I know the name Virgil, because the word on the street was that Virgil was in that shop and he would buy and not ask any questions."

Masse said Gloria would have no problem getting rid of the property. "I could bring our split, which would be 50 percent, and give it to her and her people would give me what it was worth. I thought at the time it might be the coin shop," Masse said.

The police didn't bother to ask Masse why she would get 50 percent when Dale Herbst and Bob Hord operated as ten percenters for the same information. What was different about Gloria that warranted her getting half? Why would career criminals like Masse and DeSantis make such a terrible deal with a law student? The detectives didn't ask how Gloria enforced that bad deal. There was no logic to the story other than that it gave them Gloria.

Masse continued by telling the police that Gloria knew the layout of the Davies' house, told him of a silverware set worth eight thousand dollars and believed the gold was buried in plastic pipes in the yard. He noted he first asked his wife to work with him on this job, but when she wouldn't help him, he discussed the gig with DeSantis.

Steve and Gloria talked at Neva's house more than once, Masse continued and then finally they decided to dress up in wigs and go to the house to see if Mrs. Davies would open the door. He noted that Gloria borrowed Neva's strawberry blonde wig. Masse started to talk about the day of the crime when Machen interrupted him.

"Let's skip talking about the robbery and the shooting of Mr. and Mrs. Davies and pick up after the crime had been committed," Machen said. "We're trying to develop time frames for the planning sessions and we can go into more detail at a later time."

Masse nodded. He understood. They wanted more on Gloria.

"The next day Joanne and I went up into the hills to get our property. We put it in the trailer and went home. I called my cousin and asked her to sell some coins for me. Then Gloria called and wanted to meet. Joanne and I went over to Neva's and met with her. We told her we knew nothing."

Machen looked at Brown and smiled. With what Masse was saying, they had more than enough on Killian. It was time to arrest her—again.

| 11 |

The Second Arrest

Gloria sat crossed-legged, tucked in behind the desk in the back of the office at Brian's. His accounting books were open on her desk and she sipped her morning coffee, carefully balancing the work orders against the ledger. Within days of her release almost a year ago last April, she'd gone back to work and resumed her life best as she could.

She had moved out of Virgil's house and rented a cozy one-bedroom apartment with Brian near the shop and across the street from a local park. They could see the park from their windows and in the evenings they took walks through the greenery, holding hands like newlyweds. They returned to living and working together, doing their best to move forward as if nothing had happened.

But something *had* happened and a leftover sickening feeling left Gloria overeating and drinking a little too much. The arrest had shattered her life as well as her belief in the legal system and it left her vulnerable, insecure and damaged. It also made her decide to continue to postpone finishing law school. The case had made her notorious and she felt like hiding. She'd been all over the newspapers and in Judge Grossfeld's courtroom. Keeping a low profile seemed to her like a very wise idea. She had decided to work for Brian, save money, recoup the legal fees that caused her to empty her bank account and then take the bar exam. Slowly she would recover from that dreadful arrest and those four and a half months in jail and rebuild her shattered life. Nevertheless, even though she tried to feel like everything would be okay, there was always a nagging feeling that the catastrophe wasn't really over. She couldn't understand why, but she felt the cops were too vicious from the moment she was in custody until they let her go and she felt they might be back.

Almost like a self-fulfilling prophecy, as she was putting down her coffee mug she heard the outer office door open. She glanced up to see Sergeant Hash walk in, followed by two hulking detectives. Her mind blanked out as Hash walked up to the counter and peered down at her petite frame behind the desk.

"Gloria Killian, I have a warrant for your arrest."

Gloria gulped and looked up at Hash's stern guise. She vowed not to cry.

"I have to go tell Brian I'm leaving." Slowly she stood and turned toward the repair shop.

"We'll be right behind you; don't try anything," Hash said, maneuvering behind her, the other two cops trailing them.

She entered the repair shop. Brian's huge Rottweiler leaped forward, straining his chain while emitting a low rumbling growl. The dog had grown very attached to Gloria and was extremely protective of her.

"Control your dog or I'll shoot him," Hash said, reaching for his gun.

"Please don't hurt him," Gloria pleaded with the cop. "He's on a chain; he can't get to you. Just stay out of his reach."

She walked up to Brian and calmly told him she was under arrest again. He lowered his head and held back tears. He didn't want the cops to see him as weak.

"Call Ken," she whispered as Brian leaned in to kiss her good-bye. She turned and approached Hash. Quickly he spun her around and handcuffed her hands behind her. The dog howled in protest, his chain clanging and straining, watching the three cops fall into formation around Gloria. They marched her out of the shop then down the street. She could hear the dog wail and saw the curious eyes of neighbors watching her. *These guys don't miss a trick*, she thought. *Anything to humiliate and upset me!*

They placed her in the back of the police car. Her mind was racing.

"You want to talk?" Hash asked her.

Talk? she thought. *Look what cooperation got me last time.* "What am I charged with?" she managed to ask.

"First degree murder."

Murder. That meant the death penalty again. Gloria had feared this moment from the time she was released and the actual moment felt worse. Here she was, back in a police car, handcuffed and being dragged off to jail again. She invoked her right to counsel then was driven directly to the downtown jail and processed in. She went through the same debasing process of fingerprints, mug shots and strip searches as she had the first time she was arrested. Using her one phone call she called Brian and found out that Ken Jaffe's phone had been disconnected. Since Gloria's last arrest, Jaffe's wife had been murdered, compelling Jaffe to move out of state. She asked Brian to call Neva, who would undoubtedly have the lawyer's current information.

She hung up the phone, was led to an empty cell and locked inside. Gloria sat on the floor, stunned, incredulous that this was happening again. It's one thing to live in fear of something happening, but quite another when it happens. She was back in a jail cell, arrested for murder, with the death penalty hanging over her head again. *The death penalty,* she thought, horrified. *Could I really be in such a place where they would kill me for something I didn't do? Was everything I learned about fairness and justice a lie?*

Holding back her tears, she saw a grey tail whip around her cell bars. It was Chief, a huge jail cat who roamed freely though the facility. He wriggled through the bars and into Gloria's cell. She reached out to stroke him and Chief purred noisily. It seemed to Gloria as if the cat was reminding her that she had survived this ordeal before and would do so again. This time, she wasn't so sure.

The next morning Gloria was transferred to the Branch. This time she went on the chain like everybody else, rather than shackled and belly chained like a shunned animal. Her arrival at the Branch was like Old Home Week. She stepped off the bus only to be greeted by a smiling corrections officer (CO).

"Hey, we really need a trustee. Are you ready to go to work?"

"Okay," Gloria replied. The officers quickly processed her in, took her back to her assigned cell and told her she would be working the swing shift. It was as if she had never left.

Within days Gloria was brought downtown for arraignment. But she had no lawyer and no idea what the charges were against her or why she was arrested again. *What could they possibly have this time that they didn't have before? What kind of evidence could they have collected to bring me in again?* She informed the judge that she had been unable to contact her lawyer. He postponed her arraignment for a week. Without a lawyer she was stuck in a legal limbo that gave her no information about her situation. She didn't have access to the paperwork or information about her case. She called Brian and Neva, desperate to reach Jaffe, but with no success.

A week later and back in court, she still was without counsel.

"You have forty-eight hours to reach your lawyer or the court will appoint counsel," the judge told her. But two days later she found herself back in court alone. She had been unable to reach Jaffe.

"I'm appointing Ray Thielen as your counsel," the judge said. "Mr. Jaffe can substitute in when he becomes available." Gloria watched as a tall, dark-haired, well-dressed lawyer crossed the courtroom to stand next to her. The lawyer smiled down at her and told the judge he was ready to proceed. Thielen was well spoken, projected self-confidence and had the poise and attitude associated with defense attorneys. He was a handsome man, a forty-year-old husband and father.

They read the charges against her and they were the same as before: murder, attempted murder, robbery, burglary and grand theft auto. But something was different on the prosecution side. John O'Mara, the head of the Major Crimes Division of the Sacramento DA's office and her former prosecutor, had passed the case to one of the homicide attorneys, Christopher "Kit" Cleland, who had been the prosecutor in Gary Masse's trial. Gloria looked over at the tall, striking man on the opposite bench. Something felt strange. *Why a new prosecutor?* she wondered. *What is going on with this case? Why did O'Mara back out?* She desperately wanted to speak with Jaffe.

After the arraignment, Thielen stepped back into the holding cell to talk to her. Ray Thielen was a very successful criminal defense lawyer who'd been practicing in Sacramento for years. He handed her his business card: He was the son in the firm of Thielen and Thielen. He seemed capable, but she wanted Jaffe back, badly. For days, she, Brian and Neva tried to get through to Jaffe. Finally Brian reached him. Jaffe's wife's death had left him grieving and feeling emotionally unsettled. A large death penalty case was too much to take on, he told Brian, but Gloria should go through the preliminary proceedings with Thielen to give him time and save her money. There would be plenty of time for Jaffe to step in if needed.

Gloria sat uneasily in the tiny attorney's room at the Branch, the Rio Cosumnes Correctional Center. She was nervous and afraid as she waited for Thielen to show up with the court documents she'd been waiting to read for weeks. She'd finally find out what the case was against her and why they re-arrested her. She'd finally find out why she was back in jail.

Thielen walked in stern-faced and handed Gloria a thick document.

"Take a look at this, please," he said and sat waiting, staring at her across the tiny table. Gloria picked up the papers. It was a book-like deposition of Gary Masse. She had heard that he'd been convicted.

Her eyes widened and she felt a hollow sickness in her stomach as she flipped through the reams of papers. She didn't know whether to laugh or scream as she pored over each page of Masse's statement that claimed she had masterminded the Davies robbery and spent hours with him planning the crime and working out the details. She was incredulous. *Had Masse lost his mind? How could anyone believe this insanity?*

She looked up at her new lawyer in shock. "It's just not true."

"Are you saying all of this isn't true?" Thielen looked at her, confused. This case was not going to be easy.

"Yes," she replied firmly. "It never happened. I didn't do this!" Gloria was devastated. She wished Ken Jaffe was there. He believed in her and he knew the truth. Thielen had no handle on the case, no history and no understanding of what had happened and it would be up to her to explain everything to him. She would have to try to explain how she didn't even know these people and didn't understand why this was happening to her.

"Then what's going on?" Thielen asked.

"Let me review his statement and I'll fill you in," Gloria said. "I never like to talk here. Ken told me he believed these rooms might be bugged."

"Okay," Thielen said. He stood and gathered his papers. "We'll talk later." He left her with Masse's statement to read and mark up for him. Gloria walked back to her cell carrying Masse's tome, her mind racing in circles. What was going on? She was determined to break Gary Masse's statement.

Whenever she wasn't working as a trustee, she sat in her cell going over and over every single word in the statement. She used highlighters marking lie after lie, but kept her written comments extremely vague, just in case someone read what she wrote in the margins. Sometimes in big cases, snitches sneaked into other people's cells, read their case materials and reported back to the cops or prosecutors. With her life on the line, Gloria was taking no chances.

Masse's statement was terribly incriminating against her, but it was also vague. There were no dates, no times and no specifics, just ramblings about meetings, many of which took place in the parking lot of a retail store she had never heard of. It was all too confusing and upsetting. She was facing the death penalty in a case where she knew none of the perpetrators and nothing made sense.

One week later Gloria was back in court for another arraignment hearing. She stood in the hallway waiting to see the judge when the bailiffs brought two men into the hall next to her. They were both short, with dark hair, moustaches and dour expressions. Gloria wasn't about to make direct eye contact with these men even though the bailiffs were there to protect her, but she wondered who they were.

She was led into court with these two men who stood at the defendants' table next to her.

"Who they heck are these guys and why are they with me?" Gloria whispered to Thielen.

"Don't worry about it," Thielen said, patting her on the shoulder. Gloria looked at him, disbelieving. "Don't worry about it? My life is on the line."

As the arraignment was read aloud she learned the men's names were Stephen DeSantis and Robert DeSantis. They were being charged along with her in the Davies murder. Gloria knew Stephen DeSantis had allegedly been the perpetrator of the crime along with Gary Masse, but she had never heard of Robert until that day. They were all subject to the death penalty, but she felt more baffled than ever. Her head was reeling and she couldn't figure out why the case kept changing so much.

The entire situation was making her depressed, angry and confused. Often she worked extra hours at the Branch to make the time pass and keep her grounded. In a complicated criminal case, there are long periods when nothing happens in court and the defendants must wait for their court appearances. While she didn't expect her lawyer to come to the Branch every week just to hold her hand, most of her days were spent in limbo, just waiting. She found it very hard to keep from being overwhelmed by fear or anger or sadness. Brian and Helen came to visit each week. She had her books, spent hours drawing animals and her trustee's job kept her busy, but her mind never quieted and she rarely slept well.

One evening in the recreation room, Anna, a petite Latina inmate, hesitantly approached Gloria and asked her if she would review a letter. Anna explained she was writing to her judge but her English was poor and she was afraid that the letter contained many mistakes. After reading the letter a few times, Gloria finally figured out that Anna was asking the judge to modify her sentence to a lesser amount of time, because her mother had been in a car accident and could no longer care for Anna's children. Gloria knew the judge would never be able to understand the poorly written letter, so she offered to rewrite it. With Gloria's assistance, Anna was granted her modification and sent home. This first success brought other inmates to Gloria's cell door and she began to write letters for her fellow prisoners asking the courts for modifications of sentences, concurrent sentencings, dismissals of pending charges and other legal issues. She put her legal education to use and busied herself with other cases to avoid thinking about her own and the death penalty that loomed.

Being social made Gloria feel less like a pariah. The less time she had to think about what awaited her, the better off she was. One of the first women Gloria befriended at the Branch was named Gloria Waid, a quiet, shy blonde who was a similar age and charged with dozens of counts of child sexual abuse against her own children. On her first day back from the Sacramento jail Gloria asked Waid for a cigarette and was generously given half a dozen. There were only twenty-two rooms in this wing of the jail and Gloria and her new friend were on the same side, so they went to showers and recreation together. The women developed a close friendship.

The two Glorias began addressing each other as *alter* and *ego* to avoid name confusion and to create a little levity in the glum jail. Gloria didn't believe the charges against Waid. She told Gloria that during the time she was allegedly sexually preying on her children she had been recovering from a broken back, unable to move and taking painkillers with only vague memories of the days in question.

Gloria wanted to help this woman. She believed this was another travesty of justice, not much different from what was happening to her. While Waid was provided with a criminal defense lawyer for her case, she received no attorney for family court. Gloria wrote some of Waid's motions for the juvenile dependency court, which later served as a basis for Waid's successful appeal.

But Gloria's case moved very slowly and for people held over for murder with no bail, the limbo feels like forever. After more than two months, the court finally held a preliminary hearing. At the hearing it would be decided if she and the DeSantis brothers would be bound over for trial. It was similar to her preliminary hearing the year before: There was no real evidence. Then they brought in Gary Masse.

Masse took his seat on the stand, appearing tired and confused, unable to look Gloria in the eye. She watched the proceedings in absolute shock and listened to Kit Cleland lead Masse through his story:

How he and Gloria first met at Neva's, then at the parking lot and how she set the whole robbery up. Gloria stared at Masse and Cleland. She was shocked that anyone would believe a man like Masse, least of all the court. She thought Masse's statements barely made sense and the phrase he used most often was, "I don't recall."

The hearing left her an emotional wreck. She returned to the downtown jail in anger, unable to sit still, sleep or eat. She stomped from one side of the cell to another, filled with rage. Suddenly she noticed a body curled up on a lower bunk with a blanket pulled over its head. The blanket rose and a bleary eye peeked out from under it.

"Damn, woman," a gravelly voice whispered from under the blanket, "why don't you chill out? Nothing is going to happen tonight."

"I'm sorry," Gloria said. "I didn't mean to wake you."

"It don't matter," replied the disembodied voice. "I'm kicking, so I'm gonna be up all night if I don't get into my care package." Gloria understood that *kicking* meant being deprived of heroin, but *care package* was mysterious to her.

The woman stood up and the blanket fell away to reveal a small, attractive woman with dark blonde hair and badly bloodshot eyes.

"I'm Nicki," she said. Gloria had heard about Nicki from other inmates at the Branch. Supposedly she was a very nice person and a major heroin dealer.

"Pin for me, willya, sweetie?" Nicki asked and sat down on the toilet. Gloria knew what she meant and moved over to the bars to watch for cops coming down the hallway.

"Okay, got it," Nicki said and stood up over the sink to unwrap the tight little balloon she had pulled from her vagina. Nicki explained to Gloria she'd come in to start a sixteen-month prison sentence and to ease the heroin withdrawal symptoms she had smuggled in some tranquilizers. *Wow,* thought Gloria, *now that is planning ahead.*

The women talked for the next few hours and Gloria learned about Nicki's criminal life as a drug addict and dealer. A cop shoved some dinner under the cell door, which to the women looked like horrible slop, and they rejected it immediately.

"Here we go," said Nicki, producing a stash of cookies and chocolate bars. Gloria didn't want to think where they might have been hidden and graciously accepted a share of the goodies. As the night wore on, Nicki handed Gloria a tranquilizer.

"Here, sweetie, you've got to get some rest before court." Gloria gratefully took the pill and went to sleep. The next morning Nicki was already awake when the lights came on.

"Good morning," she said to Gloria, who had finally gotten a good night's sleep. "Here's your breakfast." She handed her a coffee and another tranquilizer.

At the next hearing, Gloria watched Cleland cleverly lead Masse though his story, and she felt that Cleland was presenting as little hard evidence as possible. She anticipated that she and the DeSantis brothers were going to be bound over for trial.

She looked at the guys sitting next to her, grungy career criminals with extensive rap sheets. She knew one thing—if she went to trial with them she was done for. Just being in the same courtroom with these men was going to hurt her case. There would be guilt by association. She thought about what she could do to sever her case from these thugs and get a separate trial, but she would need to present solid legal grounds. Counties liked to try multiple defendants together to keep down the costs. She felt she and Thielen needed to proceed with this quickly.

After her hearing Gloria was returned to her downtown cell. This time she and Nicki were housed with another inmate who had just come in from the Branch for a hearing. The inmate told Gloria that Waid had been sentenced to thirty-two years in prison for child abuse and some of the female inmates had behaved poorly toward her and said some very nasty things to her. In both male and female prisons, child abusers are considered the lowest of the low.

Gloria spent only one more night in the downtown jail and as soon as she returned to the Branch, she made sure the inmates would not abuse her friend. She flexed her trustee muscles and marched up and down the hallways telling the other inmates that they had best behave nicely to Waid if they ever hoped to see so much as a bar of soap in the next six months. She couldn't abide cruelty to her friend. Her conviction and sentencing horrified Gloria. She knew her friend was innocent, as was she. If this could happen to Waid, what could happen to her?

With Gloria and DeSantis now both behind bars, Cleland and the Sacramento Sheriff's Department had to find other witnesses besides Masse to bolster their case, because they had no concrete evidence against Gloria, only Masse's testimony. There were, however, others who looked like they too might be involved in the case. Masse had said his wife Joanne was initially involved in the Davies robbery and participated with him on other robberies by getting people to open their doors. He also implicated Virgil Fletcher. Who better to use as witnesses against Gloria than people who had a vested interest in seeing her take the rap?

Sure enough, just days after Gloria's arrest, detectives brought in Joanne Masse to back up Gary's claims.

Joanne knew Gary was trying to cut a deal and she wanted to help him for her children's sakes. In her view, her relationship with Gary was over as soon as he went to jail. Within weeks she started a new relationship with another man who had a shady record, but if Gary got out early it would be good for the children.

She reiterated that Gary met Gloria at Neva's, but this time she didn't tell the cops that she had met Gloria at least ten times, like she did the first time she spoke with detectives. Interestingly, for someone who said she had never been in the Davies' house, Joanne described it in great detail.

"As you enter the house, you go down a hallway that descends into another hallway. You turn right and it goes into a dining room and off the dining room is a kitchen. To the left is a living room which faces into the backyard. If you turn to your left going down the main hallway, you would go into the bedroom area. The house is fully alarmed and this includes the gates to the backyard."

Joanne told the police she and Gary received calls from Gloria, but she did not mention any meetings like she did in her initial statements where she said they met numerous times. The police didn't confront the differences in the testimony. Joanne was giving them what they needed to convict Gloria and that was just fine with them.

"She would call and ask for Gary or he would answer and talk to her for a short time. They did most of their talking at Neva's. He would go over there and buy dope for me from Dale Herbst. I was using speed.

"Early on, Gary talked to me about going up to the front door to get them into the house. I told him that he should go get Gloria since she wanted the property so badly. I'm sure, at least for a while, Gary thought I would help. I never agreed to get involved, but I never refused either."

Police never asked what that meant or about the numerous robberies she did with her husband in the fall. They did not, for instance, ask her about the robbery that Gary told them about weeks before the Davies robbery, in October, when Joanne knocked on the door of an elderly woman, told her that her car was broken down and asked to use the phone. When Gary tried to push his way past her, they found the elderly woman had a gun and Gary and Joanne both ran.

The police didn't ask, because they had already promised Joanne and Gary immunity against any crimes they had committed. All that remained for them to seal the deal on this immunity was to testify against DeSantis and Gloria.

It was also important for the police to establish that Gloria continued her involvement with Masse and DeSantis after the crime was committed. Joanne reiterated that Gloria met with Gary and her after the robbery and wanted her share of the loot. Joanne also admitted to the police that she sold a tea set from the robbery to Bob Hord for a couple of hundred dollars and drugs.

"Bob Hord talked to me one day and said that I should watch out for Gloria and her people," Joanne claimed.

But the cops didn't ask her who Gloria's "people" were. They never asked Gary Masse that seemingly important and obvious question either. Nobody seemed to know who Gloria's "people" were, where they lived or why they were to be feared. They were never named or even shown to exist. It made no sense that career criminals would fear a law student with no criminal record.

The day after Machen interviewed Joanne, he brought in Virgil Fletcher for questioning. Machen and Brown believed he was involved, but there was no concrete proof. Masse didn't directly implicate him; there was no direct evidence against him so there was no way they could arrest him even though many people, including the victim, blamed the crime on Virgil. What they needed him to do was corroborate Masse's testimony to implicate Gloria.

They asked him to take a polygraph. Fletcher agreed and suddenly changed his story. According to his new version, Gloria, whom he'd described in his initial interviews as a nice woman and a law student involved with his friend Brian Byers, was now a loose woman who propositioned him, was likely a prostitute and certainly was looking both to date Ed Davies and to set him up.

Fletcher told police that Gloria asked him about Davies and said he wasn't surprised the woman was looking to date the married man who was more than twice her age.

"She asked me where he shopped for groceries, 'cause she was wanting to meet him. She said she wanted to go out on a date with him and she asked if he went out with young women. I said I had no idea and I didn't know whether the man stepped out on his old lady or not. I thought that she was going to hustle him."

When the police talk turned accusatory about Fletcher's possible motives in the crime, that maybe he had told Gloria about Davies' loot and had something to gain, Fletcher backtracked.

"Question is: If you didn't tell her, who did? Who would have had that kind of information if not you?" Machen asked.

"Calvin and Charlie," Fletcher said. "Calvin Duffy worked for Davies and Charlie Duncan sold him gold and silver."

But Machen didn't buy it.

"Okay, you are involved in it more than you say you are," Machen told Fletcher. "We know you BSed us in the past. It's gonna be even more incumbent on you to tell us the truth now, because we don't trust you now."

They had reason to be so distrustful. The results of Fletcher's polygraph examination report for this interview were very clear: deception was indicated. The polygraph examiner noted that the test series consisted of relevant questions interspersed with irrelevant and control questions. The questions where the polygraph indicated that Fletcher was lying were:

> Q. Were you knowingly involved in any plan or arrangement to rob the Davies?
> A. No.
> Q. Prior to the robbery of the Davies, were you involved in any plan to steal valuables from them?
> A. No.

> Q. Do you recall giving Gloria Killian specific
> information concerning where Davies kept his sil-
> ver and other valuables?
> A. No.
> Q. After the robbery of the Davies, did you know-
> ingly receive any of the property stolen from them?
> A. No.

"It is the opinion of this examiner that Fletcher was not truthful in his answers to the relevant questions," the polygraph examiner wrote in his report.

Cleland ignored the polygraph findings and put Fletcher's name near the top of his witness list. It mattered not that Fletcher was pegged a liar by the polygraph or that he had a record. He was going to put Fletcher on the stand even if he had to refer to him as an unindicted coconspirator. His was the only testimony that put Gloria with Ed Davies. There was no one else to make the connection he would need for a conviction.

The weeks in the Branch became months. Waid was sent to prison in Chino and Gloria felt scared and alone. She couldn't believe she'd spent eight months in jail with the death penalty hanging over her head like the sword of Damocles. There was no end in sight. She knew death penalty cases always took longer to try, but she longed for her time in court. She was sure no one would believe a drug addict like Masse.

One morning in her ninth month of confinement, Gloria awoke to a crackling voice on the intercom speaker. "Get up, Killian. You are going to court."

Gloria groaned, figuring it was a mistake. In the past year she had seen so many errors in the court system and people being pushed around like pieces on a chess board.

"I don't have a hearing scheduled," she said to the wall. There was silence for a few minutes and the speaker crackled again.

"I checked. You are on the list."

Gloria groaned again. Like nearly all the inmates, she hated "dry runs"—times when inmates were taken down to the courthouse and left to sit in the holding tank all day, because they didn't actually have a hearing. She got dressed, caught the chain and was hauled downtown. About 11:00 A.M. the bailiff pulled her from the holding tank and led her into a courtroom.

Thielen was waiting for her and her codefendants weren't there.

"What's up?" she asked Thielen, who was grinning.

"It's your bail hearing."

"Bail hearing?" It was the last thing she expected to hear. "Did they drop the death penalty?" she whispered, excited and bouncing on her toes.

"Shush," Thielen said, handing Gloria a copy of a decision handed down in the California Supreme Court in the past forty-eight hours. The decision in *People vs. Carlos* removed a certain category of offenders from the imposition of the death penalty. It held that it was necessary to be intentionally involved in a killing to get the death sentence. Since Gloria had never been accused of being intentionally involved in the homicide, she fell under this new ruling. Gloria scanned the document and knew right away she could be eligible for bail.

Her thoughts were spinning.

The judge banged the gavel and she turned her attention to the bench, recognizing Judge Ronald Tochterman, a middle-aged man who had a brilliant legal mind and considerable courtroom skills.

Thielen addressed the court, telling the judge that Gloria had been arrested in the same place twice, had no criminal history and should be released on a reasonable bail.

Gloria barely listened to Thielen and watched Tochterman intently, unable to read anything on his emotionless face.

Then it was Cleland's turn. He was full of spit and vinegar, adamant that Gloria was a danger to society and a cold-blooded killer and that there was no way that she should be let out on bail. He blustered his outrage until Tochterman held up his hand indicating that he had heard enough. Cutting Cleland off in midsentence, Judge Tochterman set Gloria's bail at twenty-five thousand dollars, banged his gavel and called the next case.

"I'll call Brian and let him know," Thielen said, smiling and giving Gloria a quick hug. She walked back to the holding tank on the arm of the bailiff, barely able to contain her excitement. She might actually be getting out.

The rest of the afternoon in the holding tank felt like forever. She paced back and forth in the tiny courthouse cell, the minutes feeling like hours, the hours like days. She could go home on bail, but there was no one she could tell. There was no phone and no way to contact anyone. At times she felt so frustrated she wanted to chew on the plaster and then suddenly she felt overwhelmed with such intense joy she wanted to jump up and down.

By the time Gloria got back to the Branch in the late afternoon everyone knew that she had been granted bail. It seemed everyone was excited for her, even the cops. The officer on duty told her that she could stay out to use the phone for a few minutes.

She went back to her cell and couldn't sit still, waiting for recreation release when she could get to the phone again. Suddenly, the speaker on her wall crackled: "Roll it up. You are being released."

Gloria leapt off her bed and raced to the wall, frantically pushing the intercom button. "What did you say?'

"You heard me, Killian," replied the anonymous voice with a chuckle. "Roll it up. Your people are here to get you."

"People?" she wondered aloud. *I have people? Brian is here!* she thought. Whirling like a dervish, she raced around the cell gathering her things and stripping the room so the next trustee wouldn't have any extra work to do. The guard unlocked her cell and led her down the hall to process out. The paperwork took only a few minutes, but Gloria was too dazed to pay any attention to it. The officer opened a door and gently nudged her through. There was Brian. He was smiling. He held his arms open and she fell into them.

"Oh, I'm free, I'm free!" she exclaimed. Brian led her outside and into the car where his parents were waiting for them. She hugged them and chattered on the drive back to town, asking questions and babbling. Less than twenty-four hours ago she was facing the death penalty and now she was free. Brian's mom told her that they had put up their house to guarantee her bail and Gloria was finally silenced. *What amazing people,* she thought. *How supportive and caring.* She couldn't even begin to find the words to thank them.

Brian's parents dropped her and Brian at their friends' apartment. The couple, who had immediately accepted Gloria into their lives, partied, shopped, barbequed with Gloria and Brian and had supported them throughout Gloria's ordeal. They arranged an impromptu coming home party for her. The four of them jumped around, hugging each other with tears of joy streaming down their faces. Other friends dropped in and out, ate pizza and drank beer.

As the day wound down, Brian pulled Gloria to the side of the room.

"I've got a tiny bit of bad news for you, honey," Brian said. Gloria looked at him, waiting. "You've got to be in court at 8:00 A.M. tomorrow."

"Whatever for?"

"I don't know," said Brian. "Ray just told me we had to be there."

Gloria was nervous, scared and confused. *What is this all about? What could be happening now? What could the judge have in store for me?* She understood how little power people really have in the judicial system when they are fighting for their lives and how people get pushed around like pawns. Gloria puzzled over the information, trying to figure it out, but it didn't make any sense. She had learned from being in jail that her best move would be to dress respectfully and show up on time. One thing she knew for sure: Being late for court could get her bail revoked and she wasn't about to let that happen. All night Gloria tossed and turned, waking up hourly for fear that she had overslept. At 6:00 A.M. Gloria got up, made coffee, took a shower and dressed.

Gloria arrived at court to find the same scene she had left less than a day before: Judge Tochterman sitting on the bench staring down at a very angry looking Kit Cleland.

"All right, Mr. Cleland, what exactly is the big emergency here?" Tochterman demanded.

Cleland rose to his feet roaring that Gloria was a vicious criminal and a flight risk who would no doubt leave the country to avoid prosecution and that the judge needed to withdraw bail.

"Did the defendant go berserk last night?" Tochterman asked, angrily interrupting Cleland's tirade. "Did you pull her off an international flight?"

"No," mumbled Cleland, "but this bail should be raised to at least half a million dollars."

Gloria's heart sank. Cleland knew quite well that no one Gloria knew had that kind of money.

"You know the rules, Mr. Cleland," Tochterman said, fixing a scathing look on the angry DA. "There is absolutely no basis for this hearing. Unless the defendant has done something to warrant a change in circumstances, you have no right to an increase in bail. I am impressed that this defendant never moved or changed her life in any way after her release. She was arrested in the same place both times—at her job. Her bail remains as previously set and you would do well, Mr. Cleland, to avoid bringing frivolous motions into my courtroom. The motion is denied and defendant is free to go."

Tochterman banged his gavel for emphasis and told his clerk to call the next case. Gloria and Brian walked outside into cool crisp air holding hands and grinning. It was nice to see Cleland chastised. She savored the moment. Gloria grasped Brian's hand tighter than she ever had. Even the slightest human contact, holding his hand, touching his back, his hair, gave Gloria exquisite pleasure. She sneezed as the pollen drifted off the cottonwoods that put her through so much suffering, but this time she smiled. She was free—for now.

| 12 |

The Sword of Damocles

Kit Cleland looked angry and dismayed watching Gloria Killian skip out of the courtroom, free on bail. Eventually he would concentrate on her, but right now he had a more pressing target: the DeSantis case. He wanted to send that killer to the chair. So much hinged on Masse's testimony. Cleland had to make sure Masse would be consistent and tell the jury the same things he told the detectives. Having put big-time snitches in custody before, Cleland knew career criminals and drug addicts like Masse weren't always the most reliable witnesses, so it was doubly important to choose an investigator to babysit Masse. He chose Tom Brown, a decorated police officer with years on the Sacramento force. Brown was measured and quiet yet charming, observant and shrewd, with enough street grit to make Masse feel comfortable with him. Masse was their star witness and without him, DeSantis could end up with life imprisonment and Killian would walk.

Cleland instructed Brown to treat Masse more like a star athlete they needed to recruit than like the convicted murderer he was. Brown took him to restaurants for expensive dinners and on numerous outings with family and friends. His number one aim was to keep Masse happy, cooperative and on point.

When he wasn't with Masse, Brown investigated the DeSantis case. A number of leads, from Virgil Fletcher, Gary Masse, Dale Herbst and Gloria, converged on Darlene Larsen, who had seemingly disappeared. Did this former girlfriend of Herbst, whom Gloria claimed set up her home invasion and left nude self-photos with Virgil Fletcher, have something to do with this case? Brown needed to find out.

It had been almost three years since Darlene's split with Dale Herbst but Brown soon located her. She'd moved west, right outside Sacramento, and gotten married to a local businessman. The petite, dark-haired forty-year-old former biker chick now had embraced the role of a suburban housewife.

The tall, mustached cop with the thick brown hair and steel-rimmed glasses smiled pleasantly across his office desk at Darlene.

The experienced cop chatted her up as if they were lifelong pals talking old times. She wasn't in any trouble or a suspect in anything. They wanted to know about DeSantis and, of course, if she knew anything about Killian's involvement. She had given information to the police before—in drug circles it was rumored that Darlene was a HIP (undercover drug taskforce) snitch—so talking to yet another cop was no big deal.

Darlene told Brown that she had lived with Herbst, her former boyfriend, who made his money off drug sales and other criminal activity. After a contentious breakup, she moved in with Killian. They got along fine for a couple of months, but when Gloria was robbed, she fingered Darlene as the person who set her up and they had a falling out. They stopped speaking in September, but two months later, Darlene was still trying to get back with Herbst and often hung out at his mother's.

Brown told her Gary Masse had heard she went out with DeSantis.

"Yes," she told Brown, "I met him at Neva's, but he was using another name that I can't recall. We went on a date that night and the next morning he took me to breakfast and bought me new clothes."

Brown didn't ask why DeSantis bought her new clothes after a "date." Her legal or illegal activities had no bearing on getting what they needed on DeSantis and Killian. Darlene was getting what Joanne Masse was getting: a pass on any illegal activity as long as she talked about DeSantis and Killian.

Larsen told Brown that on their next date, DeSantis asked her if she knew anyone she could set up for him to rob and she replied no.

What Brown didn't ask was why DeSantis would ask her that sort of question or if she had ever set up people for robberies before.

Larsen told the smiling, friendly investigator that after DeSantis' second visit to her home, she read about the Davies robbery and homicide. She said it horrified her and she called Herbst, upset to read that Gloria was involved. But Dale told her Gloria had nothing to do with it.

"Herbst told me that he, DeSantis and Masse had planned the robbery and no one was to be hurt. He said DeSantis and Masse jumped the gun and did the robbery for themselves."

This wasn't what police wanted to hear. It directly contradicted Cleland's theory of the case, exonerating Killian and implicating Herbst. Brown continued the interview. Right before Darlene left, Brown asked her if she knew Virgil Fletcher.

Darlene paused for a moment. "Yes, I know him. I sold items to him at his coin shop."

"Did you ever see him out of the coin shop?" Brown asked.

"No," Darlene said. She didn't mention whether she'd given Fletcher the nude photos of herself that the police had found in a search of Fletcher's home. She didn't tell him that she and Fletcher were more than casual acquaintances. She said she'd never been there though Fletcher claimed she had hung around his house, making sandwiches for men like Calvin Duffy who were doing some minor construction on Virgil's home. Fletcher had also testified that Darlene was a prostitute. Brown didn't ask her about that either.

Brown gave his report to Cleland, who seemed to react with anger and dismay. This didn't help his case at all. Cleland had a witness who put Herbst and Hord, the ten percenters, with Masse and DeSantis in the Davies robbery. Not Killian. He ignored the testimony that exonerated Gloria and did not pass the information on to her attorney.

Ever since a fire had devastated their small apartment while Gloria was in the Branch, Brian had been sleeping on a small bed in his shop. But after being in a cell for eight and a half months, Gloria wanted to live in a home and a place of their own. She spent days fixing up a new apartment in an old building across the street from the shop. She bought curtains, carpets and bedding to make it feel like home. Their friends bought them a small black cat. Gloria tried to pretend that it all would be okay.

But it wasn't.

Gloria began to drown her almost-paralyzing fear in excess food and drink. The constant flow of conflicting emotions about the upcoming trial and the fight for her life was more than she could bear. She was angry. Angry at Masse for all his egregious lies, at the prosecutor for doing this to her and with herself for being an idiot.

But Gloria had no idea how to deal with the anger constructively. Anger had never been allowed in her childhood home. No outbursts, no yelling, not even any discussions. She was raised to suppress anything that might be painful, emotional or inappropriate. She did at first what she did as a child: She ate. And now that she was an adult, she drank. Brian pounded beers while she drank a bottle of wine a night. Drinking blocked out the conflicting and agitated voices in her mind.

There was the one that said, *This is crazy. I'm innocent. The system works, wrongful convictions don't happen and I'll be exonerated.* And then there was her mother's voice, the one that said she was never good enough. She was a bad girl, a fat girl. She deserved this and should be punished for being a disappointment.

There were times she felt guilty about leaving Gerry the way she did, about hurting him, about the insanity with Kent Finch, her lover. Maybe this was God's way of punishing her for not being good enough for her mom, for leaving her husband, for quitting law school, for making mistakes. Even though she had nothing to do with this crime and these criminals, she thought maybe she deserved to be sent away for being a bad person. She was so lost, so scared, so emotionally frozen. The only thing that quieted her mind was to eat. And drink.

Within six months the petite one-hundred-twenty-pound woman put on thirty pounds. Distraught and unable to fit into any of her clothes, she bought speed. For a few weeks at a time she took speed and abstained from overeating and drinking. But soon she returned back to the physical and emotional roller coaster, frozen, scared, stuffing herself with booze and food. The bright, intelligent law student had disappeared into a puffy mess.

In the first few months out on bail, before she went into total denial and fear, she realized that if she was tried with DeSantis it would be over for her. She needed to have her case severed from his. She and her attorney Ray Thielen had discussed this, but he said there were no grounds and he didn't seem to be focusing on this issue. Gloria racked her brains for grounds as she was desperate to free herself from a trial with the killer.

One day in court she was standing in the hallway near Gaila DeSantis and some other DeSantis family members when she overheard Gaila say something about the robbery. *That's it*, she thought. *That's the way to get severed*. If she and DeSantis were tried together and Gaila was called as a defense witness, it would violate the marital privilege to make her testify. Gloria knew that Gaila loved Steve and would not want to do anything to hurt his case. She was certain DeSantis would invoke the privilege, thus depriving Gloria of her constitutional right to present witnesses in her defense.

She raced over to Thielen sitting on another bench and told him her theory of what to do. Gloria was shocked when the handsome attorney showed little enthusiasm.

"I don't know if that's possible," he said weakly.

But Gloria was certain that she was correct. After the hearing, she ran downstairs to the law library in the basement of the courthouse. Four hours later she walked out of the law library feeling triumphant. She had found the cases needed to support her theory. She was due in court again the next day and she was determined to discuss her work and research with Thielen. If he was unreasonable, she thought it might be time to file a Marsden motion and get another lawyer.

The next morning Gloria and Thielen sat on a bench outside the courtroom as she explained her research to him and told him what she wanted. She also asked him if he really wanted to represent her, letting him know that she expected a vigorous defense. Thielen murmured assurances, telling her he'd have the severance motion filed within forty-eight hours.

These past few days have been fun, she reflected, *working on a legal matter instead of focusing on all the issues in my case.* She so missed the law she loved. She missed school, the arguments, the laughter, the verbal jousting with intelligent people. Sitting in the library felt right. It made her remember why she wanted to be a lawyer in the first place. This was where she belonged, not rotting in some cell.

In September her trial was successfully severed from DeSantis'. Things were looking up, she felt.

Within the month, her former lawyer, Ken Jaffe, came to see her. She arranged to meet Jaffe for breakfast at a coffee shop near the motel where he was staying. It was a small, sunny, cheerful place, serving as an ironic contrast to their upcoming discussion of money, murder and desperation.

Jaffe walked into the coffee shop without his usual smile and bluster. His jaunty step was slower and his shoulders sagged where they were once square. He still had his scrappy attitude and his readiness to take on the prosecution, but his wife's murder had taken a heavy toll on him. Being back in Sacramento made his usually intense, bright eyes haunted and sad.

He wasn't surprised that Masse had turned once he got life without parole. Jaffe felt strongly that Masse was lying and told Gloria he'd take the case even though he hated the idea of returning to Sacramento. But this time he'd need fifty thousand dollars in cash and upfront. Impeaching Masse's testimony and defending this case properly would require lots of time and investigation.

Gloria was concerned with the changes she saw in Jaffe. She knew he believed she was innocent and wouldn't have made the trip if he didn't want to defend her, but the fire she'd seen in him was dimmed.

Still, if she could raise the money she'd hire Ken. He was the best in the business in Sacramento. She had emptied out her bank account to pay him the year before and it was money well spent. She told him she'd ask her family for cash. In the back of her mind, she knew that kind of money was out of her grasp and hiring Ken was hopeless, but she had to try.

Brian's parents weren't an option. They were far from flush with cash and had put their house up for the bail she had needed to get out months before. Brian's father and mother had jobs with modest incomes. Gloria's mother, Helen, had little in savings, was living month to month on a disability pension and had nothing left to give her daughter. Schooled to be intensely private by her introverted mother, asking anyone for money was extraordinarily difficult for Gloria, but given her dire situation she contacted her family in Washington. Her uncle Arvid had sent her a few thousand dollars after her first arrest and offered to send her more. But what he could afford barely dented the fifty grand she needed. Uncle Edgar had long since died and Aunt Louella, whom she so loved, was ailing and whatever money Edgar had left her was tied up in a trust.

Out of options, she reluctantly called Jaffe and told him she couldn't afford him. Gloria thought he was almost a little relieved, as being in Sacramento seemed too painful for him. Thielen would remain her attorney.

Gloria believed that Thielen's stability, since he was a successful lawyer and caring husband and father, would project a solid likeability to the jury, especially in contrast with what she viewed as the overly aggressive Kit Cleland.

Gloria believed her case was going to be less about whom she had as a lawyer and more about the believability of a career criminal like Gary Masse. He was a lifelong crook, his testimony was vague and his manner was consistent with a drug-addicted thug. She knew it was going to be difficult to prove Masse was lying, because reading through his depositions, he never gave any concrete dates that they met or times of meetings or phone calls. She couldn't say, "I didn't see him that day. I was somewhere else and I can prove it." Nothing was specific so there was no way to contradict it directly. But reading what he said, she couldn't believe what he was saying. More importantly, in her heart she still had complete and utter faith in the justice system. She'd studied law, because she so believed in the system and learned that innocent people aren't convicted and that is how the system works. Her wrongful arrest and subsequent release the year before helped bolster that understanding and she had convinced herself that the truth would come out and she would be vindicated.

"I didn't do it," she told anyone who asked. "There's no way they will convict me for something I didn't do."

Within weeks of her release, Thielen set her up with an investigator. The only "evidence" they had against her besides the testimony of

Masse was her trip diary datebook. Thielen told her to tell the investigator if there were any people or places in the datebook that needed to explored. The investigator was to help to clear any issues the prosecution had with the book.

Gloria knew there was nothing in the datebook prosecutors could use. She had used the datebook for the last couple of years, making notes on various pages in no particular order. On a page next to a grocery list was a tally of her gin rummy games with Helen, both notations occurring months apart.

But Thielen wanted the investigator to look into a few particular notations on different pages that the prosecution had marked of interest.

On one page was written, "Screen door, screen door lock? Where is garage? Brought anybody home. Always waiting in window. Don't approach at coin shop."

The prosecution maintained that these notations had to do with Ed Davies. Gloria knew that wasn't true. Virgil Fletcher had asked her to find a man, Herb Dawson, a contractor to whom he'd loaned money and who had skipped out, refusing to pay him back. Gloria had worked as a skip tracer and a process server at one time and was good at finding people and observing them. Often, people who are being served a summons know it and try to avoid getting the summons. A process server often has to observe the person he or she is serving so the process server can serve the person without the person running away.

In the first few weeks Gloria knew Fletcher, he had asked her to find two men, Dawson and Luther Hainey, a convicted felon. Fletcher had told her Dawson, who lived in a house in South Sacramento, was ducking him and he wanted to storm the house and get back the money he was owed. He told Gloria that Dawson had been avoiding him and when he went to find him, his wife always saw Fletcher from the window and told Herb to run. So he asked Gloria to go to Herb's house, see if the screen door was latched, if his wife was a lookout and if he could get into the garage. She made some notes in her book and told Virgil she would get there when she had time.

Gloria told the investigator to try to locate Dawson.

The next things the prosecution noted as suspicious were a group of notations: "grey hair, tinted glasses, height, cloth, gloves, tape, rope, scanner."

Gloria did not remember whom she wrote about with grey hair and tinted glasses, but she knew the cloth, gloves, tape and rope were for gardening. She needed cloth, tape and rope to tie up the chrysanthemums in the front of Fletcher's house and she needed gardening gloves. It was that simple. She didn't understand how those lists could be incriminating. Did the prosecutor think she made a shopping list of things to buy for the criminals? Did he think she was going to provide career criminals with the rope and tape they needed for the burglary? It made no sense to her at all.

As for the scanner, Herbst had told Gloria his scanner had been stolen a few months before in a home invasion and he knew that it, along with some other items of stolen property, had wound up in Virgil's shop. Gloria had set up a meeting between Virgil and Herbst to discuss the scanner. Did the prosecution think she bought a scanner for the criminals so they could monitor the police during the robbery? She laughed at the thought of criminals carrying a scanner into a robbery. This whole arrest seemed so insane, she didn't know what to think other than that the truth was so simple and the jury would surely see it.

The only notation in the book that looked potentially problematic was an address she'd written that was a few doors down from the Davies' house. She told Thielen and the investigator it must have been the address of one of the people she had served with papers. In two years she had served over 1500 people, sometimes six a day, and she didn't remember why this particular address was there. It was an odd coincidence, but she maintained that's all it was.

Gloria never heard from the investigator again. She didn't know if it was a matter of money or time, but nothing they had discussed about her datebook was investigated.

From the time she was released in February until her trial two years later, every three or four months she made an appearance in court, waiving her right to a speedy trial, postponing the dates and going back to doing her best to pretend life was normal. It played into the thoughts she had in her head that the trial would be postponed forever or at least until they would eventually drop the charges like they did before. When she went to court, she went alone. Brian was working and he couldn't handle it. Her mother never came. Gloria didn't know how to tell anyone that she was scared and wanted company in court. She didn't know how to ask for what she needed.

| 13 |

The Trial

"Help!" a woman called through the halls of the court to anyone who would listen. "Stop her! There goes the lady who robbed me."

Joanne Masse had just walked out of Superior Court Judge James J. Long's courtroom and was headed outside for a cigarette when the woman called out, pointing at her. Judge Long was presiding at a hearing with Ray Thielen, Stephen DeSantis' lawyer, Tom Condit, and Cleland on a motion to get Gary Masse sentenced. When Masse had agreed to "talk" to the police, Cleland recalled Masse's sentence and a year and a half later, Masse still had not been resentenced.

A marshal pulled Joanne Masse aside and addressed the woman who had been yelling. "What's going on?"

"I want that lady arrested."

Joanne Masse didn't recognize the woman, Elizabeth Lee. But Lee felt that she knew Joanne as the woman who, along with Gary, broke through her door, pointed a gun at her and tried to rob her several months before the Davies robbery-murder.

The marshal brought the women into Long's courtroom and over to Cleland. "I want her arrested," Lee repeated.

"Why?" Cleland asked.

"She robbed me," Lee declared. In the courtroom, Lee pointed to Gary Masse as the other robber who had come to her home and then pointed back at Joanne. Judge Long decided to hold a hearing on the matter that afternoon.

Lee told Judge Long she felt Cleland was giving her the runaround. "I want the girl arrested," Lee asserted to the judge. "She came into my home, attempted to rob me and now she's walking around scot-free."

Next Judge Long called Joanne Masse to the witness stand.

"Did you rob her?" the judge asked.

"I take the Fifth," Joanne said. "I won't answer, because it may tend to incriminate me."

Joanne Masse was not arrested and Lee went to the *Sacramento Bee* newspaper to tell her story. According to the newspaper article "Woman fails to get killer's wife arrested as suspect in robbery:"

> Masse's wife became an issue when the lawyers learned that she has never been arrested or even questioned about the Lee robbery attempt, a crime almost identical to the Davies robbery-murder… Lee testified Wednesday that she has not been allowed to view photos of the suspects nor to iden- tify possible loot taken.

Thielen acquired Lee's information, later telling Gloria what had happened and that they might use Lee as a witness in Gloria's defense.

That January, more than three years after the murder, Stephen DeSantis went on trial. Gloria, who was frightened and upset, did her best to avoid everything about the trial.

One of the issues in her case and in other cases of those wrongfully convicted is that the accused don't exactly know what they have done to bring the disaster on themselves and, as a result, become very fearful and don't act in normal ways. Perhaps in a self-defeating manner, Gloria truly believed that Stephen DeSantis' trial had nothing to do with her. She didn't know him, hadn't been involved in the crime and once the trial was severed, felt he was out of her world.

The DeSantis trial went on for months, news of it appearing in the newspapers when there was something sensational. One titillating article reported that a jailhouse snitch told the court that DeSantis had confessed. To discredit this witness, DeSantis' defense counsel brought in three incarcerated criminals who attested to the fact that DeSantis would never snitch and hated snitches.

An even more sensational story was about DeSantis' defense attorney Tom Condit bringing in Virgil Fletcher, who testified that Davies once offered him ten thousand dollars to assassinate United States Senator Alan Cranston. The *Sacramento Bee* article, "Slain Man Wanted Cranston Killed, Trial Told," by Fahizah Alim, reported:

> Condit told the court of a defense theory that Fletcher was the type of man who can arrange contract murders. The theory holds that Fletcher arranged the Davies robbery on a contract with someone other than DeSantis...
>
> [Fletcher] denied telling Killian of Davies' financial situation.

Gloria saw the piece but ignored it, just as she ignored much of what was going on around her. She was no longer friends with Virgil, so she had no idea about the things he would or would not say in her trial or had said before. *Of course he would deny telling me about Davies' financial situation*, she thought. They had never discussed it and Gloria had never even heard Davies' name until his murder.

She had no idea that Stephen DeSantis had testified during cross-examination by Cleland that he *never* met Gloria Killian, never saw Gloria Killian and that Gloria Killian had nothing to do with the Davies robbery. Cleland never told Gloria's lawyer Thielen about that testimony either. Gloria never asked Thielen if he was getting the dailies or following the trial. She wasn't thinking; she was drinking. She talked with no one about the case and trusted none of her friends. Her mother refused to ask her what was going on. On those rare occasions when Gloria cried or mentioned the trial to Brian, he inevitably said, "Honey, relax. It's not going to happen. You're not going to get convicted. You didn't do anything."

During the months DeSantis waited for sentencing and Gloria waited for her trial, Brown and Cleland treated Masse to luxuries that prisoners—especially convicted murderers—rarely, if ever, enjoy. On Cleland's okay, Brown transported Masse at government expense to visits with his family outside the jail, to dinners in restaurants and on excursions all over the city without handcuffs, giving him access to guns and treating Masse like a "buddy."

Cleland kept Masse close. Years later, Masse, his father and his mother all testified that the prosecution told Masse "not to say certain things that could have violated DeSantis' rights of discovery."

None of this information was made available to Thielen for Gloria's defense.

That summer, the court finally began its pretrial motions in *State of California vs. Gloria Marie Killian*. They submitted witness lists and discovery. In October they set the trial for four months later. *Voir dire* and jury selection would begin the upcoming January. Gloria tried desperately to pretend that everything would be okay.

Gloria was a fan of Christmas celebrations. Even though she was nervous and frazzled, she needed something to take her mind off Gary Masse and her upcoming travails.

Gloria's mother, Helen Erickson Goodwin, at Fort Bliss Army Hospital in El Paso, Texas, 1944

Gloria as a child

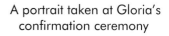

A portrait taken at Gloria's confirmation ceremony

PRIVILEGE CARD

CALIFORNIA
DEPARTMENT OF CORRECTIONS

STATE OF CALIFORNIA

STATE OF CALIFORNIA

CALIFORNIA PRISON
W23749
KILLIAN G
03-30-95

KILLIAN, G.
W-23749

PRIVILEGE CARD

The former Sacramento
County Courthouse,
with the new
jail building visible
in the background

Gloria Killian's prison
identification card

A photo taken in prison showing Gloria with Brenda Aris,
a battered woman who was imprisoned
for killing her abusive husband.
Gloria's efforts helped Brenda eventually
gain clemency and parole.

Maria Suarez and Gloria, photographed in prison at Christmastime

An aerial photo of the California Institution for Women (CIW) at Chino

Private investigator Darryl Carlson and Gloria

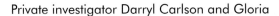

Defense attorney Bill Genego

Gloria, Joyce Ride and Mike Farrell, star of the TV series M*A*S*H and head of Death Penalty Focus, a group that advocates abolition of the death penalty

Joyce Ride and Gloria Killian at a recent science fair
on the California Institute of Technology campus

Gloria in 2004 at a program where she was given an award by Soroptimist, an international organization for business and professional women who work to improve the lives of women and girls

She bought a small Christmas tree and spent over a week decorating it with car parts and tools instead of balls and tinsel. Every day she polished and cleaned small wrenches, filters and car parts and hung them on the small tree next to strategically placed red ribbons. Brian took pictures of the tree and sent them to an auto magazine, where it and a small article about Gloria was featured. It was the first write-up about herself in a long time that she liked.

Her mother, whom she still saw regularly and who still refused to hear any talk about the case, rarely bought large gifts, but for this Christmas she gave Gloria the largest gift box she had ever received.

Gloria and Brian went to his parents' for Christmas dinner. There he presented her with a velvet box in which were small diamond earrings. He knew Gloria loved diamonds and he felt wearing them would make her feel good when she went to trial. It was the happiest Christmas Gloria could remember, despite the sense of dread.

The last week in January had been cold, even for Sacramento, and Gloria sat in the kitchen on a small metal chair reading the newspaper and drinking a cup of coffee to stave off the early morning chill. Unable to sleep, she had gotten out of bed before dawn and brewed herself a pot of coffee. She'd already picked out a red dress with four-inch suede high heels to wear and was just waiting until it was time for Brian to drive her to the courthouse. They both decided it was best for him to be at work and not sit at jury selection all day with her. He had a lot of work, but she also knew he couldn't emotionally deal with what was happening to her. Neither could her mother. Helen wasn't coming and Gloria would have to sit in court alone.

Brian drove the truck the fifteen blocks between their apartment and the courthouse. He pulled up in front of the building and they kissed good-bye.

"Want me to pick you up?" he asked her as she got out of the truck.

"Don't bother, hon. I'll walk. I'll meet you at home," she said and made her way up the steps.

She walked into the hallway leading toward her courtroom, saw Thielen and smiled. Not far from him stood Kit Cleland. As she walked toward them, Cleland refused to meet her gaze. She could feel his intense anger toward her from across the hall. She had never felt that kind of antipathy toward her before and it unnerved her. She could not fathom why Cleland reacted to her so viscerally. *Why does this man hate me?* she thought. Once again she found herself thinking, *I don't get it. I haven't done anything wrong.*

The courtroom doors opened and the parties walked inside. The small room looked typical: a judge's bench in the front, on the left the defendants and on the right the prosecution. The guests sat behind a small half wall in the back of the court. Judge William Lally, a short, round, white-haired man with a small frame and thick voice sat in the jurist seat presiding over the trial. Gloria knew very little about this judge. She hoped he would be fair.

The room was packed with potential jurors. Neither Cleland nor Thielen had a jury expert. In this period jury experts were rare, particularly in public defender cases. The courtroom was filled with mostly white, elderly people, a few young people, even fewer Hispanics and a smattering of African-Americans.

Judge Lally banged his gavel.

"Gloria Killian, please stand up." Gloria stood and felt every eye in the room upon her. The judge read the charges then asked the potential jurists, "Does anyone in this room know this woman?"

Gloria stood, feeling humiliated like an animal being stared at in a zoo. "Turn around," the judge instructed her, making sure that everyone in the courtroom had a good look at her. If any potential juror knows or has met a defendant before, he or she is automatically dismissed from the trial.

No one knew Gloria, so she sat back down. The trial was less than five minutes old and already she felt ashamed and humiliated.

"Everyone here looks like escapees from a senior center," she said to Thielen as they began the *voir dire*, the jury selection. It wasn't going to be easy.

At the end of day one, they hadn't gotten one juror. Gloria walked outside the court building. The air was cold and crisp. It was only 4 P.M., not yet dark, and she wanted time to think or at least to settle and be in quiet. She looked at the shoes on her feet, four-inch heels, and debated calling Brian. Deciding not to, she lit a cigarette and started to walk the fifteen blocks to their apartment. The walking calmed her and she stopped to buy a soda from a local grocer a few blocks from their home. Since her time in the Branch, she cherished the time she could spend alone, choosing to do what she wanted when she wanted. To Gloria, something small like buying a soda and walking home still felt like freedom.

Gloria knew that picking a jury was an art and something she was certainly not an expert on. She asked Thielen to reject the people she thought looked overtly hostile or stared at her in a condescending way.

After two weeks the jury had been selected, but Gloria wasn't satisfied. The jurors were just about all white and most were retirees. She didn't think they would understand who she was. She was afraid they might relate more to Kit Cleland and his Boy Scout demeanor, but as she watched the twelve seats fill in, she tried to project confidence that the truth would set her free.

Kit Cleland opened his remarks with guns blazing. He paced dramatically in front of the jury, full of spirit, vinegar and certainty. "Gloria Killian has the blood of Ed Davies on her hands," he said, perfectly modulating his voice. He was an excellent speaker. His years in front of juries and numerous wins in court made him quite sure of himself and confidence vibrated through every word.

He went on, described the robbery, the murder and the role of ten percenters, creating a dark world that he said Gloria inhabited. She listened feeling very surreal, wondering when he was going to explain to the jury how she became an expert in this underworld and why she could demand 50 percent when hardened criminals only got 10 percent.

The prosecution laid out its case in a very straightforward manner. First the coroner, who testified about Ed Davies' death and how and when he died. Next the police, who talked about the robbery and Grace Davies' heroic crawl to save her life.

In all of these testimonies, even though Gloria was not involved in the crime itself, Cleland always brought the crime back to her, calling her the mastermind responsible for these heinous acts. He brought in neighbors who were at the scene and had testified against Masse and DeSantis, people who had never seen Gloria before in their lives.

Then he brought in Grace Davies.

Davies, with a bullet still lodged in her head, was frail and tired. Slowly she trod to the stand for a direct examination by the prosecutor. Over the past five years Grace Davies had never identified Gloria as the woman who came to the door of her home weeks before the robbery and her husband's murder, but Cleland hammered her with questions.

He then brought Joanne Masse into the courtroom—not to testify, she would never testify; she'd be too easy to impeach. He brought her in to try to establish that she was not the one who knocked on the Davies' door in the weeks before the robbery. He'd been working hard to discredit the idea that Masse, Cleland's main witness, would be testifying against Gloria to protect his wife Joanne, the mother of his children. Cleland felt he knew what Elizabeth Lee had to say and how similar the crimes had been.

Cleland positioned Gloria, who had put on over twenty-five pounds since the crime, next to the thin Joanne Masse. He moved close to the frail and hard-of-hearing Mrs. Davies. "Ms. Davies, do either of the two ladies look familiar in terms of the person who came to your door before January ninth and asked to use the phone—or, excuse me, December ninth and asked to use the phone?"

"I think Ms. Killian's build was about the same as the person that came to my door."

"How about the build of Ms. Masse?"

"She is too slender," Davies replied.

During Thielen's cross-examination he asked Grace, "Do you recall having looked at a photographic lineup in February after you had been released from the hospital?"

"Yes," Grace Davies responded to Thielen's question.

"And do you recall whether you were able to identify anybody in the photographic lineup?"

"The first lineup, well, I guess that was the only one at that time. No, I wasn't."

"Specifically I'm talking about a photographic lineup in which there were pictures of five different females."

Grace Davies confirmed she had seen the women's photographs and hadn't identified the woman who had come to her door prior to the robbery.

"Mrs. Davies," Thielen concluded his questioning, "as you sit here today, can you say with any degree of certainty whether or not Ms. Killian is in fact the lady that came to your door at that time?"

"Not with any certainty. No."

During Cleland's redirect examination, he asked Grace Davies, "Could she be the lady that came to your door?"

"She could be, yes."

Ray Thielen jumped out of his seat and asked the court if he could ask a question. The judge agreed. "Mrs. Davies," Thielen asked, "could she also *not* be the lady that came to your door?"

Mrs. Davies replied yes.

The numerous times Grace had seen Gloria previously, when Gloria was thirty pounds lighter, she had never made a connection to her. In his direct examination of Gloria, Thielen brought that out.

"Miss Killian," Thielen began, "did Mrs. Davies, during the court proceeding, identify you as a lady who came to her house sometime prior to December ninth?"

"No, she did not," Gloria responded.

"In August when you went to court, during that court appearance did Mrs. Davies identify you as the lady who went to her door sometime prior to December ninth?

"No."

Mrs. Davies still had not identified Gloria as the woman. Year after year, time after time. But at Gloria's trial Cleland implied that Davies' lack of identification of Gloria implied guilt.

Yet Cleland knew who had come to the Davies' door. In his trial, Stephen DeSantis had testified under oath that it was Joanne Masse in a wig and a disguise who went to Grace Davies' home.

At DeSantis' trial, defense attorney Tom Condit had asked, "After the first meeting you said you had with Gary Masse, did you ever discuss with Gary Masse what possible ways there were of committing the robbery that he suggested?"

"Yes," DeSantis had replied.

"Any idea how many meetings after the first one that was?"

"I'd say about three, four or five."

"I see. And when you discussed that with him I take it you exchanged ideas with Gary Masse about how you could get into the house and how the robbery would be committed?"

"Yes."

"And you explained—can you explain what was discussed between you and he about that subject?"

"Well, he said he had went over once with his wife one time, using a wig and something about the woman answered the door and wouldn't let them in the house."

Following Grace Davies' testimony, subsequent testimony came from the Sacramento Sheriff's Department: Joe Dean, Harry Machen, Stan Reed and Ray Biondi. There was no concrete evidence, no forensics to testify about as there had been in Masse's trial. Cleland needed the police to talk about the information from confidential informants and anonymous sources that contributed to Gloria's initial arrest.

"Did the sheriff's department, you specifically, receive information from what is known in Sacramento as the Secret Witness Program?"

"That is correct," Detective Reed confirmed.

"Could you briefly describe what the Secret Witness Program is?"

"It's a program sponsored by the *Sacramento Bee* where people can submit information. They remain anonymous, pertaining to their various types of crimes."

Reed said an informant told the police that the people involved in this particular case "were two male Mexicans, one named Steve, one named Gary, and there was a female named Gloria whom he thought to be a student at McGeorge School of Law who set it up."

Cleland also needed to establish that Joanne Masse fingered Gloria as well.

"So did Joanne Masse tell you anything about plans that had gone on, planning that had gone on before the robbery and murder of Edward Davies on December ninth?"

"Yes," Reed replied, "that she had accompanied Gary Masse, her husband, on at least ten occasions to a parking lot on Florin Road where they met this female only known to her as Gloria."

"And what were the nature of the discussions that went on between Gary Masse, Joanne Masse and the female known as Gloria?"

"Well, mainly the discussions were between Gary and the female named Gloria regarding doing this older couple that had gold and some conversation that Gary was supposed to get somebody to help him do the crime."

"During your conversation with Joanne Masse, did you obtain from her a description of the person whom she was calling by the name Gloria?"

"Yes, she described her as a white female, thirty-five, dark hair with it sort of combed back, heavyset but not fat. I believe that was the extent of it."

Next Cleland asked Machen about Gloria's first arrest, the one where she said, "You have the worst sense of timing. I always get caught," as she walked to the waiting police car. Later Cleland characterized it as an admission of guilt in his closing arguments.

"So she gets in the car and on the way down to the sheriff's department she makes this curious statement: 'You have the worst sense of timing. I always get caught.' Now that's not really a Freudian slip. A Freudian slip is kind of when you mean something else, but you say something that means, that says what you really have on your mind. But it is kind of like it. When you have something on your mind and it's so boiling it kind of pops out. And that is what happened here. Out of a sense of guilt she makes this curious statement to the police."

Gloria wondered why Cleland never asked Machen why he never questioned her about this statement when she was arrested that December day. If the police believed that statement was an admission of guilt instead of the offhand quip about sex that it was, why didn't they follow up with questions about it? If it was a suspicious admission of guilt, why didn't the police ask her what it meant when they interrogated her and why was it never cited until the trial? What does *always get caught* mean to a person who's never been arrested before? It seemed to her that Cleland was grasping at straws.

After the first two days of the trial Gloria felt shell-shocked and humiliated. At home, she and Brian ate dinner and she barely talked about what transpired in court. As sweet as Brian was, he couldn't deal with anything that was going on, falling into the pattern of "Honey, it's going to be okay." Gloria drowned her emotions with a nightly bottle of wine, which was the only thing that gave her a few fitful hours of sleep. Each morning she woke up, put on the clothes she laid out the night before and went back to court. She wished she had the antidepressants her friend gave her at the jail. Listening to the cops testify had been difficult. She knew what might be in store for her with Masse on the stand. She wondered how she was going to be able to sit and watch a man she didn't even know lie about something so heinous.

On the third day of the trial Gary Masse walked into court looking like a man who just came from a picnic, not a thug taken from the halls of prison. He wore jeans and a chambray shirt and his hair was neat and combed, his beard shaved. Also missing were the shackles, chains and handcuffs mandatory for convicted criminals being brought into court. Cleland had them removed before Masse entered the courtroom. There was no way the assistant district attorney wanted him to look like the convicted felon he actually was.

Masse was Cleland's witness, so he opened with direct examination, leading Masse along a trail of lies. Masse talked about how Gloria approached him at Neva's, offering him 50 percent of the proceeds for robbing the Davies. He talked about their trip weeks before the actual robbery to the Davies' door and her subsequent calls after the robbery demanding her half.

Cleland guided him through his testimony like a mule on a chain, tugging on him just a little when he got stuck:

"Can you give us an idea of how many times you met with Gloria Killian personally, from the time you first met her until the time you finally perpetrated the crime of December ninth, roughly?" Cleland asked Gary Masse.

"I can't be sure. I know I talked to her off and on. I don't know how many times."

"Would you say that it would be more than twice?"

"Yeah, it's more than twice."

"Less than twenty?"

"Yes."

"Less than fifteen?"

"Sorry, I can't be sure. I was going over there all the time, you know."

"You can be satisfied with less than twenty times?"

"I'll say less than twenty."

"Okay." Cleland continued on. "In addition to the personal contacts that you had with her, did you have opportunities to talk with her over the telephone about this idea of robbing Grace and Edward Davies?"

"Yeah, I talked to her on the phone, too."

"And can you give me a rough idea how many times you talked to her on the phone?"

"I can't be sure of that. It's been over four years. It's hard."

"I understand. More than once?"

"I talked to her on the phone a few times, you know. I can't be sure."

Cleland knew that both Killian's and DeSantis' testimonies under oath stated they had never met each other and Neva Snyder's testimony stated that she had never seen DeSantis and Killian together at her home. But he pressed:

"And did you introduce [DeSantis] to Gloria, Gloria Killian?"

"Yes, I did."

"Where did this meeting take place between yourself and DeSantis and Gloria Killian the first time you got together?"

"Neva Snyder's house, I believe."

"And approximately when was that in relation to December ninth that the three of you got together for the first time?"

"I don't know if it was a month earlier. I can't be sure at this time."

"More in the range of a month?"

"Yeah a month or more. I can't be sure."

Masse was even vague about Gloria going to the door and the attempted robbery.

"Did you ever go over to the Davies' residence or drive by the Davies' residence with Killian and DeSantis for the purpose of checking it out?"

"I can't—I can't be sure of the three of us were together just to check it out or not."

"Did the three of you go over there for any purpose?"

"Yes, we did."

"And could you describe what that was?"

"That was to rob the people."

"All three of you?"

"Yes."

There was never any mention of dates or times when he and Gloria supposedly met or phone records of the numerous times Masse said that Gloria called him. Everything was vague: meetings, phone calls, times or who her "people" were.

"And did you really have any idea who, quote, her people were, unquote?"

"No, not for sure."

"But whatever it was, you were fearful of them?"

"Yeah, at the time. I was—my mind was pretty—a lot of things were going through it."

Cleland never mentioned in court, told Ray Thielen or gave Thielen the transcripts in discovery that DeSantis had contradicted everything Masse said about Killian. From the trial of Stephen DeSantis:

"Prior to December ninth, had you ever spoken with Gloria Killian?"

"No, I hadn't," DeSantis answered his defense attorney's question.

"Had you ever heard her name mentioned prior to December ninth?"

"No."

The most damaging of part of Masse's testimony, one that could legitimize what he said in the eyes of the jury, was whether or not he had a deal with the prosecution and why he was moved to "tell the truth."

Thielen tried to bring to light the fact that Masse had a deal, but the slippery criminal was as evasive about that as he was about the times and places he talked with Killian.

"What was your purpose or intent in asking to speak to the sheriff's officer after having been sentenced?" Thielen questioned.

"To bring the truth out."

"Was it your intent to better your position as far as what your actual sentence was going to be?"

"You could say that."

"Pardon me?" Thielen wanted to clarify.

"You could say that."

"Do you say that?"

"Well, I'm saying, for me, telling the truth would show exactly what position I played in the whole thing."

"As you sit here now as a witness in this case, do you expect that if Ms. Killian is convicted you will not serve a sentence of life without the possibility of parole."

"No, I don't believe I will," Masse stated.

Thielen continued to press about a deal.

"During the conversation, did you strike a bargain with the officers as far as you receiving a lighter sentence?"

"No, there weren't no bargain made."

"Was there a reference to twelve years, the term of twelve years during the conversation?"

"Yeah, I said twelve years."

"And in what context did you say twelve years? What did you mean by twelve years when you said that to them?"

"Well they asked me how much time do I think, for my part, for what I played in it. I told them twelve years."

"And what, if anything, in your mind did you think they expected in exchange for giving you a twelve-year sentence?"

"Objection," Cleland interrupted. "That assumes a fact not in evidence that they had some sort of authority."

"Mr. Masse," Thielen continued, "did you expect these police officers to assist you in getting an ultimate sentence of only twelve years?"

"That's a hard question to answer. At that time it was just, I was going in the dark, you know. I couldn't expect them to do anything. They wouldn't give me nothing in writing. In other words, what I was telling them was, you know, I was just doing it on my own with nothing to hang onto. Just like right now. I'm floating. I don't know what is going to happen. I can't tell you that."

"Do you expect Mr. Cleland to go to bat for you at the completion of your testimony if Miss Killian is convicted?"

"If Miss Killian is convicted or not, you know, they don't have nothing to do with it. It's what, you know, the truth, you know. I had to go with the truth, bring the truth out...You know, it's hard for me to answer the way you—the way you say it. You make it sound like if I don't...I don't, you know. Don't make no difference if I, like, for them, you know, to make it good, look good for the prosecutor. It's going to help me more."

Neither Gloria's mother nor others came to support Gloria. Alone except for her attorney, Gloria sat in her chair listening to Masse and thinking, *This is insane. I don't believe anything this man says. How can anyone else? It's too crazy. Who would believe someone so vague?* She tried hard not to peek at the jury to see how they were reacting to Masse. Thielen had told her not to look at the jury and not to react to Masse's testimony at all.

Occasionally, though, she couldn't help glancing over at the twelve men and women who were in control of her fate. Their faces were calm, almost placid, and didn't seem hostile or angry like Cleland's, but she felt their blank stares echoed a lack of understanding of all that was going on and she made no eye contact with any of them.

After two days of testimony from Masse, Cleland called in his other witness, the man who was to corroborate Masse's testimony and help supply Gloria's motive for the robbery and subsequent murder: Virgil Fletcher.

Gloria hadn't seen Fletcher since her second arrest and was happy to be as far away from the shady coin shop dealer as possible. She had no idea he had taken a lie detector test months before and failed it.

Fletcher was squirrely on the stand, with more statements of "I don't know" and "I can't remember" than Masse. When Cleland asked him direct questions about Gloria, he repeatedly said he couldn't recall, so Cleland took out the transcript of the conversation with Brown and Machen where he failed the lie detector test and used it to "refresh" Fletcher's memory.

When Cleland asked Fletcher about Ed Davies, he suddenly knew very little about the man whom he bought a hundred dollar bottle of scotch for and who had offered him ten grand to kill Senator Alan Cranston. Cleland never mentioned how odd it was for a man Fletcher hardly knew to offer him money for a murder. Instead, Cleland pressed Fletcher on Gloria, asking about her relationship with Davies and her reaction to his murder. Fletcher responded that he remembered little. Cleland then had him read his testimony from the DeSantis trial.

"Did you ever tell Gloria Killian that Davies could be a sugar daddy?"

"Mr. Cleland, if you will read that yourself, you will see that the word *sugar daddy* was put into my mouth."

"Oh, it was?"

"Yes, it was. And then I said, 'Okay, if that is what you want to call it, fine. We will call it a sugar daddy.'"

"Do you want to back up further, Mr. Fletcher?"

"Okay, fine."

"Let me ask you this: Did you ever tell Gloria Killian that you thought Mr. Davies was a wealthy man that she could pick up on?"

"I told you and the rest of them that I have told Gloria that Mr Davies was the only man that I knew of that came in there that had money. That's a matter of record there."

"Uh-huh."

"And that I didn't know whether she could pick up on him or not. And still to this day I don't think she was serious. She was just asking silly questions and I—I still don't believe she had any intentions. Because she never met the man as far as I know."

"Well, what were all these silly questions she was asking you?"

"She just asked me if I knew of anybody who had money. And I said I didn't know of anyone, but that was the only man that ever came into the shop that even looked like he had money. Boy, I'm telling you, when you make a remark like that it sure gets pushed out of shape, huh?"

Then Cleland asked him if he read the July transcript:

"On July first, did you make a statement that Gloria Killian asked you where Ed Davies traded?"

"She may have, sir."

"The question is," the judge cut in, "did you make the statement at the time that you were interviewed? Is that what you said at the time? Not what you remember today."

"Oh, okay. It is very possible that I did, sir."

Fletcher agreed that he probably made the statements that past July that Gloria asked if Davies went out on his wife as well.

"And did you make a statement in July that Gloria Killian asked you if he had plenty of money?"

"I don't recall her asking that at all, sir."

"Well, did you make that statement in July?"

"They had it down there that I did make it, so apparently I did."

Cleland didn't bring up that Machen, at the time, told Fletcher that he was a suspect and told Fletcher the police thought he was involved in the planning of the robbery and the fencing of goods. He also didn't tell the jury that Fletcher failed a polygraph test that day.

Thielen assembled a small defense. Gerry Killian attested to Gloria's stellar character and the fact that she was once much thinner. Kent Finch affirmed that she had worked for him as a process server for the times she had stated. Calvin Duffy said he never saw Gloria before. Elizabeth Lee told the court that Gary and Joanne Masse tried to rob her in her home weeks before the Davies robbery. Charlie Duncan stated that Virgil's former girlfriend brought stolen goods from the Davies robbery into the pawn shop and that Virgil had introduced him to a man named Herb Dawson at the shop.

Finally, Thielen put Gloria on the stand. She was surprised he didn't run through his questions with her before putting her on the stand, coach her or practice with her at all. She was very nervous. She had been taught to answer questions as honestly and succinctly as possible. As nervous as she was, she knew one thing for sure: She had nothing to hide.

Point by point, she told the court she didn't know Gary Masse, didn't plan the robbery, had never met DeSantis and was no way involved in the robbery. She confirmed she knew Neva Synder, Dale Herbst and

Darlene Larsen but stated she had no idea what they did or what a ten percenter was.

She never once said or did anything that contradicted her plea of innocence.

On his cross-examination, Cleland remarked that her request for a lawyer after she'd been arrested—even though she spoke to detectives for two hours—was an example of hiding her guilt.

"Now, did you have something to hide when you told the officers you didn't want to talk to them anymore?"

"No," Gloria responded, nervous at first of Cleland's aggressive style.

"Wasn't it a fact that because Virgil Fletcher had not been arrested you figured you could have done the same thing and when you couldn't talk your way past them you decided not to say anything anymore? Isn't that what happened?"

"No. I refused to talk to them anymore, because they placed me under arrest. It was obvious that they didn't—"

"Didn't you feel like, 'Hey, wait a minute. I can explain this'?"

"There's no point to continue to talk after you have been arrested."

"How do you know that?"

"From law school."

"You learned that in law school?"

"That is the first piece of advice you learn in criminal law. It is best to have an attorney present."

"Uh-huh. Well, why didn't you—my question remains though. If you had nothing to hide, why didn't you explain to the officers further, try and explain to them further so that they would understand that you had nothing to do with this crime?"

"I object, Your Honor," Thielen interjected, "that the question is argumentative."

"Yes," Judge Lally replied. "Would you both approach the bench?"

Outside the hearing of the jury, Judge Lally continued. "Kit, I just have some concern about pressing. I just remember some case that said if someone wants to avail themselves of their right not to, say, testify or raise the Fifth Amendment, that to do so is not to be used to presume that they are hiding something."

"I understand that. The way it has been developed by them, I feel there is some redress."

"I think you are treading on very dangerous ground and you could end up with a real problem."

"I understand."

"I thought it was just best to mention it before we got any deeper," Judge Lally cautioned.

The court's warning that he was doing something improper didn't stop Cleland. From his cross-examination of Killian and into his closing arguments, he contended no fewer than eight separate times that Killian had something to hide by becoming silent on arrest. He was desperately trying to impeach her.

Cleland's closing arguments were masterful. He did everything he needed to impeach Gloria's character, disagreed with everything she said and held Gary Masse up as a confessor and truth teller. Repeatedly he reiterated he and Masse had no deal and that Gary Masse was telling the truth.

Cleland cited Killian's notebook entries as circumstantial evidence of planning the robbery and murder. He was eloquent and very clever.

"Ed Davies' blood is on her hands and she is trying to wash it off," he began. He continued with his statement, building his argument. "…when it became time for her to take her final examinations at McGeorge School of Law, she didn't go to school…She changed and radically turned her life in a different direction and took up with a new crowd: Neva Snyder, Dale Herbst, Robert Hord. In case you have forgotten these names, Herbst and

Hord are the people that go around and find out about people who can be robbed in exchange for ten percent of what is taken in the robbery...

"She hooks up with this guy Fletcher, stays at his house, asks him out, all these silly little questions that Virgil Fletcher is so reticent to tell us about...But finally it comes out that, 'Yes, she wanted to know if I knew of any man that was wealthy and the only man I knew of was Ed Davies...'"

But Cleland's case was nothing without Masse's testimony and he hammered his argument at the jury again and again. "...there is always the suggestion, as Mr. Thielen keeps trying to bring up, that Gary Masse is going to get something for what he has to tell us. Well, right now Gary Masse hasn't gotten a darn thing except a little hope that maybe by trotting out the truth for once in his life Judge DeCristoforo may be impressed to the point where his sentence may not be quite as harsh as it otherwise might be...He was telling it like it is, because he has to tell the truth. That's the only hope he has. And I submit to you that Masse's testimony has a ring of truth to it. Just subjectively. You sit here and listen to the guy, you know that is what happened."

Gloria left the courtroom shaken and afraid. Cleland was good, very good. And her lawyer was inexperienced in this kind of trial.

She walked home in silence and waited for Brian. He came home minutes after her and she smiled at him and opened a bottle of wine. There was nothing left to say. It was just time to wait. She prayed that the truth would prevail.

Gloria was sitting in Brian's shop, doing the books like she always did, when the call came that the jury had made a decision. She ran across the street to the apartment and put on a green ultra-suede dress and a pair of gold high heels that she had saved for this occasion.

Brian drove her the short trip to the Sacramento courthouse in his truck and sat watching Gloria for a moment. He let her out at the courthouse steps, giving her a peck on the cheek, pretending it was just another day.

"Call me when it's over and I'll come get you," Brian said, trying to sound cheerful. He watched Gloria walk up the steps, her back to him, silent. She never turned around.

"We'll go out to dinner, too," he yelled out before she disappeared behind the huge courthouse doors. "To celebrate."

Thielen was waiting for her. She looked at him and he shrugged— he hadn't heard a thing. They walked in silence into the courtroom and took their usual seats at the defendants' table. Opposite them stood Kit Cleland, smiling and glad-handing, full of hubris. He was very proud of the job he'd done and she could see it on his face, even though he refused to look directly at her. Having already put Masse and DeSantis away, Gloria would be the last gem on his personal Triple Crown.

The courtroom was silent as Judge Lally began the proceedings. Gloria watched as the men and women who held her fate in their hands filed slowly and solemnly into the jury box. Standing, but unsure how long her legs would hold her, she tried to look a number of jurors in the eye as they took their seats. None would meet her gaze. Sweat began to pour down Gloria's face and chest, staining her dress. Her heart started pounding. All eyes in the courtroom turned to the judge as he handed the verdict to the court clerk. He paused for a moment and looked out at the court, avoiding Gloria's nervous gaze, just as the jurors had. Then Judge Lally turned to his clerk.

"Would you please read the verdict of the jury as it pertains to the charges contained in Count One of the information and inquire of the jury if this is the verdict?"

The clerk stood and began reading.

"In the Superior Court of the State of California, in and for the County of Sacramento, the *People of the State of California versus Gloria Marie Killian*, Case Number 66894, Department Twenty, verdict.

"We, the jury in the above entitled cause, find the defendant, Gloria Marie Killian, guilty of the crime of violation of Section 187a of the Penal Code of the State of California, murder in the first degree."

Gloria was stunned and speechless.

"Ladies and gentlemen, is this your verdict?" the judge asked.

"Yes," the jury foreman replied.

"Please poll the jurors," Judge Lally instructed.

Gloria watched the jury in frozen silence as they were polled one by one.

"Yes, guilty," each responded in turn.

Each time a juror said the words, Gloria felt like she'd been stabbed through the heart. She could barely stand; her chest felt closed down. The bailiff moved behind her, making sure she couldn't run or hurt herself or to catch her if she fainted. Once her breath returned, the bailiff took her by the arm and pulled her to the side of the courtroom.

"Take off your belt," the bailiff ordered. "We can't afford a hanging."

He handcuffed Gloria's hands behind her back. The jury watched in silence as her dress fell limply around her waist. She stared at the jurors, incredulous, as they glared at her with the contempt one gives a pariah. A murderer.

Look! her thoughts screamed. *Look what you've done to an innocent woman!*

| 14 |

Hard Times

The officer walked a somber Gloria in silence to the holding cell at the county jail, opened the heavy steel door, locked it behind her and walked away. Alone, Gloria sat down on the cold metal bench unable to calm her racing mind. *How could the jury find me guilty of something I haven't done?*

She felt no sense of time or place and the dank jail cell became a vortex of swirling thoughts for what seemed like hours. The surprisingly kind voice of a female cop snapped her out of it.

"Would you like to use the phone? You can use it for as long as you want."

Stunned, Gloria looked up and saw the familiar face of Officer Everett, traveling phone in hand. Everett, whose visage had worn a menacing scowl when she strip-searched Gloria hours before, now had a softness forming around the corners of her mouth as she pushed the phone through the bars.

"Can I get you anything else?" Officer Everett added. Gloria shook her head no. Tentatively she lifted the receiver and dialed Brian's number, her hands moving slowly as if through mud. He answered on the first ring. He had been waiting. He already knew of her conviction. Everyone did. It would be front-page news.

"Are you okay, honey?" Brian asked before Gloria could even breathe out a hello.

"Yes," she said, choking back tears. But in seconds pain and sadness overwhelmed her and tears streamed down her face.

"Please call my mom and see if she's all right," she croaked out between sobs. "I just can't deal with her right now."

"Of course, honey. I'll take care of everything," Brian replied. "My folks are here and they send their love."

"Make sure they have my bail exonerated," she said. Even in her distressed state, Gloria was lucid enough about legal matters and wanted to make sure Brian's parents regained clear title to their house.

The moments on the phone and the time in court all fell in on her and she felt a wave of exhaustion that made holding the phone seem almost impossible. She staggered backward toward the bunk in the cell.

"Brian, I have to go," she whispered. "I'll talk to you later."

"I love you," Brian replied.

Gloria hung up, put the phone down and collapsed on the bunk. She closed her eyes, her suede dress crushed up against the cold, hard wall. *My life is over* ran endlessly in her mind for what could have been minutes or hours when Officer Everett approached the cell again.

"Are you okay?" she asked with an unusually kindly affect. "Are you hungry? Would you like me to move you to a cell where you would have some company?"

"I'm fine, thank you," Gloria said. Within the hour, when the solicitous Everett popped back in, inquiring about her welfare yet again, Gloria finally understood the reason for her concern.

She had heard stories about how, at times like these, many first-timers going to prison killed themselves by hanging themselves in the cell or worse. Gloria knew, as Everett did, that she was facing a twenty-five years to life sentence, most likely spending the rest of her life in prison, which could cause a horrible scenario. Everett probably was concerned about the liability and the paperwork.

"I'm fine," Gloria said. "You don't have to keep checking. I'm not going to do anything." Sure enough, Everett left her alone to a fitful night of half-sleep.

The next morning she found herself back on the chain and back at the Branch. Though she hadn't been there in two years she noticed that the deputies, who had known her on and off over the past five years, were going out of their way to be kind to her. One guard brought her a cup of coffee as she stepped off the bus. Another greeted her with sadness in her eyes.

"I'm sorry, Gloria," she whispered as she walked Gloria to her cell. Gloria could easily handle the gruffness and cruelty of the guards, but after everything she'd been through, it was kindness that broke her down and brought tears to her eyes.

In the California criminal justice system it can take anywhere from ninety to 120 days for sentencing, so Gloria knew she'd be at the Branch for a while. So did the staff and even though this time she returned there a convicted murderer, she was quickly asked if she wanted to return to work.

"Sure," Gloria said, smiling, thinking about the irony of the whole situation. Killer or not, to them she was still their dependable trustee. Just as she did in the years before, she gave out phones and tampons and cleaned the unit.

Brian and Gloria's mother Helen came to visit, bringing books and magazines. Thielen came too and they discussed the appeal and next steps. Neither of them knew which lawyer the State would assign for her appeal.

Thielen told her he ran into Harry Machen a day or two after her conviction. He wanted Thielen to ask Gloria if she was now ready to make a deal.

"Deal? What? What does that mean?" she asked her lawyer, painfully aware that she was facing a mandatory sentence of twenty-five years to life. What could she tell them that she hadn't already?

"Tell them the truth and they will help you out on the sentence. That's what Machen said."

"I did tell the truth," she said quietly. "No one believed me." Gloria decided not to talk to the police or to ask for any sentencing deals. Even after her conviction, knowing what she faced, she strongly maintained her innocence.

Within sixty days she was brought in for sentencing. Belly chained and shackled on the arm of a kindly guard she knew from her time in jail, Gloria was escorted into court next to Thielen. On the other side of the courtroom stood the beaming Kit Cleland. This final sentencing marked the end of his very successful prosecution. He approached the judge.

"May I address the court, Your Honor?"

Gloria was surprised. *What does Cleland have to say now?*

First Cleland reminded the court that Gloria had never been in trouble or arrested prior to this case. He reiterated that she was a law student from a good background with great potential.

Gloria didn't know where he was going with this. *Surely he isn't looking for leniency?*

Suddenly Cleland's face set into a hard sneer. He looked past Gloria then turned toward Judge Lally and stated that Gloria's involvement in this heinous crime was evidence of real evil and that she should be punished most severely. Cleland paused dramatically then requested Gloria be sentenced to a greater term.

Gloria looked at the judge who seemed to be nodding in agreement with the prosecutor. As Gloria stood shaking before him, Judge Lally pronounced a sentence of thirty-two years to life. There was a stunned silence in the courtroom broken only by the guard's involuntary gasp of shock.

Gloria had expected twenty-five years to life, but this new sentence rendered her immobile. She stood frozen until the guard gently led her away.

Cleland picked up his papers, smiling. He had put all three murderers away for a long time.

The Branch chaplain brushed back her hair and stood at the cop shop waiting for Gloria. The petite prison chaplain had already heard about Gloria's sentencing so she stayed past her regular hours, waiting to talk to her. She liked Gloria and knew she might need some comfort now.

The guard walked a still-stunned Gloria back into the Branch and led her the dayroom. The chaplain walked in, put her arms around her and looked at her with a knowing smile.

"I don't believe you will do this time. There will be a miracle for you."

Gloria heard her, but the words didn't register. Thirty-two years? She was sure she would never again be free.

Several officers came into the dayroom where Gloria sat with the chaplain and quietly asked if she needed anything. One whom Gloria was friendly with set a cup of coffee on the table and patted Gloria on the shoulder. It seemed the unnecessary harshness of Gloria's sentence had repelled even the cops. They had come to know her during her months in the jail and had drawn their own conclusions about her. Other inmates who were in the dayroom came over to give Gloria a hug and tell her that it would be all right and she would be okay in prison. To Gloria it felt like no one at the Branch seemed to think that her sentence was fair, least of all her. The whole thing was unreal and she felt lost and hopeless.

After sentencing it was just a matter of time before Gloria would be transferred to the California Institution for Women at Chino (CIW), also known as Frontera, at the time the state's only maximum security prison exclusively for women.

Prisoners were normally transported to prison approximately two weeks after sentencing, so Gloria knew that she had one week left at the Branch and time for one last visit with her mother and Brian. She called Brian the night after her sentencing and asked him to bring her some cash on his visit so that she would have some money in prison. Brian told her he and Helen would come the next night. They never got the chance.

"Roll it up, Killian," a disembodied voice barked out of the speaker in her cell. She looked at the clock, which read 4:00 A.M. "Roll it up; you're going to prison."

The indignity of having no say over anything you did annoyed her. If they had only notified her, given her a chance to say goodbye to her mother or Brian. She was going to a prison over seven hours away. It would be very difficult for Helen, who was on disability, to get there. Gloria didn't know when she would see her mother again. And she was broke. She didn't have any money on her books other than one dollar, which would not meet her needs in prison. Gloria opened her mouth ready to protest. Realizing the futility of it, quietly she began putting her hygiene items and meager art supplies into a plastic bag. She had protested her innocence and it had done no good. So she "rolled it up" like the good little prisoner she had become.

Gloria then traded the RCCC pants and yellow T-shirt for the same clothes she'd been wearing when she heard the verdict and was remanded into custody: her green dress, gold high heels and silver jewelry. Slowly she changed into her street clothes, noticing that the only thing that hadn't been returned was the leather belt that had been removed in the courthouse as a suicide prevention measure. But she didn't really need it as she was given a shiny silver chain belt to wear accessorized with handcuffs on the side and a small padlock at the back.

Led out into the hallway and chained like an animal, Gloria was turned over to two large male sheriff's deputies, one young and one older, who were to transport her to the penitentiary far across the state. The older cop looked familiar to her and soon told her that he had been on courthouse duty during her second arrest. He then told her they were waiting for another inmate, June, to be transferred to a prison downstate. June was going to be committed at Patton State Hospital, a mental hospital for the criminally insane. It was the same hospital where Joseph Kennedy had his daughter Rosemary lobotomized in the 1940s.

They waited in the hallway for a few minutes until June shuffled out from her dormitory in similar chains and shackles. Gloria didn't know June but knew her story. The slim, grey-haired, fifty-five year old had suffered a complete mental breakdown and during her psychosis shot her only daughter, paralyzing the young woman from the waist down. Fortunately for June, she had been defended by an excellent lawyer and was being sent to the state hospital rather than prison.

The deputies loaded the two women into a large Sacramento County Sheriff's van, which had three rows of seats in the back that were separated from the officers in front by a metal security screen.

"Sit anywhere you want," the older officer said.

"What kind of music do you like?" the younger officer added, turning on the radio. For the first time Gloria felt relief rather than fear.

They were on the road by 6:00 A.M., heading on a journey that would take them through much of the State of California. Gloria thought it was odd and unfair that June, who had shot someone, had the hope of freedom in her future while Gloria, who had done nothing, had none. Still reeling from the guilty verdict and extremely harsh sentence, all she felt was hopeless and afraid.

Despite the grim nature of the journey, the women made it a pleasant experience by bouncing from side to side in the van and looking out the window. Occasionally one of the officers pointed out something of interest and Gloria and June craned their necks to see. When the officers stopped for snacks, drinks and meals, they brought a menu outside so that Gloria and June could select whatever they wanted to eat and drink. The only unpleasant aspect of the trip was using the bathroom. When the two women needed a restroom break, the officer pulled into a gas station and parked as near to the restroom as possible in order to unload Gloria and June from the inside door so that they were screened by the van. Unfortunately, the first time they stopped they also needed gas, so the deputy parked the van by the gas pump. As Gloria and June climbed out of the van in their shackles and belly chains, everyone at the service station turned and stared at them. Even the cashier came out of the building to stare at the two women hobbling across the concrete, forced to take mincing little steps due to the shackles. Gloria was mortified. She could see the fear, contempt and curiosity in the eyes of those who watched them. For a woman who preferred to be as private as possible, this public humiliation was the worst possible scenario.

Seven hours later, they arrived at Patton State Hospital, a series of older buildings set on beautiful, tree-covered grounds with flowerbeds interspersed everywhere. Gloria said good-bye to June and wished her good luck. After sharing the long ride together, it felt like she was losing a friend. June had helped her take her mind off where she was going and she hoped that June would soon be healthy, free and back in the world again.

Alone in the back of the van, the reality of her situation set in. As the van neared CIW, the officers stopped at a local motel to check in so they'd be sure to have rooms for the night. Unfortunately, after they left the motel, the deputies got lost and began driving aimlessly, past farms, ranch houses and cows. They zigzagged past gas stations and through small towns for over an hour. Gloria was unnerved but powerless. *What are they doing? What if we get lost and are never found again?* She felt very odd, almost anxious to get to a place where she didn't want to go.

Finally the officers got back on track and after more than ten hours the van arrived at the California Institution for Women in Chino.

At first glance, CIW looked more like a University of California campus than a maximum security prison, more like UC Riverside than like Alcatraz. Built in 1952, dormitory-like brick buildings covered the center of the 120-acre campus. Each of the sprawling, L-shaped brick cottages contained 120 individual cells, each of which housed two women. In addition, there was a small reception center building that provided short-term housing to process, classify and evaluate incoming inmates.

Pastoral grounds and dorms aside, CIW was a prison. Razor wire surrounded the entire facility and armed guards watched the inmates around the clock from two huge guard towers.

The first thing Gloria noticed when the van pulled into CIW was the smell. CIW was in the center of dairy farms and the stench of fresh cow dung permeated the air. The putrid smell, terrorizing guard towers and razor wire heightened Gloria's fear. Leaning against the hot metal in the stuffy van, she closed her eyes and quietly prayed that maybe this was all a dream, maybe no one would notice her, maybe when she opened her eyes it would all go away.

She opened her eyes to find it hadn't and she watched the deputies pull the van into the sally port, a series of gates that holds a vehicle in a cage-like space while it undergoes security checks. In stunned silence Gloria watched a guard stationed in the tower a floor above the van let down a white plastic laundry bucket. She wondered what that could be for, then watched as the older deputy got out and placed their guns in the bucket that was hoisted back up on the rope. She thought the whole scene looked more like something out of a police parody rather than a maximum security prison and snickered under her breath at the sight, momentarily relieving her tension. As the internal gates of the sally port opened, the smile quickly left her face.

The sheriffs parked near a small one-story building, opened the van and watched her struggle to walk to the reception center in her three-inch gold high heels, belly chained and shackled, her hands cuffed to the chain around her waist.

They followed her into the small, drab room, bare but for a small counter and a few metal benches bolted to the floor. Warning signs were plastered on every wall. Some read, "NO TALKING;" others, "YOU MUST ASK PERMISSION TO USE THE BATHROOM." Gloria glanced past the counter to an open door that led into another room, which was vacant. The deputies finally unlocked her waist chains and she noticed her green suede dress was soaked in sweat and hanging on her like a creased tent.

Unencumbered for the first time in ten hours, Gloria took a breath and touched her face and hair. Her long dark hair was hanging in her eyes and stuck to her face, her makeup smeared. Her wrists were bruised and swollen from the handcuffs and chains and her head hurt. The older sheriff took a small packet out of his front pocket and handed Gloria the last antibiotic that the Sacramento Country Jail doctors had prescribed for her when she got bronchitis in RCCC.

"Can I also get an aspirin and some water?" she asked him, her throat hurting and her head throbbing.

"No," he said quickly. "They'll take care of you here."

As she swallowed the pill dry, they dropped paperwork on the counter and gathered up the chains and cuffs, ready to be on their way. Gloria looked at them, filled with fear, and wondered how they could just leave her there alone. As much as she may not have liked these men, she felt like they were the devil she knew, always less scary than the devil unknown.

"Where are you going?" She followed them toward the door.

"Don't worry. You'll be okay." The older deputy patted her on the shoulder and glanced at his watch. It was 5 P.M., time for their dinner; that's why they seem so rushed. Her life was on the line and all they were concerned about was food.

"Someone will be along soon. Relax," the younger deputy said, shutting the door behind him. She heard the click of the bolt as they locked her inside.

Gloria had no idea what to expect in a maximum security prison. At the Branch people knew her. They knew she was kind, smart and a respected trustee. Here she was nothing but a convicted murderer housed with other murderers and the dregs of society. If you were a woman who ended up at CIW you were bad, a real criminal. CIW was the place they sent some of the women who had been accomplices in several savage murders with their leader Charles Manson. Here were housed the women who were considered the lowest and most dangerous in all of California. Gloria had no idea what she was in for. And she had no idea that a dangerous murderer was the way they would see her.

Alone yet again, Gloria sat on the bench and looked around the drab room, unsure if she was more scared of being alone or of not knowing what was going to happen. It was a bizarre scene. After fifteen minutes, a man lumbered out from the room in the back and up to the counter. He looked like the old bull guards in the prison movies Gloria had seen: six feet tall, heavyset with a big belly and a shaved head.

"What's your name and what county are you from?" he asked Gloria, who sat timidly on the bench.

She wondered why he asked. *You'd think they'd know who they were expecting. Do the police just drop off total strangers here?* Gloria stood up and walked to the counter.

"Gloria Killian. Sacramento County," she said.

"Good," he said, introducing himself as a sergeant and handing her a stack of papers. "Sign these."

Gloria took the papers, walked back to the bench, sat down and started reading. The sergeant tapped his fingers on the desk, impatient.

"What's taking you so long?" he said.

"I don't sign anything I haven't read."

"Well, I can see that we are going to have trouble with you," he said, his black eyes twinkling.

Gloria smiled tentatively.

"Can you sleep in an upper bunk?" he asked.

Gloria had never been in a bunk bed before and was afraid of heights. "No."

"That figures," he said, eyes still twinkling as he left the room.

Within minutes a woman wearing jeans, a blue chambray shirt with *R&R* stenciled on it, jewelry, full eye makeup and long red nails walked in. Gloria had no idea that she too was a prisoner and the *R&R* stood for *Receiving and Release*.

"Get over here," she said and roughly rolled Gloria's fingers in ink for fingerprinting, then handed her a small board with a number on it.

"Place this under your chin and don't smile."

Is she joking? Gloria wondered. *Why would I ever want to smile?*

Then the woman left and a female guard appeared. She wore a different uniform from the cops in the Sacramento jails, but she looked like almost every female guard Gloria had ever met: stocky, short-haired and angry.

"Get in here," she ordered Gloria, pointing to an open room behind the counter with a couple of showers to the right.

"Take off all your clothes and hand them to me one by one," she snarled. Gloria knew it was time for yet another strip search and removed her clothing piece by piece, handing it to the guard for searching. Then began the humiliating litany of "lift this, spread that, bend over, spread 'em and cough."

Having ascertained that her orifices held no contraband, the guard doused Gloria with delousing spray and handed her a cup of thick, clear liquid. She stood staring at the liquid, confused, profoundly sad and mortified.

"Wash your hair now or I'll do it for you," the guard growled.

Gloria took the shampoo and walked into the shower. She put her face in the water and started to weep, overwhelmed with a sense of powerlessness, a sense of shame and humiliation that made her feel like she was lower than dirt.

She had never been treated this horribly in all her life. She wasn't dirt; she was a human being. And she was innocent. She had not yet realized that no one cared, nor would they ever To them, she was a killer with a long sentence who had better get with the program quickly.

She walked out of the shower, regained her composure and waited for five minutes, dripping wet and shivering, until the guard returned with a handful of towels, two pairs of white cotton underwear, shower thongs, a comb, a toothbrush, a bedroll and a floral print muumuu, which Gloria thought even her grandmother would not be caught wearing.

"Where are my clothes and my purse? I need my contact lens case."

"You'll get your property in a few days," the guard snapped back. "Just wait here," she added, then disappeared, probably wondering where this new fish got her nerve. Here was a lifer with the nerve to make trouble, ask questions. She'd tell the staff about this one. She'd learn her place really soon.

Gloria stood in a panic. She couldn't wait a few days. She took her hard lenses out nightly, unable to sleep in them. Her eyes were dry from the ten-hour trip. Her head hurt. Soon the guard returned.

"Please, I really need to get my contact lens case from my purse. I have to take my contacts out."

"Where the fuck d'you think you are?" the guard said and stormed out.

Finally the first sergeant returned, so Gloria tried again. "Look, sergeant, I really need to get my contact lens case from my purse. I have to take them out or my eyes will be damaged."

"You need to tell your housing officer," the sergeant interrupted. "Pick your stuff up and go to the dorm."

Gloria was unable to understand the terms prisoners know so well. There is no course, no training for new inmates. There's a prison language and a prison walk and talk that's different from the outside world. Gloria was expected to know it and behave accordingly.

The sergeant walked up to her, opened the same door she came through and pushed her outside. It was already dark.

"Go straight ahead. You can't miss it," he said.

She crept across a paved area toward a lighted brick building, all the while thinking, *Why are these people leaving me wandering alone in the dark?*

She opened the double doors of the dorm and walked into a drab, beige hallway with glassed offices near the far wall. She saw a couple of guards inside the room. *Must be the cop shop*, she thought. That term, at least, she knew from the Branch. To her right was a large room with a television set, couches and chairs, empty but for a woman with white blonde hair sitting in a chair in front of the TV. Relief flooded Gloria's body. It was Jenny, an inmate whom she'd met in county jail in Sacramento. While she didn't know this woman well, she was at least a familiar face. Gloria fell onto the young woman as if she was her long lost mother.

"Oh, I'm so glad to see you. I don't know what to do."

Jenny pointed toward the glass office. "You need to go to the cop shop to check in and be assigned to a room. Don't worry," she added, "they'll let you out again."

"I have a migraine."

"Tell 'em in the cop shop."

Gloria walked up to the glass room and soon discovered that for inmates there was no way inside. An officer found her looking around and pointed to a small square opening about four feet high which she needed to bend down to talk into.

"What do you want?" asked the cop.

"I just got here and I don't know what to do."

"You want your door popped?"

Gloria had no idea what he was talking about and handed him the piece of paper they gave her in Receiving and Release. He walked back to his colleagues while she just stood there. Fifteen minutes later, he came back.

"Go to forty-four and I'll pop the door. You can come back out for programming."

Gloria stood still, having no idea what he meant.

"Go down the hall. It will be okay," he said, motioning for her to walk down a hall.

Hesitantly she walked down the hallway and heard a loud popping noise. Suddenly a door swung open. She looked inside to find a bunk bed, a small wooden closet and a wooden desk. To her right was a flat piece of wood on wooden legs. She lifted it up to find a toilet underneath it. There was no one and nothing else in the room. She put her bedding on the lower bunk and walked back to the cop shop and stood at the little window for several minutes while officers sat around the desk inside and ignored her. Finally one came to the window.

"Yeah, what do you want?"

"I need some aspirin for a migraine and my contact lens case."

The guard stared at her as if she was crazy. She looked away, afraid to meet his gaze.

"What's your name?"

"Gloria Killian," she said. The guard walked away to confer with another cop. He returned and handed her two little small paper cups.

"Put your contacts in these," he said.

"What about my aspirin?"

"You can't have any. You haven't been cleared by the doctor."

She stood in shock with her head pounding.

"Get away from the window," the cop said. Quickly Gloria moved from the cop shop and back to the TV room where Jenny was still watching TV. She sat down on the floor beside her and put her head into her lap.

"I have a terrible migraine. Can you help me?"

Jenny disappeared and returned with two aspirins and some water. Gloria continued to sit in shock and watched TV until a cop showed up.

"Lock in," he said.

Gloria stumbled to her cell, closed the door behind her and sat on the bed in the dark for two hours. Suddenly the door popped open and a slender young woman with short brown hair and brown eyes walked in with a bed roll. The two women circled each other like wary dogs but soon realized they were both terrified. The woman introduced herself as Erika. She was twenty-four years old and she had never been to prison either.

She and Gloria talked for a long time that first night. Why they were there, where they came from. Erika had been sentenced to fourteen years for her involvement in robberies that she and her boyfriend had committed. She could have gotten probation, because he was the one who committed the robberies and she was only with him in the car, but her boyfriend convinced her to tell the judge the robberies were her idea, because she didn't have a record and would get off easier than he would. He'd convinced Erika that their special love was worth her sacrifice. She hadn't heard a word from him since the sentencing.

They quickly bonded since it was obvious that neither one of them was much of a threat to anybody. They were both terribly frightened of everyone and everything else. Suddenly they heard a key in the door and they jumped into each other's arms, petrified, as a cop walked in. Neither of them knew the door could be opened with a key.

"Who's Killian?" he inquired. Gloria slowly nodded. "Cheryl Morales sent me over to see if you were okay." Gloria stared at the short, skinny, swarthy guard who smiled at her warmly.

"I'm okay," she lied, unsure what to believe. Cheryl was an inmate she met in Sacramento when she came from CIW to testify at a trial. *Could this be a trick or is Cheryl that powerful? Could an inmate order a CO to do something? What is the protocol in this place?*

"If you need anything, let me know," he said and walked out, leaving her puzzled as to what that meant. How exactly was she supposed to let him know? But she'd been awake twenty hours and was physically and emotionally drained. She laid her head on the prison-issue pillow and eventually fell asleep.

What seemed like moments later, but was actually 6:00 the next morning, Gloria was jolted awake by what sounded like machine gun fire.

She watched the door of her cell pop open and she and Erika crept toward it, curious to see what was happening.

"Breakfast in fifteen minutes," a disembodied voice yelled out.

Gloria stepped tentatively out in the hall, still in her prison muumuu.

"Line it up," a cop yelled at her.

Gloria and Erika noticed the women in the hall were forming a line and they lined up with them. Another cop marched the women down the hall into the dining room in the same building, directly behind the cop shop.

The dining room in R&R was small and filled with a few metal tables with four metal stools each. At the front of the room was a serving bar where women stood on one side and put food on the inmates' trays.

Gloria and Erika were led onto the food line. A woman placed a cinnamon roll, cereal, coffee, milk, sugar and a piece of fruit on her tray. She thought the food didn't look too bad, but she really wasn't very hungry. The inmates were seated in order, with no choice of where to sit or what to eat.

The room was almost silent except for a very handsome officer wearing black sunglasses indoors and screaming "no talking" at regular intervals, doing his best to intimidate the women and introduce them to "prison life" even though he was under five feet tall. Though they were ordered not to talk, Gloria noticed some of the women talked to each other and most of the women were dressed in street clothes. She didn't realize it at the time, but most of the women there had been arrested before and knew to pack their own clothing. At that time, an inmate was allowed to bring one trunk to prison and keep it in reception.

Gloria moved the food around her plate for the fifteen minutes they were given to eat, then another guard marched them all back to the cells, popped the doors and locked them in. There was nothing to do. No books, no paper, no pencils. Nothing. She sat silent, determined not to cry. Erika soon fell back asleep. Gloria wasn't so lucky.

Sergeant Preston sat in her office pushing papers, assigning cells. Over the years she'd been at CIW she'd seen fights, thefts, stabbings. Day in and day out she dealt with inmates who had little respect for her or one another.

"Killian," she called into the hallway.

Gloria walked into the hot office that stank of sweat and dirt and stared at the guard.

"You—Gloria Killian," Sergeant Preston glowered at her. Gloria nodded timidly.

"You're going to Killer Miller and they are going to break your arms and legs."

Preston looked at Gloria's frozen face. Her mouth was open, her eyes glazed. Preston probably thought it was a pretty strange reaction from a murderer. Maybe the woman was actually scared.

"You'll be okay if you stay out of the mix and stay clean."

Gloria nodded, filled with fear.

"Roll your stuff up. You're going to the yard right now."

She watched Gloria stagger out of the office. The guard looked like she was appraising the new prisoner. Better learn quick or they'd kill her in Miller.

Gloria walked into her old cell, gathered up her belongings and lined up in the hallway behind a prisoner who was to lead her to the yard and to her "cottage." The whole thing seemed very strange to Gloria. Sometimes they were slammed behind locked doors and barbed wire while at other times prisoners were allowed to wander around the grounds. There seemed little rhyme or reason to the schedule or anything else the prison authorities did.

She was led out of the reception center and through a huge gate topped with razor wire and monitored by a gun-toting guard in a tower. The inmate leading Gloria took her halfway down the path to a large green area surrounded by low brick buildings.

"Bye. Miller is over there," she said, gesturing toward the opposite side of the giant lawn.

Gloria's knees shook as she walked alone toward Miller, carrying everything she owned in a clear plastic bag. She found a door and stepped inside into an office.

"Hey, you can't just walk in here! What do you want?" yelled a uniformed guard, his feet propped up on the desk.

"I've just been sent from Reception Center."

"You're in the wrong place," he snarled at her then picked up the phone and began cursing into it at the top of his lungs. No one seemed to care about language or protocol or about the women. To Gloria it seemed the staff hated every one of the inmates; most did. Many of the women at CIW had been convicted of serious crimes, so the guard staff looked down on them and treated them accordingly.

In moments a tall, slender, dark-haired officer appeared and led Gloria into a group of offices in the center of the building. She had mistakenly walked into Miller A and was now being led into the infamous Miller B. Killer Miller got that name, because new inmates with life sentences were housed there and most of the offenses were homicides. Miller B was the home of convicted murderers, the new home for Gloria, a lifer, a killer, convicted of first degree murder.

Besides being home to murderers, Miller B was also the release unit for those inmates who committed criminal acts while in prison or broke prison rules. Women who had gotten disciplinary write-ups and had been sent to Administrative Segregation (Ad Seg) were released to Miller B when they got out. Going to Ad Seg was referred to as going to jail and the women who went to jail on a regular basis were pretty rough types, the kind one would expect to find in a maximum security prison: drug dealers, enforcers, thieves and violent criminals. Mixing new lifers with Ad Seg releases created huge problems on the unit, as the women newly released from Ad Seg were women who often preyed on the new lifers.

Unlike the inmates in men's prisons, many women who go to prison for homicide have never been in trouble before. Many of these murdering women are battered women who have killed their domestic partners or acquaintances; they know little or nothing about crime or street life. Gloria and many of the new lifers on Miller B were vulnerable to the career thieves and troublemakers who treated Ad Seg and prison like a revolving door.

Gloria walked into Killer Miller, her eyes wide. She was easy to spot as a new lifer and was not anxious to make the acquaintance of the women looking to "break her arms and legs." She was put into a room with a tall African-American who was wearing the prison muumuu. LaTanya, who was lying quietly on the bed, had covered the windows with blankets and kept the radio on loud. Gloria placed her plastic bag on her bunk bed, afraid to unpack. They made little conversation until bedtime, the radio blaringly loud all day.

"Radio bother you?" she asked Gloria the first night before they went to sleep.

"No," Gloria lied, too afraid to tell her that it would keep her up all night. LaTanya moved out the next morning and Gloria found herself alone in the small cell. She took a deep breath and looked around the dreary room, furnished for two. It had bunk beds, a wooden desk, a wooden closet with two doors and a toilet with a wooden lid in the center of the room. There was a small window that opened out and was screened in.

Gloria's second day in Miller was her birthday. Unable to use the phone since she hadn't been given a job yet and hadn't "earned any privileges," she was lonely and completely devastated.

Toward the end of the night, Gloria walked into the TV room where she saw China, a tall, pretty, half-Chinese woman she knew from the county jail.

"You know any way I can get to use the phone? It's my birthday," she explained to China.

"Lemme see what I can do." She walked out and returned with Ma Barker, an African-American woman with a Texas accent and a twinkle in her eye who loved to get one over on the guards. China and Ma Barker smuggled Gloria into the closet where the phone was kept. She dialed Brian, who picked up right away.

"Hi, honey, happy birthday," he said and tears of relief and joy ran down her face.

Since Killer Miller housed the toughest and most dangerous criminals, it was a close custody unit, which meant inmates were not allowed
to leave the building after 4 P.M. without an escort. The correctional
officers took the prisoners to dinner and to other appointments.

Miller B was under strict supervision and the inmates were only
allowed in and out of the unit for ten minutes on the half hour and
the hour, a system known as "on and off the red." On the red was the
ten-minute segment during which inmates could have their cell doors
opened and go in and out of the unit. Off the red was the remaining
twenty-minute segment in which they were required to remain inside
their cells or outside the housing unit.

Miller was closely guarded. Gloria quickly found out why.

There was a triumvirate of women who made it particularly trou-
blesome for the new lifers: Ruby, Ruby's girlfriend Bette and Tina.

Ruby was athletic, boyish and tough. Bette, built in the same vein,
was smaller, with bleached hair, a snaggletooth in front and a mean look
that matched her disposition. Tina was a trim, pretty woman who always
wore nice clothes and jewelry, usually stolen from other inmates. Her
demeanor was pleasant and her face attractive, but she was the toughest
of the three. These women fought with fellow inmates, stole whatever
they could and feared and respected no one. They often spent as much
time in Ad Seg as out of it.

Gloria learned who they were during her first few days when she
received her first quarterly package from Gloria Waid. The two women
had continued their friendship through Gloria's first release and trial
and Gloria felt lucky to have Waid in her life. Waid had spent two years
at CIW before her conviction was reversed and knew exactly what
Gloria would need in prison to survive.

Gloria was thrilled when she got her package. Waid had sent thirty
pounds of Gloria's clothes, makeup, perfume, hygiene items and food.

Seeing her personal items was a huge boost for Gloria and she felt almost normal.

When she returned with her package, her unit was off the red. The CO working the unit allowed Gloria to come inside but made her stand by her locked cell door until the unit was on the red. She stood for ten minutes with her clothes, food and toiletries at her feet, in plain sight of every thief and lowlife scanning the hall. Bette, Ruby and Tina looked over at Gloria and looked at each other, making a mental note of her room number.

The inmate who lived across the hall from Gloria, the biggest, baddest dope dealer and enforcer on the yard, watched as Ruby and the girls eyed Gloria's belongings and room. Gloria saw her neighbor watching the scene and gave her some cookies, trying to curry favor with at least one of the women on the hall. She knew earning the friendship of at least one of the badass women, even if she was scared to death of her, would be a good thing.

The next night when Gloria went to dinner, she returned to find her cell door wide open. Her room was empty and all the food, toiletries and clothes were gone. Gloria knew that only COs could open cell doors, so what had happened?

Gloria was devastated, crying as she ran down the hall to the cop shop and complained to the situation to the COs. There was a lot of yelling and room searches, but she never got anything from the care package back. Guards sent her to Program Services to discuss what happened with the sergeant who was in charge of handling all the incidents in Program I.

The sergeant sat in his office chair wearing his ever-present dark glasses and a pleasant smile. Gloria sat down on the chair next to his desk, curious to see what he would do or say. She was already resigned to never seeing her things again, but his suggestion for how to handle these types of violations caught her off guard.

"If you catch someone in your room, just use the door jamb to break their fingers," he told her. The doors on Miller did not have handles on the inside, so to open or close the doors the inmates needed to wrap their fingers around the edges of the doors.

Gloria sat staring at him, incredulous that the guards had no intention of protecting the inmates from one another. The sergeant looked at Gloria's shocked face and mistook her incredulity for stupidity. He got up from his desk, walked over to the door, opened it, placed his fingers between the jamb and the door and started to close it.

"This is how you do it," he demonstrated.

"But I'll get a one-fifteen," Gloria managed to squeak out. She was afraid to get a 115, a disciplinary write-up. The sergeant smiled at her naiveté and ignorance.

"All the one-fifteens cross my desk," he said with a sly grin. "And I'll be glad to take care of everything. Especially if you get Tina."

Gloria left the office dumbfounded. Apparently the cops wanted the inmates to do the job that the COs were supposed to do. Gloria knew there was no way she was going to be able exact justice on her own by breaking someone's fingers. Surviving in Killer Miller was going to be a full-time job, with no benefits.

| 15 |

Jailhouse Lawyer

California prisons are a big business, costing the state over eight billion dollars a year; however, men and women behind bars create a substantial work force, one the state likes to keep gainfully employed. "Prison goods and services include farm and dairy products, such as eggs, prunes and almonds; meat cutting; coffee roasting; manufacturing of furniture, shoes and clothing; dental and optical services; and much more, including a knitting mill run by the California Men's Colony in San Luis Obispo," reveals the article entitled "California prison factories generate $150 million in sales each year, new UC Berkeley report finds," by Kathleen Scalise.

At the time, work programs in the California prisons were not mandatory and inmates scrambled for open positions, getting paid only fifty-seven cents per hour on average, if they were paid at all. According to a University of California, Berkeley report, "A main goal of prison work programs is to provide 'a positive outlet to help inmates productively use their time and energies'...[and] to instill good work habits, including appropriate job behavior and time management." But for those behind barbed wire, the reason was different: If you didn't work, you didn't have privileges.

Two weeks in CIW without a job left Gloria without privileges, which meant she was not able to use the gym or the phone. But finding a job was not an easy task. There were no help wanted signs posted anywhere or any job listing service. Soon she found that like anything else in prison, if she wanted to find out something, she needed to ask the inmates.

She had sat alone in the TV room for three weeks, depressed and trying to figure out what to do, when she heard the law library was looking for a clerk.

A law library! Gloria was thrilled but afraid to get her hopes up. She'd noticed right away that if the COs saw you wanted something, they tried their best to make sure you didn't get it. But she missed the law, the smell and feel of books, the hours reading texts and helping people. She had to try.

The next day she walked through the prison circle barely able to breathe the foul, stagnant, inland air, thick with chemicals and cow shit. Twice in her first month she went into spasms where she could hardly breathe; being outside at midday was proving to be a health hazard. She prayed it wasn't asthma but was desperately afraid it was. She'd heard prison medical care was a nightmare.

She found her way to the Education Building, a one-story, long brick building behind Miller. The first room on the right was labeled *Law Library*, but the reality was far from its label. Inside she saw a jumbled mess of books, magazines and people congregating in the center of the room chatting, not reading. On her left was a door marked *Library* and that room held another mass of shelves and books with a long low counter in front and a glassed office in the back.

Gloria walked into the library and stood at the counter until a middle-aged woman walked out of the back office. Gloria tried to size her up. Was she staff or an inmate? Inmates could wear street clothes, high heels, even jewelry. If you could keep it from being stolen, you could wear it.

"I'm Bess Ryan, the librarian," she said in a curt southern twang, her hands folded in front of her. Her no-nonsense manner quickly told Gloria this woman wasn't going to wait long to find out her reason for being there.

"I'm interested in applying for the law clerk job," Gloria said. "I was in law school before this...happened."

The librarian peered at Gloria, unsure she was telling the truth, but her eyes belied her pleasure that a well-dressed, articulate, tattoo-free woman was applying for the position.

"What is your sentence and how long have you been here?" Miss Ryan asked, not wanting to train a short timer.

Gloria told her and was surprised that the librarian never followed up her questions with anything technical or legal. She left unsure whether she would be hired, but a week later, when Gloria went to ask if she got the job, the librarian handed her a signed job form and told her to give the Classification Committee the paperwork.

"I usually get the girls I want," Miss Ryan said, smiling. Gloria prayed the committee would allow her to work for this friendly woman.

The Classification Committee met every Tuesday in a small office in the back of the mailroom of the Education Building. Space was so scarce that inmates were kept herded like animals in lines outside the building, in the heat or the rain, pushing, shoving and tired of waiting. She was nervous, holding her ducat tightly in her hand. She wanted the job, but didn't have much hope: The Classification Committee was known for not giving inmates their requests.

"Killian," a gruff voice from inside the office yelled and she was shoved through a small door into a tiny room jammed with men around a conference table. Two men, the classification lieutenant, who was a slender, middle-aged man and another lieutenant, who was a young, good-looking blond with a permanent sneer, wore guard uniforms, whereas the other three men were in street clothes. Gloria's assigned counselor motioned for her to sit next to him and introduced her to the younger lieutenant, an education supervisor who was there to take notes.

Gloria's counselor read aloud a summary of Gloria's probation report and when he reached her education section, he looked at the other men and smirked.

"And she claims to have attended law school."

They started to snicker, even laugh. The younger lieutenant intimated that Gloria was lying only to be seconded by the classification lieutenant who said, "Well, if it was true she wouldn't be here."

Gloria had already learned better than to speak up or argue. She would have wound up in the kitchen.

"Why don't you have proof you attended law school in your central file?" asked the lieutenant.

She had no clue how to get any information into her file, so she just shrugged, said, "I don't know," and meekly handed the slip the librarian had given her to the still smirking lieutenant. The staff and administration always laughed at her when she said she went to law school. Being laughed at and ridiculed was part of daily life in prison.

The lieutenant read the paper for a moment and handed it to the recording officer.

"Put her in there," he said to the officer then turned to Gloria. "Now get out."

Gloria felt like she'd been hit by a two-by-four from all the hostility in the room, but she skipped over to the library and gave Miss Ryan the news.

Two days later she reported for work, nervous and excited. Miss Ryan showed her the law library, a huge room with white walls, free-standing shelves placed haphazardly and three desks set up in the center of the room for the law clerks. There were no partitions between desks, so there was no privacy to discuss legal issues.

At one desk sat Curtricia, a slender and beautiful African-American in her thirties, hip, cool and very in-the-know about all things at the prison. Patricia, who sat at a second desk, was obese, ill tempered, lazy and bossy, but she had been assigned the lead law clerk slot and took her title very seriously. Being the lead law clerk didn't mean she knew more or did more; it meant that it was the slot that was open when she went to the Classification Committee. Lead positions throughout prison were not always assigned by merit or even earned in some cases. If that was the job that was open, that was the position assigned.

Immediately Gloria noticed there was no sense of order or logic to the arrangement of the law books that were shelved, many being out of order, with the wrong reporters and in the wrong series. Supplements to volumes were misfiled, out of date, not kept up to date or missing.

She also realized that the law library was in a separate room from Miss Ryan with no staff supervision. It was absolutely against prison rules for there to be an area of inmate activity with no staff supervision, but somehow the law library had slipped through the cracks and over the years had become a den of iniquity, a chaotic area with inmates running in and out of the room and hiding behind the shelves to make out or deal drugs.

Gloria spent her first week getting the books into correct order and developing a system that the women could use to find what they needed. Curtricia was more than willing to help her, freely admitting that she had no idea about ordering the books but was happy to have some semblance of organization in the library. Patricia refused to do anything that involved moving out of her chair.

"I ain't movin' nothing," Patricia said, placing her hands on her prodigious hips. "I graduated from Hastings Law School and I ain't gonna do none of this."

Gloria looked at Patricia in shock. She knew Hastings as a prestigious school and had serious doubts that this woman was a Hastings graduate. Patricia's egregious lie was Gloria's first introduction to one of the truths about prison: People can tell you the most outrageous lies with an absolutely straight face.

No sooner did Curtricia and Gloria get the books in order than Ryan told them that because of the lack of supervision they were moving to the main library and they would have to move every book themselves.

Soon Gloria discovered that most of the women in CIW had no understanding of the legal system, why they were there, how long they had to serve and what they needed to do to get out. They had been through trials and motions but were totally ignorant of their rights and the law. She was going to try to change that, at least as much as she could.

Gloria found the legal issues in the prison fascinating, intrigued by the myriad of issues, administrative policy and prison regulations. Most of the inmates came in with just questions, especially since she was new, but word spread quickly that there was someone really smart in the law library.

One day, a delicate, sweet-faced, petite Hispanic girl walked into the law library, barely able to cover the expanding bump in her midsection. Rosa Barbosa had been convicted of robbery while in the early stages of pregnancy and didn't want her child born in prison. She asked Gloria if there was any way she could get out earlier. Gloria understood Rosa wanted a modification of her sentence for an earlier release. Under California law it was possible to modify a sentence within the first 120 days but the reality of it happening was highly unlikely.

Rosa told Gloria her pregnancy was classified high risk, so Gloria had Rosa collect medical evidence to show the court she needed advanced medical care. She also instructed Rosa to compile letters from home and other materials in support of her case. Once she had a packet of evidence ready, Gloria wrote Rosa an elaborate cover letter to the judge citing Rosa's remorse for the crime coupled with her desperate desire for a healthy baby and promises that she was going to turn her life around.

To Gloria's surprise and Rosa's delight, the judge modified Rosa's sentence and released Rosa on probation, a victory no CIW law clerk had ever achieved.

After getting the good news, Rosa ran out of the library screaming with happiness. The word that Gloria had gotten her out was all over the yard in minutes. In a month, Gloria had gone from the new fish in Killer Miller to the town genius. Lines soon began forming at her clerk station.

While many inmates, like Rosa, had legal issues that dealt with their cases, one of the most interesting, challenging and fun parts of Gloria's work in the law library dealt with the disciplinary write-ups inmates received from guards if they misbehaved or for offenses like having contraband and fighting. Through her research Gloria learned that all inmates and staff were required to follow Title 15 of the Administrative Code of Regulations. In this book every rule and regulation of prison life is described in detail. Most of the women believed that they had to plead guilty to the charges. This didn't seem right to Gloria, especially if the inmates hadn't done anything wrong. Gloria observed the women at CIW hadn't grasped the idea that they could stand up for themselves. It seemed prison staff could do anything to anybody anytime they wanted; the only question was would they get away with it.

The staff had been very lax with their paperwork and Gloria seized the opportunity. If the staff did not follow the rules of Title 15, the inmates could not be punished, much like being waived the fine on a parking ticket that's made out incorrectly. With Gloria's guidance, inmates soon were pleading not guilty and beating their disciplinary hearings. Word got around that things could go an inmate's way "if you had the right lawyer." That lawyer was Gloria.

Gloria sat at her desk one day as a tall, thin, toothy, young black girl walked in.

"You Gloria?" she asked.

"Yes, what can I do for you?"

"I'm Ducky and your roommate sent me," she mumbled, holding out a crumpled bunch of papers. Ducky was a typical inmate who used jail as a revolving door, unable to make it in the straight world or even in prison. Uneducated, without any vocational training, she faced hardships wherever she went.

Gloria took the paperwork. Della, Gloria's roommate, had told her about Ducky who was always being punished, sometimes for things she hadn't even done. As Gloria read over the documents she snickered to herself. The officer who had written this 115 had incorrect grammar, spelling and citation of the rule violation. Gloria wasn't sure what infraction Ducky supposedly committed, but she felt sure she could beat this on appeal. She asked Ducky a few questions about the supposed incident and then smiled.

"Come back tomorrow and I'll have your appeal finished."

"Really?" said Ducky disbelievingly. "You can do that?"

"Oh, yeah," Gloria said. "I can definitely do that! And just a couple of words of advice: Never plead guilty until you talk to me. Okay?"

Ducky nodded, a little unsure.

"And you'll come to see me if you get in trouble so we can plan your defense."

She shook her head again. Gloria realized she needed to drive the point home.

"And you're never to plead guilty again even if they catch you with the head in one hand and the axe in the other."

Ducky smiled her toothy smile. She finally got it. And she never lost a hearing again.

The person who left Sacramento a total mess was little by little finding her footing. Once convicted and her fate settled, instead of climbing back into the bottle or a bag of chips and hiding, Gloria's inner strength, the one that got her into law school without a college degree, was slowly returning in the law library.

Gloria learned it was to her advantage to spend as much time as possible at the law library, because it took her mind off where she was and why and the stress of her appeal. Three months into her sentence she had received a letter from the Appellate Project informing her that Julian Macias, the lead attorney for Stephen DeSantis, had been appointed for her appeal. Immediately she felt that was a conflict of interest. In Gloria's opinion, if Macias had information that would help Gloria but hurt DeSantis, he would be ethically bound to help DeSantis since he was the first client and was facing death. Gloria wrote Macias a letter asking him to withdraw from the case. Weeks later she received an affidavit filed by Macias denying any conflict and alleging that he could do her appeal without compromising his previous client. She was furious. She filed a motion with the appellate court requesting the withdrawal of Macias' appointment based on the conflict of interest. The state public defender, who was now representing DeSantis, also filed a motion in the appellate court requesting his withdrawal based on the same conflict of interest. Gloria hoped the appellate court wouldn't allow a conflict of this nature to proceed.

As Gloria waited to hear the appellate court's decision, her job and the legal work were the only things that kept her feeling sane. On her daily breaks she went outside the library to look at the people around her, feeling like an alien observer, like she'd been snatched up and dropped off on another planet. The library was the only thing that got her out of bed in the morning. She was often frightened and didn't sleep well.

Night after night she thought about what happened and it crushed her that she couldn't figure out her case or what had happened and was unable to help herself. She read every case, every decision and every statute that ever came down but couldn't find anything that would help her. So helping others became a priority. As she continued to organize the law library and secure successes in cases, she convinced herself for a short while that she was in prison because it was her mission in life to go there. She helped many women at the prison and did research and legal work for the administration, which was previously unheard of, but the work helped her rationalize a reason for the disaster that had befallen her. The horror of spending life in prison was so great that if she couldn't find a reason for what had happened, she felt she wasn't going to survive. Working all the time also helped her ignore the meanness and ugliness of her situation, the sense of powerlessness with which she lived.

To her dismay, the appellate court didn't allow her motion and Macias remained her lawyer. She worked hard on her appeal in the law library and sent Macias a letter citing the issues that she thought could be raised in her appeal. He never responded to her letter or her calls.

A few months later she received a copy of the appeal Macias drafted and it was just as disappointing as she felt it would be. There wasn't a winning issue. Macias had raised a Dillon/Lynch argument, which is about the proportionality of the punishment to the participation in the crime. Twenty-five years prior it might have been a great argument, but now, Gloria felt it was a waste of time.

But she, like many lifers in prison, had learned to live a state of duality, fluctuating between hope and hopelessness. When she read Macias' appeal she knew she would lose, but she put it out of her mind and made herself think she'd win and go home in a year, telling herself daily she could stand anything for a year. It was the only way to survive.

The law library became Gloria's purpose and she, in turn, made the library something it never really was: a place when inmates could get sound legal help. CIW was divided into four separate areas: Reception Center (RC), Mental Health Yard (SCU), Administrative Segregation (Ad Seg) and General Population (the Yard). Access to the law library was limited to the women on the Yard, although the clerks could receive written requests from the other areas. These written requests were called blue slips (they were actually the color white), but while being delivered they could be and were read by other inmates and guards. That made for planning a 115 defense against a guard particularly difficult.

Gloria strode into Miss Ryan's office, who she'd come to know over the past few months as a fair, honest and kind woman. The two had become friends.

"There's a problem with the blue slip system," Gloria told Ryan, explaining to her the lack of confidentiality.

"And you'd like...?" Miss Ryan said, smiling and waiting to see what her clerk had in mind.

"Since we're not meeting the legal requirements set forth by the US Supreme Court, I suggest I develop a schedule so that I could physically go to the special yards every week or two so that everyone has the opportunity to get the legal assistance that they need and to which they are entitled by law."

Ryan looked around the neat, organized new library and the firebrand clerk she had in front of her. She stepped out of her comfort zone and made a decision to take it up with the staff. It wasn't received well. Most of the custody staff felt that all inmates were scum who deserved nothing, but Ryan pushed the change through and from then on, the special yards had direct legal services.

What was particularly odd for Gloria was that she lived two distinct prison lives. During the day, she went to work in the library and was treated with respect, as a human being doing an important job.

At nights and on weekends, she was surrounded by custody staff who mostly treated the inmates like they were less than human. She was yelled at, cursed at, made fun of, abused and refused basic services, all for what seemed to be little more than the guards' amusement.

Her inmate clientele, almost all of whom were more used to prison life than she, also didn't have boundaries or treat her with respect at first either. Many of them had been abused and mistreated from childhood, so they often compensated by being loud, aggressive, demanding and disrespectful. They approached Gloria in the yard or in her cell to ask legal questions or get advice. In the beginning she was scared and eager to please and didn't set any limits but soon became bombarded.

One morning a woman came to her unit at 7:00 A.M., having been sent by another inmate. Gloria, told it was an emergency, ran to the second woman's unit, but it turned out she only wanted Gloria to file a ninety-day demand for trial on a pending misdemeanor.

Gloria snapped, letting out some of her bottled-up anger. It was her first big step in dealing with her anger and disappointment and in regaining her self-respect. She went to the law library and wrote out rules and set limits on her time, specifying what she would and would not do outside her work hours. It didn't make her very popular, but it was not about being liked anymore. She no longer had to be the "dog in the meat house," as her mother used to call her. Gloria was starting to make a life for herself and she stuck to her rules. Soon she found that when she stuck to her rules the inmates followed.

A year and a half after Gloria had been sent to CIW, the Appellate Court denied her appeal and affirmed her conviction. She now faced a conundrum. She could appeal this denial to the California Supreme Court and raise the issue of Macias' conflict of interest. She figured she had a fifty-fifty chance of winning, but the only thing she would get would be a new appeal with a different lawyer. She had no new information that would make a difference, no new evidence. It was still a matter of the jury believing Cleland and Masse over her. If she lost a second appeal, she might be barred from filing a new appeal later due to the rules against multiple appeals. She decided not to file another appeal, preserving her right to go back to court when the day came that she had something to work with. It wasn't much hope, but it was better than nothing.

In addition to the stress of her appeal, she also decided to end her relationship with Brian. She had called him several times since she had arrived at CIW and their talks were strained and emotionally painful. She was filled with guilt and sadness for him, wanting to give more than she could behind bars. She heard from Gloria Waid, her friend from the Branch whose wrongful conviction for child abuse was overturned and who was back in Sacramento, that Brian was very lonely and despondent since she'd been sent away. Gloria loved talking to him every week and the sweet and loving letters he wrote her, but she felt the situation and distance was destroying him. She wrote him and expressed that he needed to move on, that she loved him dearly and that she wished him well. She tried not to cry as she posted it.

| 16 |

Solitary Confinement

The smog that surrounds the air at CIW is one of the worst in the state. Smack in the middle of the Inland Empire, CIW gets no ocean breeze and the stagnant air hangs heavy over the entire area. Add in that CIW lies in the center of a region filled with chemical plants and farms; lung diseases are common. Within months of her arrival at CIW, Gloria developed allergies and asthma. She was admitted to the prison infirmary multiple times until she was finally put on cortisone therapy to help with her allergic reactions.

One day she went to the infirmary for treatment of a migraine headache. The very busy doctor on duty, who at first believed she was "faking it to get out of work," prescribed her ibuprofen, totally unaware that the two medications, cortisone and ibuprofen, were contraindicated. Gloria took the pill the doctor gave her and laid down on her bunk in her cell.

Six hours later her roommate, Della, returned and found Gloria close to death. All color had left Gloria's face, she was bloated and her face was swollen. When someone touched her skin, it began to peel. She was unable to stand without help, having lost her sense of balance, and she had a constant knife-like pain in her left side.

"Get the nurse! Quick!" Della screamed down the hallway, afraid to leave Gloria alone. A nurse's aide ran into the room and she and Della helped Gloria to her feet. Gloria's body was so swollen her own clothes didn't fit. The nurse's aide and Della dressed her in a larger muumuu and carried Gloria to the nurse's station.

"What's wrong, Gloria?" another nurse asked, staring at her, clueless.

But Gloria was too sick to answer. She sat silently, going in and out of consciousness. Occasionally she babbled incoherently. The supervising nurse walked into the nurse's station and circled Gloria. She stared at the bloated, confused inmate and said she couldn't find anything wrong. What Gloria needed to do was "sleep it off" and in case Gloria didn't feel better in a few days, the supervising nurse made a doctor's appointment for Gloria for the next week. She was ordered back to her cell.

The following evening, Gloria got worse. She began to hallucinate and moan. She still couldn't walk and when she could say something, it made no sense. Della ran to the cop shop and clamored for the watch commander. If Gloria died she wanted the administration to know what was happening.

"You better come quickly! Gloria's dying."

The watch commander raced down to Della and Gloria's cell.

"Look at her," Della said indicating her bloated, incoherent roommate lying on the cot. "Gloria needs to go to the hospital."

"We can't override medical authority," the watch commander said. "She needs to stay here."

"But she might die," Della protested.

"There's nothing we can do."

The watch commander left. For three days Della kept vigil at Gloria's bedside as Gloria suffered intense pains and hallucinations. No one in the medical ward would come to see Gloria, so she couldn't be approved to be taken to the hospital.

Finally Gloria's fever broke. A week later, when she got strong enough to walk on her own, she went to the library, looked up her symptoms and told the medical staff that what they gave her had poisoned her kidneys and she could have died. They were nonplussed.

If the medical staff wasn't going to listen, she would talk to administration. She marched into the watch commander's office.

"You need to change prison policy," she told him. "Medical care is bad enough, but the cops need to be able to send women to the hospital even if medical sends them back to their cells. I could have died."

The watch commander knew Gloria was right and brought the issue up with the warden, who soon changed the policy. But Gloria knew that wasn't enough. What happened to her was just the tip of the iceberg when it came to the horrific medical care at CIW.

Doctors and nurses in the medical office generally thought that inmates lied about their conditions to get out of work, so many women were denied the most basic medical care, misdiagnosed and refused medication. Gloria knew of a woman with severe asthma who was told by the CIW nurse that she was faking and denied help. Fifteen minutes later the woman collapsed and died at the nurse's feet. Gloria knew of another inmate who returned from surgery at a local hospital then died in the CIW infirmary where no one noticed until the food trays started to pile up next to her bed. A woman in the psychiatric unit starved to death and staff didn't notice until the day they were transferring her to the infirmary. The officer pushing her in a wheelchair said he didn't understand why she wouldn't talk to him, having missed the fact that she was dead!

Gloria's good friend Anita had slipped while working at CIW and broke her wrist. Custody staff picked her up, packed her arm in ice and towels and took her to the hospital where her wrist was put in a temporary cast. The doctors told her to come back to the hospital in forty-eight hours when the swelling would be less and they could set the wrist.

But medical care in prison is not that easy. No inmate goes to the hospital in a non-emergency without a written order from a doctor, so Anita wasn't taken back to the hospital.

One morning Anita walked into the law library, her arm in the temporary cast for over a week, and showed Gloria her blackened, tangled mess of an arm. She was in agony, as no pain medication had been prescribed. Gloria was frantic, but luckily she had an appointment with the chief medical officer that day and she promised to tell him about Anita's arm. Gloria described Anita's situation to the officer, but nothing happened. Every day for a week, Gloria went to the medical staff, the watch commander, the program administrator and anyone else she could think of, in an attempt to get Anita the medical care she required.

Finally, after twelve days, Anita was taken back to the hospital where doctors had to re-break her wrist with a mallet to set it. The wrist never healed properly, even after several surgeries, and Anita was eventually paroled from prison with a crooked wrist.

When the *Orange County Register* learned about these incidents, it sent a team of reporters and ran a series of articles about the horrific medical conditions at CIW, including the dead inmates.

The newspaper articles caught the eye of State Senator Robert Pressley of Riverside County, who initiated an investigation into the horrors of prison medical care; he was curious why the inmates called the infirmary "The Killing Fields" (TKF).

His investigation made tensions at CIW run high. Pressley sent investigators to talk with staff and inmates, but all were scared to speak up. The administration didn't like politicians coming in to tell them how to do their jobs and the medical administrators were attempting to cover up the gross inadequacy of the medical care. Some of the line staff, COs and nurses were sickened by what was happening and wanted to help the situation by talking to the investigators, but, like the inmates, were scared of retaliation.

The senator had been told about a smart law clerk who knew what was happening in the infirmary. Gloria was nabbed by the guards as she took a break outside the library.

"Killian, come with us. You're going up front." Going up front meant going to the Watch Office in the administration building, which was never a good thing.

"Why?" she asked. But her question was met with silence as two COs marched her away. She walked toward the admin building in the dark, wondering what she might have done wrong.

One officer took her into a small office where two well-dressed men in suits sat waiting. The guard left and the men in suits handed Gloria their cards.

"We're special investigators with Senator Pressley's office and we're here to talk about the medical care, the deaths and the cover-ups here at CIW," one of the men explained.

"How did you get my name?" she asked.

"From your friend, Anita. Can you provide us with confidential information on the medical facilities here? You don't have to be afraid. We will protect you."

Gloria knew better. If the staff were scared, she had reason to be scared, but she knew she had to do something to try to stop the mis-treatments in the CIW medical facility.

To protect herself from retribution, she came up with a plan to notify the senator's people in case something "happened to her" and she started feeding the senator information through her friend, Officer Bradley, who was able to sneak information out of the prison. Through Bradley she began to regale the senator with horror stories and the facts to back them up. A few weeks into the investigation, Bradley contacted her.

"What's the name of the woman who miscarried in her cell and was told by the nurse to put her dead baby in a shoebox until the nurse got around to seeing her?" Officer Bradley asked.

Gloria told him.

"Thanks. You know, this is my last shift and I'm never coming back. I'm afraid someone is going to kill me. Be careful," Bradley cautioned and quit that same day.

The next evening while Gloria and Della were watching TV, their cell door flew open. One of the COs, steroid huge and mean as snake, sneered at Gloria lying in her pajamas.

"Get up, Killian. You're going up front."

"Let me get dressed," Gloria said, standing up.

"Just put your robe on. Let's go."

As Gloria put on her red silk robe, the CO grabbed her arms, handcuffed them behind her and frog-marched her out of the unit. Another cop handcuffed Della and took her out of the building by a different route.

In the years she'd been in prison, Gloria had never been arrested, handcuffed or sent to jail. She was frightened. The CO with Gloria shoved her into the institutional investigator's office, sat her on a stool and left her there, handcuffs tight against her wrists.

She waited fifteen minutes until Lieutenant Henderson sauntered into the room. Henderson circled her then grabbed her arm, lifting her off the stool.

"I'm not talking to you, I'm not interrogating you; I'm just locking you up and I'll deal with you tomorrow," he said.

Refusing to show any fear, Gloria calmly said, "Fine." In her three years she'd never been sent to Ad Seg until now. It was July 14, Bastille Day, France's national holiday commemorating the storming of the Bastille fortress-prison, and she was going to jail. She smiled to herself at the irony.

Henderson stared at her and they waited silently for a CO with a cart to drive the two of them to Ad Seg, housed in a building across campus. She was booked into the prison jail and placed alone in a cell. A *Keep Away* notice was posted on the door, stating that no one was to talk to Killian without the approval of the lieutenant. As with all of her other arrests, she had no clue what was going on. She didn't know how long she would have to stay in the solitary cell or how she was going to let someone know she was there.

But then voices started coming through the pipes.

"Hey, Gloria, we know you're in here. Do you need anything?" her fellow inmates in Ad Seg called through the pipes.

"Gloria, it's me, Glenda." Glenda Virgil, Gloria's best friend at the time, was a battered woman who had killed her abusive husband and been placed in Ad Seg for a recent infraction.

"Glenda!" Gloria called back, relieved to hear her voice. "I need to get word to my unit that I'm here and to make a call first thing in the morning."

"Let me see what I can do," Glenda said and sent Gloria a book and some candy via the fishing line. Inmates in lockup passed things from one cell to another by tying string around the item and pulling the string from one cell to the next. Gloria looked around the cell and thought, *Well, I've really gone and done it now.*

Via the fishing line, Glenda got a message to Gloria's unit that Gloria was in Ad Seg. Gloria's friend Marcia knew to call Anita if anything happened to Gloria. Anita would call the senator's people directly.

The jail doors popped loudly at 6 A.M. and Marcia raced to the telephone, convinced the person who had signed up for the first phone slot to give her the time and called Anita. Seconds after Marcia hung up the phone Henderson cut the phone lines in the unit. The plan, however, was in already in motion. Anita called Senator Pressley's office and the senator called the CIW director of corrections, who called the warden. The warden called Lieutenant Henderson, who had no intention of releasing Gloria: "Killian is in protective custody for her own safety."

That bogus message zipped around the phone tree until it got back to Anita, who knew otherwise and called the senator's office. "There's no way that's true," she told the senator's staff. "Gloria's the last person in the world who would need protective custody. They just want to punish her for talking to you."

Once again the phone tree lit up, getting back to the senator who ordered the director to let Killian out. The director called the warden and ordered Gloria's immediate release, but Henderson and the staff were reluctant to let her go.

After two days in solitary confinement, Gloria was handcuffed, taken out of Ad Seg, put into a van and driven to the administrative building. Back in Lieutenant Henderson's office, Gloria was made to wait, unwashed, cold and shivering.

Finally Henderson entered, slammed the door and malevolently circled Gloria. "Tell me about the call you got from the CO," Henderson demanded. Gloria just stared at him.

"Are you going to tell us?" he asked again.

"I'm exercising my constitutional right to remain silent," Gloria said, watching the lieutenant do a double take.

"What did you say?" he stammered.

"I said I'm exercising my constitutional right to remain silent."

"Will you make that statement on tape?"

"Sure," she said and watched as Henderson whipped out a small tape recorder from a drawer in his office.

She repeated the same words to the tape recorder and was taken back to Ad Seg, unaware that Henderson had been ordered to release her hours ago. He returned her to the same solitary cell and slammed the door behind her. She was scared and wondered how long they could keep her in Ad Seg without having charged her with anything.

She sat afraid for hours until another officer came to her door holding a file. "I have your release order here and I want to be sure you actually get out now. I'll be right back."

The CO took the paperwork to the sergeant, returned to Gloria and personally walked her out of Ad Seg and across the yard to her housing unit, where everyone was agog with curiosity.

She stumbled over to the sergeant at the cop shop a mess, her hair matted to her face, the sagging, sweaty Ad Seg muumuu hanging from her, but she was relieved to be out of solitary confinement.

"I'm exhausted. Can I get my door popped?"

"Forgive me for mentioning it, Killian, but you could use some makeup."

"No, what I could really use is a drink," Gloria said and stomped down the hall to her cell. In the next few days officers and inmates who had never bothered to speak to her previously went out of their way to talk to her. Her time in Ad Seg and subsequent release, together with what was happening with the medical issues, had given Gloria a new level of respect.

Soon after Senator Pressley filed a report in the State Senate to initiate reforms in prison medical facilities throughout the state.

In her first few years at the law library, Gloria made it a point to reach out to every prisoner organization in the state to find resources and made requests to every law school in the state to create a Law Project at CIW. Since she'd started working in the law library, it had been a dream of hers to create a Law Project for the women where they would have access to lawyers and law students. Legal Services for Prisoners with Children (LSPC) contacted Gloria to ask if she was willing to find out how many women were at CIW for killing or injuring their abusers. The legal profession was just beginning to look at the issue of domestic violence cases, but nobody knew how many of these cases existed.

It was an unspoken rule among inmates that you did not ask people why they were in prison and Gloria knew there were risks inherent with asking women why they were there.

Before LSPC approached her, Gloria had already met battered women at CIW. The inmate who lived across the hall from her had been, along with her twenty-one-year-old son, sentenced to life without the possibility of parole for the murder of her abusive husband. At first Gloria thought the woman was a disgusting mother who destroyed the life of her son for her own selfish needs, but Gloria soon realized she had no understanding about the domestic abuse cycle and the toll it takes on all the family members who often band together to end the torture that they can no longer endure. In the three and a half years Gloria had attended law school, not one word had been spoken about battered women.

Gloria knew nothing about battered person syndrome or about how the law didn't allow testimony about the victim's abuse of the person who killed him. She didn't know that a woman and her children could be beaten and abused for years and when the woman took up arms against the abuser, the history of abuse wasn't allowed to be entered at her trial. She also had no clue that there were unfair laws and that battered women who killed their abusive husbands were never let out of prison. She was amazed to find how the number of battered women at CIW quickly began adding up and climbed to over three hundred. She knew that many legal organizations were working to change the laws about battered women and decided she wanted to be a driving force within the prison walls to change California laws and the treatment of battered women. She felt this issue was too important to ignore.

The last lifer she approached was Maria Suarez, by far the sweetest woman Gloria met in prison. Gloria didn't know her very well but often saw her running on the track when she was there also.

Gloria approached the shy, thirty-five-year-old, dark-haired Latina and asked about her case. Maria stared at her and then a tear slid down her beautiful face.

"I have never told anyone," she said.

She and Gloria walked over to the cement handball court and sat down. Maria told her a horrifying story of kidnap, rape, torture and witchcraft. Gloria was even more horrified to learn that Maria was innocent of any crime and had been convicted from the false testimony of a codefendant who made a deal to protect his wife. Gloria could relate. She vowed to help Maria Suarez get out of prison.

Ironically, just a few months before she met Maria, Gloria met the woman who would help her change the destiny of many battered women in the state: Brenda Aris.

Brenda was a few years younger than she, in shape and attractive, five feet seven inches tall with long brown hair. She seemed quiet and reserved, so Gloria struck up a conversation with her while walking around the track at the recreation field, which both women did regularly.

Gloria liked the shy woman and several days a week they met on the field and walked and talked. Gloria, always the chatterbox, found it fun talking to a woman who laughed at her stories and agreed on the absurdity of prison regulations. A few months into their friendship, Brenda told Gloria they could no longer walk together. It wasn't because she didn't like Gloria, Brenda explained. It was that she didn't understand everything that Gloria said; she used too many big words and Brenda wasn't comfortable talking to her. It made her feel stupid. Gloria was stunned and her feelings were hurt, but she didn't know what to do. She knew that Brenda was a battered woman who had self-esteem issues, so pressuring her to find out what was really wrong wasn't going to help. Sadly, Gloria had learned that prison was not the best place to learn to heal. One may think that with all the time for introspection, inmates would use the time to grow, heal and deal with the issues that put them there, but that was rarely the case. If anything, prison hardened inmates and made them less aware and open for healing.

A few months later Brenda's unsuccessful appeal was published in the *Daily Appellate Report* and despite the fact they were no longer talking,

Gloria took that section of the paper to Brenda. Gloria made it a practice when a woman's case was published to take the copy of the paper to her so that she didn't have to worry about the other inmates reading it and spreading it all over the yard. Gloria was a little hesitant about approaching her, but Brenda thanked Gloria and asked Gloria to sit with her and explain the court's ruling to her. Brenda was an uneducated, young, battered woman who had killed her abusive husband and hers was the first published case Gloria had seen really delve into the issue of battered women in prison.

The loss of Brenda's appeal brought the women back together. A few weeks later, Brenda approached Gloria in the library and asked her what she could do since she lost her appeal. They soon started spending more time together and eventually Brenda opened up and told Gloria her story.

Brenda met Rick Aris when she was sixteen. He was twenty-three, tall and good-looking and seemed worldly. His possessiveness seemed cute. When she got pregnant, he wanted to marry her. She refused. When he told her parents about the baby, they urged her to "do the right thing," which meant marrying the baby's father, so she did.

On their wedding day, Rick thought she had looked through his things and slapped her. When he found out it was his mother looking for cufflinks, he begged Brenda for forgiveness, but a brutal pattern of accusations and beatings had begun and soon the violence escalated. Rick was an ex-felon who was unemployed for most of their marriage and often stole Brenda's welfare check. They had three daughters in four years, all before Brenda was twenty-two. Rick beat her the day before she was to undergo a hysterectomy, because he was furious that she could not give him a son. He never allowed her to work, because he was obsessively jealous. Brenda lied to family and friends about her injuries. Once, Brenda's mother secretly moved her out of town, but Brenda returned, because she was unwilling to keep her daughters from seeing the father for whom they yearned.

One night, Rick held a party for a friend who was headed to jail. As usual, he got drunk and beat Brenda in front of the partygoers and then passed out. Brenda knew he would beat her again as soon as he woke from his drug-induced stupor. When she went looking for ice for her bruises, she saw a gun on her neighbor's refrigerator. She knew the pattern: she'd be beaten again in the morning. She returned home, gun in hand, looked at her husband and saw a madman. She fired five bullets into him as he slept.

In her trial, four years before she met Gloria, the judge had barred testimony that Brenda suffered from battered person syndrome and subsequently convicted her and sentenced her to fifteen years to life in prison. Brenda still suffered from the abuse with nightmares that haunted her throughout her years in prison.

Gloria knew how difficult the issue was to understand. The California Evidence Code did not permit a defendant to present evidence of "prior bad acts" by the victim. In their trials, the battered women could not say why they were in fear for their lives and acted as they did. Their husbands might have beaten them repeatedly for years, but this information was not allowed to be disclosed in court. They were not given fair trials. Gloria realized that the best course was to educate the public and portray these women in a sympathetic manner and that Brenda's was the perfect case with which to do this. She thought about what to do for a while and started a letter-writing and public awareness campaign to bring attention and publicity to Brenda's situation. She became so involved in writing articles about Brenda and working on her case that she began to dream that Brenda's husband was chasing her.

Gloria's intense letter campaign attracted local and national attention and soon the media began to focus on Brenda's case. Gloria and Brenda received letters from total strangers that read, "I never knew that someone like you went to prison for what you did." Gloria prepped Brenda for interviews and the shy, quiet Brenda learned to come across smart and sweet. Gloria expanded Brenda's media blitz to include as many politicians as possible, coached her for every interview and wrote everything that was requested of her: articles, speeches and letters.

In the months that followed, several of the other battered women approached Gloria and she wrote letters for each of them, which were used to expand the campaign for clemency for battered women.

Altogether Gloria wrote over six thousand letters. Each letter had to be written individually, because the prison charged ten cents for a copy and no one could afford it.

Gloria had finally found her footing and this issue gave her something to fight for, something she believed in. Until she had her army of battered women around her, she felt very alone. These women became her family. Gloria vowed to change the way the world looked at battered women and to change the way the courts viewed them as well. She was determined to have these women who were serving life sentences released. She was going to get them out.

Gloria was no longer the same woman without a voice who had watched, afraid, as the lies of a murderer put her in prison.

Finally, after eighteen months of hard work, a group of lawyers and law students from the University of Southern California came to CIW, interested in interviewing the battered women as part of the initial effort to help them. Almost every battered woman at CIW brought Gloria's name up during their interview as the person who'd assembled their information and given them a voice. A couple of the women were so traumatized by their situations that they could not do interviews without Gloria present in the room with them, holding their hands and prompting them about their cases. After the hearings, Gloria spoke with the USC lawyers about creating a Law Project for the women at CIW.

Although there were some highs, the bulk of prison life was a succession of lows and around her five-year mark, Gloria crashed and fell into a deep depression as many lifers do. She became so despondent she could barely function and refused to leave her cell except to go to work. She stopped exercising, stopped running, snapped at friends and staff and went into a deep, silent, black hole of despair. She was convinced she would never get out of CIW and didn't want to live anymore.

One of Gloria's friends who was sentenced to life without parole saw Gloria sink into a dark depression. She and her roommate, Carol, decided to help Gloria.

Both knew about life in prison. Carol had been at CIW for twenty years and was serving a life sentence. She was sweet-faced and kind. She knew about hopelessness and how to help Gloria regain her faith. For months, every evening after work Gloria's friend and Carol dragged Gloria across the yard to their housing unit and walked her around the housing circle for hours, talking her out of thoughts of suicide and despair. It took months, but Gloria came out of it, even then understanding the irony that a murderer had saved her life.

| 17 |

White Knights

Joyce Ride is a formidable woman. The widowed mother of two grew up in the small Minnesota town of Detroit Lakes, not known for producing feminists or activists of any kind. Detroit Lakes is known for being the only place in the United States that boasts of 425 lakes within 425 miles.

After years as a California housewife raising two daughters—one the noted NASA astronaut Sally Ride—and with her husband teaching at Santa Monica College, the petite white-haired woman with piercing blue eyes yearned for something to do, but with her background and at her age, she was unsure what.

Joyce read a book entitled *The Last of the Just*, a story of integrity and persecution that culminated in the Holocaust. Growing up in Minnesota, Joyce knew little about the specifics of the Holocaust. She read the book again. And the woman who never cried broke down in tears. She gave the book to her friends and discussed it in her church groups. The prejudice and injustice revealed in the book made her more than sad; it made her angry. Joyce started a group in her church to talk about prejudice, injustice and feminism. Eventually she met a nun from the local Catholic diocese who volunteered at local jails counseling incarcerated women. Joyce asked her to speak to the group about underprivileged women and life in jail. Her work with the poor, uneducated, often Black and Hispanic women who ended up in jail inspired her. She knew in her heart that the nun was speaking to her. It was the bookend to her encounter with the Holocaust book, a defining moment. Within days she asked to meet the nun at the jail to find out exactly what she did and how she could help.

Soon Joyce was a weekly visitor at the Sybil Brand Institute, the Los Angeles county jail for women. She listened intently as the prisoners talked about themselves, their lives and their families. She also joined a new organization called Friends Outside, whose mission was to assist children and families of prisoners and current and former prisoners with the immediate and long-term effects of incarceration and to act as a bridge between them, the community at large and the criminal justice system.

The soft-spoken but iron-willed Ride visited ten to fifteen women a week, making it not a full-time job but a way of life, her driving force. If an inmate needed someone to call her mother, feed her children and make sure her grandma was sleeping on a bed instead of towels on the floor, she asked Joyce Ride. If an inmate or her family needed food, help at home or contact with the outside, Ride was there to help. She worked tirelessly to aid these women who were awaiting trial or jailed.

There were many times the women proclaimed their innocence and sometimes they asked Ride to help them get out, but she never took up the cause for anyone. That was not her mission. It was part of the mandate of Friends Outside never to ask prisoners about their crimes or their guilt and she was, she says, "well trained." The members of Friends Outside were there to help, not pry, not judge. In fifteen years Joyce went from a volunteer to the head of the board of Friends Outside. She was also a feminist, albeit a quiet one, never one to spout rhetoric.

What she really found abhorrent was the plight of battered women. Jails were filled with women who'd been physically abused. Women who were abused and beaten into submission and often forced into a life of crime went to jail for the crime or worse, killed their abusers and lost their freedom forever. It angered Joyce. She was aghast at both the laws and the treatment of the women.

After her husband died, Joyce took up the banner full time. She planned to go to a conference in Texas that was going to feature a symposium on battered women in prison and Ride wanted to learn as much new data as she could. Dora Ashford, a woman she'd met at Sybil Brand a few years before when Ashford was awaiting trial for killing her abusive husband, had recently been compassionately released from CIW after serving three years for his murder. Ride phoned her. Ashford, a bright and capable woman who had been caught in the web of an abusive relationship, told Joyce of a woman she had met at CIW who helped her, a law clerk named Gloria Killian who had written articles on battered women, thousands of letters, and was working with USC. Joyce asked for Gloria's address and wrote her for some information.

Gloria responded with a packet of her articles and information on battered women. To Gloria, this correspondence was just another way to get attention for the cause.

Impressed with Gloria's extensive knowledge about battered women, Joyce wrote her a thank you note. They began exchanging letters and eventually Joyce asked Gloria if she could visit her. In the last twenty years Joyce had been to jails numerous times but never to CIW, a women's prison housing people found guilty of murder and locked up for life.

Gloria went to talk to the Friends Outside representative at CIW who had a small office in the back of the mailroom.

"You ever hear of this Joyce Ride?' she asked at her meeting.

The representative smiled at Gloria. "You're kidding, right?"

"No. She's been writing me this past year and she wants to visit me. Is she legit?"

The representative told her that Joyce was not only the board president of the organization, but also well known in Los Angeles circles for her work with women in the jail system. She told her about Joyce's daughter Sally, the astronaut. The information made Gloria very nervous. She felt she had been in prison so long she wouldn't know how to talk to a "normal" person face-to-face. Writing was one thing, but real social contact was another.

A day later, Joyce Ride drove her car into the parking lot of CIW for the first time. She looked around at the guard towers and the barbed wire and was horrified. She'd driven the long journey through the hot countryside by herself, wondering what Gloria was truly like.

Joyce slogged though the indignity of the visiting process, annoyed by the invasive searches and endless paperwork. Finally she made it into the visiting room where she waited for Gloria with the other visitors. She looked around and saw that the bulk of the inmates were African-American or Hispanic, some missing teeth or lacking care in other obvious ways. She was surprised when a small, pretty, well-kept, blue-eyed woman nervously approached the other side of the door. Joyce's name was called and the door was buzzed open. Joyce walked toward Gloria.

"Hi, Sally," Gloria said nervously.

"Hi, Gloria, pleased to meet you. I'm Joyce," Joyce said, graciously glossing over Gloria's error.

The two women made small talk. Joyce didn't ask any personal questions and did not inquire why Gloria was there or what her offenses were.

Gloria mentioned that her family was Norwegian and Joyce was surprised by the coincidence. She'd never met a fellow Norwegian in custody before. And this woman seemed smart, very funny and very well informed. Joyce, always reticent to talk, let Gloria, a natural chatterbox, take the lead. Gloria talked about Brenda and Maria Suarez and the hundreds of women she was trying to get released. When visiting time was over, Gloria promised to send Joyce more packets of information. They thanked each other when the visit ended and it was time for Joyce to drive the two hours back to Encino.

Gloria returned to her cell thinking, *Well, that was interesting. Some quiet, older lady who didn't talk much and wants more information on battered women.* She didn't yet see the fire in Joyce's eyes and mistook Joyce's cool, aloof manner as indifference toward her, so Gloria was quite surprised when she soon got another card from Joyce asking if she could come back.

Over the next year, Joyce visited Gloria every three or four weeks. They discussed women in prison and issues of battered women and initiated strategies of how to help them get released. She and Gloria both intensely believed that the battered women, most of whom never had committed a crime but when threatened, killed their abusive partners, didn't deserve to be in prison for life. Joyce also laughed with Gloria. She sent her books and magazines to read and over the year they developed a friendship and rapport. The reserved Joyce listened to the loud and funny Gloria, who had a dry, smart sense of humor like Joyce's late husband and was extroverted like him, too. Gloria, despite her surroundings, was fun. Many times, after Joyce left, she wondered about Gloria and her case. She didn't look like a criminal or act like one. Something didn't seem right.

The women had been visiting for over a year when one spring day, while they enjoyed some lemonade, Joyce blurted out, "Just why the hell are you in here, anyhow?" She saw Gloria flinch. Had she been too rude? Then Gloria laughed.

"I hope I didn't offend you," Joyce said nervously.

Gloria laughed, shaking her head. "I just never heard you use the word *hell* before. Or ask me a direct question."

Joyce listened intently as Gloria told her about the crime during which Ed Davies was murdered and his wife gravely injured, the allegations, her arrest and trial and that she was innocent but had lost her appeal. Joyce didn't say much, just took in what Gloria told her and thanked her for her honesty.

Joyce drove home believing Gloria had told her the truth. She didn't look or behave like someone who would plan a robbery or murder and she had met quite a number of those women over the past years. She went to church that Sunday and talked to a fellow parishioner she thought might know something about hiring a detective. The name the parishioner suggested was Darryl Carlson.

The next time the two women met, Joyce quickly got to the point. "Would you mind if I hired an investigator to look into your case?" she asked Gloria.

Gloria was stunned. Here was a stranger offering to help when in six years even her mother had never come to visit her.

Gloria told Joyce that an investigator who had done some work for her after her appeal had found absolutely nothing. "Don't waste your money," Gloria told her. "I don't understand why this happened, but there is nothing to investigate."

Joyce listened politely and, as was her wont, then went off and quietly did exactly as she intended to do in the first place: She called the investigator.

Darryl Carlson, a six-foot-four Swede, bore a striking resemblance to the popular wrestler Hulk Hogan. Handsome and with a chiseled physique, Carlson started his career on the enforcement side of the legal system as a member of the border patrol in south San Diego.

Filled with swagger and a sense of purpose, Carlson worked the law for years, but soon found there was too much deemed black and white in what he was doing. He felt there were too many issues, too many grey areas, but he loved to investigate, so he started working as a private eye and for years traveled the world, finally finding his way back home to southern California.

Joyce made an appointment to see him. Sitting down at the desk opposite the imposing man, she once more got right to the point.

"I want you to go to CIW to talk to my friend, Gloria Killian. She's in prison there. I have a sense that something is wrong. Would you investigate?"

Carlson looked at her. He knew through a friend about the organization Friends Outside and Joyce's position, but he had no clue about her relationship with Gloria. He let her continue.

"Her case is in Sacramento, so you're going to have to go up there," Joyce told him. Carlson wasn't thrilled with the thought of going to northern California. As a private eye, he knew Sacramento was a small town compared to Los Angeles. Its judicial system was tangled like a hornet's nest and he'd been stung there before.

"Well, I'll need to talk to Gloria first. We need her cooperation," Carlson told her.

"I'll take care of that," Joyce said, standing. "I'll let you know when you can visit." Carlson watched her walk toward the door, secure, smart, focused.

"Excuse me, but who's going to pay for this?" Carlson asked. "I charge seventy-five dollars an hour plus expenses. It's going to cost."

Joyce turned around slowly and smiled. "I'll take care of that, too. How much do you need to start?"

"Five hundred."

Joyce wrote out a check and left.

Days later, Joyce met with Gloria, but the small talk was over.

"I've hired an investigator," she said. "His name is Darryl Carlson and he'll be out to visit you soon."

Gloria had no idea what Joyce's financial situation was and would never think of asking. Neither women knew what this case could end up costing, but Gloria believed it might be expensive.

"I don't want you to waste your money, Joyce. I told you. I hired an investigator years ago after my appeal and he found nothing. Please don't waste your money."

"It's not your decision," Joyce told her calmly. "Injustice annoys me." She was sure that her friend, who never wavered in proclaiming her innocence, truly was innocent. She knew that Darryl would be visiting Gloria in a few days. She hoped Gloria would be cooperative, but Joyce's mind was made up.

A few days after Joyce's visit, Darryl Carlson sent Gloria word he would be coming to see her that day. Gloria walked into the visiting area, searching the waiting room for him. She was a little nervous. As she scanned the people on the other side of the glass, a handsome blond man caught her eye. *Wow, is that Hulk Hogan?* It was a definite possibility as the prison did get the occasional celebrity visitor, but she was shocked to learn it was Carlson.

Gloria and Carlson found an easy rapport. It had been a while since Gloria talked to a man who could make her smile.

Carlson was a talker, so it was no surprise that he and Gloria spoke for almost three hours at their first meeting. He believed her version of the story right away and said he'd be glad to work for her, but Gloria told him she didn't want him to pursue the case, because she was still concerned about wasting Joyce's money. Darryl felt differently about Gloria's reticence and believed she was simply afraid to hope. He had seen people in prison grow hard, but Gloria was different. He felt she been so disappointed by the justice system in her case and thought nothing could be done and so to invest money and time and then have nothing happen would be more than she could bear.

Carlson returned to meet with Joyce.

"She didn't want me to open up the case," he told Joyce. "She told me everything she knew, but she's afraid to hope. The truth is a powerful thing."

Joyce paused for a short moment.

"Gloria's not your client; I am. Gloria's not paying you; I am." She took out her checkbook and wrote Carlson another check for five hundred dollars and sent him on his way with a short admonition. "Spend wisely, Darryl. God is watching."

The fibers drifting off the limbs of the cottonwoods that line the rivers in Sacramento cluttered the air when Carlson made his way into the *Sacramento Bee* library. Gloria had told him to take tissues, just in case, because allergies were always bad for her this time of year. He smiled at her concern as he wiped his nose and sat down on the heavy wood benches and began to thumb through old newspapers. He wanted a feel for the city and its goings-on before the Davies murder. He believed Gloria was telling the truth and she was innocent. His job was to find out how this whole thing happened.

The first thing that grabbed his attention was the inordinate number of home invasions of elderly people that happened at the time in the general area. It felt to him that there might have been some kind of ring of criminals targeting the elderly.

One article had a blaring headline: "Woman fails to get killer's wife arrested as suspect in robbery." Carlson turned to the story. "Elizabeth Lee said she solved her own robbery Wednesday," the *Sacramento Bee* article read. "Lee said she recognized the murderer, Gary Masse, as one of two persons who broke through her front door in October, pointed a handgun at her and tried to rob her. She said she recognized his wife, Joanne Masse, as the other robber when she spotted her in a corridor outside the courtroom."

Carlson kept reading. Masse was there for a hearing to decide whether he should be sentenced before the trials of DeSantis and Killian. Lawyers for DeSantis and Killian contended the prosecution had worked out a deal with Masse and wanted him sentenced. But

Carlson was really shocked when he read what happened after Lee saw the Masses, went to prosecutor Kit Cleland and told him she wanted Joanne arrested. Cleland did no such thing. He told Lee to "back off" and that she "would be getting into something she shouldn't get into." Joanne Masse took the fifth and was never prosecuted.

Carlson called Joyce Ride.

"I got a sense Masse was covering for his wife," he told Joyce over the phone. "And I think he definitely had a deal. I'm gonna find it."

Carlson started to wonder. *Did Masse or a friend give the anonymous tip to the newspaper hotline about Gloria? Was Masse's testimony predicated on saving his wife? Is there any paperwork that documents Masse's deal?*

Carlson's years in police work told him what he felt must be true: that Masse must have made a deal for both himself and his wife. With a deal he would get a reduced sentence and she would go free, but Carlson needed to find more proof. He firmly believed they both had lied, so he decided it was time to visit another man he believed might be lying.

Carlson drove his rented car up a dusty dirt road to a small farm outside Sacramento. He pulled up to a rundown house and found a heavyset man rolled up in a chair on the front porch, his arm in a make-shift sling, his white beard streaked yellow from tobacco juice. A shotgun was balanced on his prodigious gut and he was surrounded by eight snarling Dobermans.

Slowly Carlson got out of his car and judiciously walked toward the man in the rocker. The man stood. He was hunched over and he limped toward Carlson, who was still nervously making his way toward the house. He knew if this man felt any trepidation, he'd have his dogs rip him apart.

"You Darryl Carlson?" the man called out in an exaggerated Texas twang, sounding like a good ol' boy.

"Sure am," Carlson said, smiling.

"I'm Virgil Fletcher," the man said, smiling back. "Come on in."

Carlson and Fletcher took a seat in his dirty, tattered living room. The last fifteen years hadn't been kind to Fletcher, who was old and sick. Carlson thought it must have been a long time since Fletcher received company, because he appeared disheveled and dirty and talked a blue streak. He told Carlson he knew the Sacramento cops pretty well and went on to say that he had friends on the force and for many years ran a bar in town, knew the cops and the thugs.

"Yeah, some of those guys would steal a pig or a cow or bring in a side of beef to pay me," Virgil said, chuckling, recounting the good old days in Sacramento. "And I shouldn't tell you this," he said, moving in closer to Carlson, "but if the cops had a guy they wanted to get rid of, they would put a bullet in 'em through and through. I had a lot of friends in the cops."

Carlson asked him about Charlie Duncan and Ed Davies.

"When Charlie was in the front I knew everything what was going on in the shop. I'd sit up there in this little room in the back with a red light. It had a peephole and I could look through that peephole and see whoever was out there and what they was doing. I could see the people who didn't believe in banks."

Carlson knew exactly what Fletcher was alluding to but wouldn't say. He thought the old coin shop dealer was playing with him, putting on the old country boy demeanor, and later he told Joyce, "You have to be pretty smart to act that stupid."

He asked Fletcher specifically about Davies' criminal past.

"Sure, I knew Ed Davies was a gun runner. When Senator Cranston was cracking down on gunrunning on the border, Ed offered me ten grand to put a contract out on 'im."

Virgil went on and on, talking about how his friends were cops and how smart he was and said very little about Gloria, but Carlson read between the lines.

Why would Davies offer Fletcher money to kill someone unless he was a criminal with a network of crooks at his disposal? Fletcher wasn't afraid of the police because of his long affiliation with them, proven by the fact that he was never arrested.

They talked about many different things, with Fletcher treating Carlson like a long lost friend. He asked Carlson to do him a favor. "You know, I was born in Texas on the day Bonnie and Clyde were killed right in Texas. If you could find me the newspaper on that date, I'd be real appreciative," Virgil said.

Carlson was surprised at the request but smiled and said he'd try. As Carlson was about to leave, Virgil Fletcher made one more interesting comment.

"You know, it ain't what you know. It's what you can prove."

Carlson left, sure this man was involved in the setup of the Davies robbery, and went right to the county court where Kit Cleland was still a feared prosecutor. No one would talk. He then went to the Sacramento Sheriff's Department and got the same silence.

"The community is silent about this case and even defense lawyers don't want to speak about it," he told Joyce. "I get the feeling it's an embarrassment."

He even went to talk to the cops. Lieutenant Ray Biondi had left the force by then, but Carlson visited him at his home and asked him why he left the Killian case the second time she was arrested. He had been very involved in bringing in Gary Masse, but when O'Mara reassigned the case, Biondi left it. Darryl was not surprised when Biondi hedged his answer about whether the celebrated cop thought Killian guilty.

"I don't know, but I know Stan Reed thought she was," was all he would say.

The more he learned, the more Carlson felt full of the fire of injustice. He was sure Virgil Fletcher knew much more than he was letting on.

He then went back to the courthouse and started to dig around, spending hours looking through file after file in the case. Finally he looked in another court, Department 14, in the files of Masse's sentencing judge. And there it was. He found a letter from Kit Cleland to Masse's sentencing judge dated eight months before Gloria's trial. His eyes opened wide as he read it:

> I am writing at this time to make a record of my planned recommendation to the Court when Gary Masse is ultimately sentenced. I want it to be clear that my present position is unaffected by the outcome of the DeSantis trial...
>
> While Gary Masse's criminal conduct cannot be condoned, his cooperation, in my judgment, deserves consideration by the Court in determining the appropriate sentence. To that end, the People plan not to object to a renewed William Motion to strike the special circumstances.
>
> In taking this position, I make the assumption that Mr. Masse will conduct himself properly while incarcerated and will continue his cooperation by testifying truthfully at the trial of Gloria Killian.

Here was, in Carlson's opinion, concrete proof that Cleland had made a deal with Masse before Gloria's trial. The "striking of special circumstances" meant to Carlson that Masse would get a maximum sentence of twenty-five to life instead of life without parole. Carlson felt Cleland gave Masse a way to get out of prison if he testified against Gloria Killian.

Cleland's statements at her trial that "Gary Masse hasn't gotten a darn thing except a little hope" and "we have nothing to do with the time Gary serves" were misleading and explained why Masse talked about twelve years. He thought he would get a twenty-five-year sentence without special circumstances and he'd only have to serve half to get parole.

Cleland had written the letter and told the court clerk to hold it until Masse was sentenced, but it was obvious that Masse must have known he had a deal. Why write it then if not for a deal? Masse knew if he said what he believed the prosecution wanted him to say about Killian, he'd be able to get out of prison.

Carlson thought this information alone would be enough for Gloria to claim her trial was unconstitutional and, through a writ of habeas corpus, demand release or a new trial. But he believed this letter was only the tip of the iceberg in a case that looked very dirty and filled with lies. Carlson wrote a twenty-page report and presented it to Joyce.

In his report he said he was convinced that Gloria had been set up by Masse to protect his wife and get a deal. He believed Virgil Fletcher was instrumental in setting up the Davies robbery and helping to get rid of the proceeds. His experience in law enforcement told him this case broke all the rules of what he knew to be true about the criminal element.

He noted in his report that the Gloria Killians of the world do not "hang out" with the Stephen DeSantis types and that the idea of them being "crime partners" and her getting half of anything was, to Carlson, ludicrous. How would someone like her get a guy like DeSantis to hand over anything? Carlson wrote:

> So when the proper tools of evidence were not there and the case against Gloria was shown not to be a case in accordance with the proper court procedure, they simply fixed it with the trained seal testimony of Gary Masse…But, anyone can see that Gary's testimony is heavily laden with the input of embedded commands given in a subtle manner by clever people who "knew" that Gloria was guilty.

Carlson was the first who found real evidence about Masse's deal and was convinced that Cleland misled the court when he said that there was no agreement about a new sentence for Masse. Carlson was the first to find the missing puzzle pieces and pleaded with Joyce to initiate further investigation. He was now on the team that Joyce had created and was sure Gloria Killian was innocent.

Carlson went to see Gloria, told her of his findings and gave her a copy of his report. For the second time in years she felt like someone new really believed her. Carlson told her of the evidence he'd uncovered of why Masse told the lies about her on the stand. The evidence of the deal meant she had always right about it, but what upset her just as much were the comments from Lieutenant Biondi.

After reading his report, she sat in shock across from Joyce and Darryl in the visitors' room, not knowing whether to laugh, cry or celebrate.

"I'm just so stunned that some of the cops weren't even sure I was guilty," she said. "They destroyed me just because they could."

Gloria eyes started to tear and she began to get very angry. *This wasn't just an outrageous mistake*, she thought. *Maybe these people who sent me to prison, maybe these law men and prosecutors, maybe they are the real monsters.*

Joyce was convinced she wanted Carlson to continue investigating no matter what the cost. She and Carlson were sure what he conveyed of his findings was just the beginning and that if they kept digging, they would find enough evidence for Gloria to vacate her conviction and be granted a new trial. What they didn't know was that a new mountain of evidence was days away from being dropped into their laps and would come from a shocking source.

| 18 |

Death Row Revelations

The thick, grey, putrid air that swirled around the 275 acres over-looking the San Francisco Bay that make up San Quentin State Prison had been making Stephen DeSantis sick, frail and weak. He'd been on death row for ten years and wasn't breathing or eating well. His mind was a jumbled mess of incoherent ramblings. The lime green gas chamber down the hall from his cell block loomed large in his thoughts and over the years, DeSantis had gone from being a strong, hearty man to a weak, sickly, paranoid mess. His wife had been pregnant during his trial, exposed to indignities and searches that made him crazy to think about. She had since divorced him and taken their child out of his life forever, a loss he still felt he couldn't endure.

The East Block is a giant five-story cage with wet cement walls, filled with the rattling screams of tortured inmates with no hope. DeSantis was housed in this filthy, noisy section of the facility and he hated every minute of it. He couldn't believe or stomach what his cousin Gary had said and done. DeSantis had always maintained that it was his cousin, in a drug-induced stupor, who pulled the trigger and that Masse gave statements to Cleland so Stephen would be put in the gas chamber. He wanted to appeal what he claimed was his unconstitutional conviction in an attempt to save his life. Since he'd lost his habeas appeal in the California Supreme Court and exhausted all constitutional relief in state courts, he was taking the next steps by filing for a new trial in federal court. Maybe in the federal courts that weren't connected to Sacramento he'd have a chance. He knew they hated him in Sacramento and that the odds had been stacked against him ever since he was a child. He was convinced that if he didn't get off death row soon, he was going to die at the hands of the COs.

The federal court had recently appointed him new lawyers who he hoped would help overturn his conviction and maybe even help put his lying cousin on death row in his place. He heard that his two new lawyers, Scott Williams and Mary Louise Frampton, were in Sacramento reviewing his trial records and court files for the case. He hoped they would find something soon; he didn't know how much more time on death row he could take.

Scott Williams and Mary Louise Frampton had been civil rights lawyers since the 1970s when they opened their Fresno, California, law firm: Frampton, Hoppe, Williams and Boehme. Williams was a local California boy who went to college at Stanford but went east to Boston to law school. Frampton was from New York City and went to Brown and then Harvard. The two met in the East, then travelled West, picked up more partners and in time, their civil rights defense firm became well known and well regarded across the state. Williams and Frampton had spent years trying cases in front of judges and filing habeas petitions in federal courts. They regularly heard impassioned pleas from federal judges imploring experienced lawyers like them to take on the post-conviction death penalty appeals, which so few lawyers wanted to do, because it was time-consuming work and put an emotional strain on the attorneys involved. It was one thing to try to get someone out of prison; it was another to make a last-ditch attempt to fight a sentence when the person was scheduled to die.

But Williams and Frampton strongly believed that the death penalty was unconstitutional. They agreed to take their first death penalty case as the court appointed federal lawyers for Stephen DeSantis.

The workload was heavy. Not only did they need to go through all the files for DeSantis' case, but they needed to read through all the court proceedings for Masse and Killian as well. They had to familiarize themselves with every aspect of the case before they talked to DeSantis and talking with him wasn't going to be easy, for he and they were aware that his life was on the line.

Early in his study of the case, Williams made a routine request, asking that Kit Cleland, the district attorney in these cases, turn over his personal files. Williams was shocked when he received a note from the attorney general, representing Kit Cleland and the state, that objected to the request and said that Cleland was refusing to turn over the files.

That had never happened before and Williams filed a motion to get the files, but the AG and Cleland fought back. Over the next nine months, a lengthy battle ensued which culminated in the judge issuing an Order to Show Cause for Cleland to hand over the documents. He set a hearing to determine why Cleland was so resistant and told him if he didn't show up with the documents, he'd be charged with contempt.

Cleland did show up, contrite, controlled and charming. Watching Cleland's gracious and polite behavior with the judge, Williams was immediately aware he was a highly skilled lawyer. He'd watched many other prosecutors in his time and knew that the best of them had learned when it was appropriate to be outraged in front of a judge and when it was advantageous to be quiet. Observing Cleland in action, Williams and Frampton knew who must have controlled the courtroom in their client's trial and in Masse's and Killian's as well. They were up against someone to be reckoned with.

They felt that Cleland's reasons for not handing over his files were instinctual rather than legal. Williams believed the prosecutor, a man in the business of putting people to death for murder, simply didn't want to be second-guessed. He didn't know if Cleland was hiding anything or not, but to Cleland, not giving up his files was a matter of principle and likely a bit of ego as well.

Not getting cited for contempt was also a matter of principle and finally Cleland gave his personal files to DeSantis' new attorneys. Williams and Frampton did their due diligence and went through it page by page, even thought they'd seen much of what was in the files before.

As they worked their way through the papers something caught Williams' eye: a handwritten letter from Gary Masse to Tom Brown, Cleland's investigator and Masse's handler, written two weeks after Gloria Killian's sentencing. He paused and took a deep breath when he read: "I feel that I am getting screwed and as far as I'm concerned, there was a verbal agreement of no more than twelve years....I gave you DeSantis and Killian. I did my part all the way to the end. I even lied my ass off on the stand for you people."

It was a direct admission that Masse had lied in court and, equally important, Williams felt it showed that Cleland knew it. Williams doubted anyone had seen this letter before, certainly not Gloria's appellate attorney, since Cleland fought so hard to keep it hidden. Williams needed to talk to Gary Masse about this new evidence and then to Gloria Killian.

Three months after Carlson found Cleland's letter asking the judge to change Masse's sentence, Gloria received a letter from Williams. He told her he was representing Stephen DeSantis on his death row appeal and had new information for her; he and his partner Mary Louise Frampton wanted to come down from Fresno to interview her.

Gloria had mixed feelings about the whole thing and wasn't very trusting, especially not of any lawyer representing one of those dirt-bags, Masse or DeSantis. She didn't answer Williams at first and soon received another letter from him, this one with a more autocratic tone, informing her that they were coming to interview her, like it or not.

That made Gloria angry. One thing she knew about being in prison was that no one from the outside could push you around or make you talk to them, so she quickly informed Mr. Williams by return mail that they would not be meeting or discussing anything. She asked herself, *What can they do to me? Send me to prison?* Gloria then gave copies of the letter to Darryl Carlson and Joyce Ride.

Carlson called Williams, who refused to give him the details of what he wanted to talk to Gloria about, but made the private investigator comfortable enough to agree to try to get Gloria to agree to see Williams, who also promised that Carlson could attend the meeting with them.

Two weeks later, Scott Williams and Mary Louise Frampton arrived at CIW with Darryl in tow. The two lawyers looked professional and well dressed, but Frampton kept coughing; her asthma was acting up. Gloria knew exactly how she felt, because in the ten years she'd been at CIW she'd developed similar breathing problems.

The group sat in the small visiting room like card players around a table, sizing up one another and not saying much. They were all wary, not because anyone had anything to hide, but because everyone had so much at stake.

After the initial stare-down, Carlson broke the ice by bringing everyone cups of coffee and treats from the vending machine. Gloria smiled and relaxed just a little. Williams and Frampton needed to know what Gloria knew and if she was at all involved, but Gloria didn't know their motives. Neither Williams nor Frampton believed Gloria was guilty, but they needed to hear directly from her the story of how she got caught in the web of lies.

Williams and Frampton listened carefully as Gloria told them what had happened from her point of view. They found her bright and articulate, albeit on her guard, as the years in prison had taught her to be wary. Gloria spoke not only about her case, but also of her work for battered women and as an attorney behind bars. She had a strength and confidence that belied her status as an inmate.

Williams was puzzled by this smart woman who certainly didn't behave like any inmate he'd met before. He'd read through the case numerous times and Gloria's alleged participation in the Davies robbery-murder had always been a mystery to him, partly because of the lack of any hard evidence and partly because he'd interviewed DeSantis extensively and DeSantis consistently held fast to his statement that he never met the woman or so much as heard her name before his arrest.

When Gloria was finished telling her story, sadly neither Williams nor his partner had any greater understanding of how she got pulled into the case as they did before they met her, but they believed in her innocence.

Now it was Williams' turn to tell her a little more about Gary Masse. He and Frampton told Gloria that they had found numerous letters from Gary Masse expressing that he'd perjured himself and there was evidence withheld by the prosecution. The letters they found and the subsequent conversations with Masse supported everything that Carlson had found. They now felt they had more concrete evidence that Masse had made a deal that depended on his lying on the stand about Gloria's involvement. But there was more: When Williams had gone to talk with Masse in Mule Creek where he was imprisoned, Masse told Williams that the story about Gloria's involvement in the crime was a joke. Masse didn't know her; she wasn't involved and he wouldn't even recognize her if she walked in right then.

Gloria was stunned and ecstatic. After all the confusion and horror she'd endured wondering and agonizing about what had happened to her, here were letters, the proof that she had searched for that she was innocent. Masse had lied for a deal. Williams also told her of more evidence they found in discovery indicating that Virgil Fletcher had proceeds from the robbery in his motor home and in his house.

Sharing what he found with Gloria, Williams felt he couldn't do anything further to help her. He already had a client whose life he had to save using much of the same information, but he told Gloria he would be glad to make all the files and evidence available to her lawyer.

Gloria's legal mind began working. She knew she could file a writ of habeas corpus in the California Supreme Court, as she had never filed a writ after her first appeal. With this new evidence, she'd be able to fight for her freedom, bringing an end to the prison nightmare she'd endured for ten long years.

When Williams and Frampton left, Gloria and Darryl again raided the vending machines, toasting with cupcakes instead of champagne. They couldn't help grinning while trying to be discreet. Gloria was far too smart a convict and "legal beagle" to let the word about this get around.

But she couldn't wait to tell Joyce, who came the next day, what had happened. She already knew. "Well, then," said Joyce, "time to get you a lawyer."

When Joyce Ride walked into William Genego's Santa Monica office, Genego was more than a little curious. He had gotten preliminary information about Ride from friends at USC. He knew about Friends Outside, he knew about Sally Ride and he even knew a little about Gloria. But he had no idea why Joyce was so invested in this case.

She sat down in his tenth-floor office on the corner of Wilshire Boulevard, the Pacific Ocean gleaming outside his window, and told the bearded, no-nonsense attorney about the woman she met at CIW whom she believed was innocent. She candidly told him he was the first of five attorneys she'd be interviewing for the job.

She was quick and to the point, something he admired. Neither Bill nor Joyce relished small talk or inane pleasantries. Quickly she told him about Gloria, Carlson's investigation, the contact by Scott Williams and Masse's letters.

This case sounded interesting to Genego and from what Joyce said about Williams' findings, it seemed there might be grounds for a habeas. It was also interesting that the case involved a woman, which would be a first for the forty-year-old bachelor dating a fellow lawyer who would become his future wife. He thought this case might be a good one for them to work on as a team, giving two busy lawyers time to spend together, even if it was work.

Genego was also intrigued by why Ride was advocating for Gloria. Here was someone who was paying for a lawyer for someone else, not a family member, just someone she met in prison whom she felt was unjustly treated. How could he not reciprocate for that act of kindness? He told Joyce he was interested.

Joyce never went on any other attorney interviews. She hired him on the spot and didn't flinch when he told her his fee was $250 an hour.

She wrote another check, they shook hands and Bill Genego agreed to see Gloria.

CIW was a new kind of prison for William Genego: it was the first female penitentiary he'd visited. He'd been to countless other prisons all over the United States in his capacity as one of the best defense attorneys in California, and when it came to post-conviction appeals he had few peers.

He pulled his briefcase out of his car and strode into the reception center, looking forward to meeting the woman he'd heard so much about. Gloria and her tale of wrongful conviction had piqued the craggy, brilliant lawyer's interest.

It had been five years since he left teaching at USC, where he helped start the prestigious USC Law Center's Post Conviction Justice Project with his mentor. Most recently, in his private practice, he'd just finished an important case that left him flush with cash and the pride of accomplishment. Earlier that month, Genego, with the cooperation of a fellow attorney, won the freedom of a young Marine unjustly imprisoned for a murder he didn't commit. The vindication was a big victory for Genego. He decided that Gloria's case would be his next challenge. If there was one thing Genego savored, it was a challenge.

Genego grew up a poor Irish boy with an Italian name on the wrong side of town outside Rensselaer, New York. It was a tough life for the youngest of the Genego clan, whose parents were hardworking people and not academics. His mother and father held GEDs, worked blue-collar jobs and didn't quite know how to manage their whip-smart son. Genego found small-town life tough yet boring and he left home as soon as he turned eighteen to make his way downstate to the Big Apple. He started out working odd jobs part-time and going to Manhattan Community College, his high school grades too low for a four-year school. But soon the young man put his head and heart into his studies. Within two years he was at New York University and two years after that at the top of the class at Yale Law School, an editor of their prestigious law review.

At Yale he became interested in criminal law, particularly post-conviction work. In his second year in law school he filed a habeas petition in the federal court of appeals and in a rare breach of protocol, Genego, the student, was allowed to argue in front of the court. He won, which was an extremely rare event at the time. So rare that when the judge published his decision, he cited an article written by Genego and fellow law students as one of the bases of his decision.

Genego learned that he relished post-conviction work. While he knew it was a zero-sum game—pending trial you can negotiate a sentence, post-conviction you win or lose—he liked to be a maverick and liked to beat the odds. He also liked to take on cases he believed he could win, so he needed to talk to Gloria. Without her cooperation, her case would not be winnable.

On the day they were to meet, Genego walked into the attorney interview room at CIW where Gloria waited for him, left arm tied to her side with bandages. Gloria had recently incurred a severe rotator cuff injury, exacerbated by what she felt was the poor medical treatment at the prison. She was in pain and a little cranky, but she did what she always did when she met a new person: talked about her work in prison and what she was doing to help other prisoners, even to a lawyer who was there to talk about her case. She talked about battered women, the horror of prison medical services and the USC project.

To Genego, it was all a little strange and a little off-putting. Gloria seemed more comfortable talking about what she did in prison rather than how she got there.

She knew she was babbling, but deep inside Gloria didn't know how this big-time lawyer was going to be paid. What if Joyce was spending all her savings on her? Could she let Joyce do that? Deep down she was also afraid, much like she had been with Darryl Carlson the investigator, that he wouldn't or couldn't help her. She had no idea that Joyce had already hired him. As much as there was new evidence, Gloria felt beaten up by the judicial system, railroaded by her trial and the worthless appeal. She'd been innocent and had spent ten years in prison. All this legal work would be an ordeal that would cost money, time and hope. It was the hope that frightened her the most.

Genego, on the other hand, recognized right away what she was feeling. He had seen people in this stage of a case before and knew there was a part of her that was afraid to allow herself any hope of getting out, but he was confident in his assessment of the case. She did not strike him as a home invasion co-conspirator, a criminal tied up with the likes of Masse or DeSantis. Even before they talked, he could see the differences from reading the transcripts. Now he was assured she was smart, erudite and didn't talk or carry herself like a convict. But she wouldn't commit to having him represent her.

Awkwardly they danced around the issue, Gloria refusing to ask Bill to represent her and Bill not pushing her. As he was about to leave, still unsure if he was on the case or not, there was a problem with the institutional count and no one was allowed to leave visiting until it was cleared. Bill and Gloria had run out of things to say to each other, yet remained trapped in the noisy and crowded room. Gloria uneasily tried to make small talk with this incredibly smart man who had a low bullshit tolerance.

The next day Joyce returned to Santa Monica only to find Genego waiting in his office to return her check.

"I don't think I can do this," Genego said. "I got the distinct impression she didn't want me to represent her and as much as you may want to hire me, I can't do it without her cooperation."

Joyce nodded, still silent, waiting for Bill to continue. But what could he say? Before it grew too uncomfortable, Genego added, "I surmise the reason might be that Gloria doesn't want to allow herself any hope. It's tough to lose."

Joyce listened. His objections meant little to her. She liked him. "I have to talk to her," she said, refusing the check. "And you need to go back there."

Genego agreed to go back, but it took an additional visit after that before Gloria opened up about her case. Unfortunately, she didn't know much more than she knew before and the little that Scott Williams, DeSantis' lawyer, had told her. It would be up to Genego to review the thousands of pages of documents Williams had and see what they could use for her habeas petition. Genego told Gloria he would contact Williams, get the paperwork and begin his search for the specific evidence he needed to get her conviction overturned and free her from prison.

Lauren Eskenazi had just gotten out of the University of Southern California, Gould School of Law and needed a job. The women's studies major had gone to law school so she could work on women's issues like abortion, egg donation and surrogacy. Defense law wasn't her first choice, but when a fellow attorney told her Bill Genego was looking for someone to assist him on a post-conviction case, he suggested her with the caveat, "He's an excellent attorney; don't screw it up."

The tall, dark, curly-haired twenty-seven-year-old Eskenazi wasn't intimidated by the intense veteran lawyer with the disarming smile and she loved the idea of post-conviction work. He hired her on the spot, gave her Scott Williams' information and told her to get everything, read everything and make notes. She grabbed a bunch of colored pencils and pens and got to work. For months Eskenazi read through over thirty thousand pages of transcripts. After she'd outlined everything and was informed on the case, she passed it to her boss. The ball—and Gloria's fate—was in Bill Genego's court.

Within weeks, Gloria, Bill and Lauren sat down in the CIW visiting room. Gloria liked Lauren right away. This was her first big case after law school. Bright, funny and warm, she was much different from the serious, down-to-business Genego. Eskenazi made Gloria feel at ease with Bill and helped her open up.

For hours and hours that day and in upcoming weeks they went over everything that Gloria knew, every single detail of the case and the trial. Bill and Lauren felt that Gloria sounded more like a lawyer than a convict and it made it even more unbelievable to them that she was incarcerated.

"How did this happen to you?" Bill finally asked her.

Gloria paused and looked at him, thinking about all that had changed in the decade she'd been in prison. How she got her strength back, how she finally recovered from all that had happened to her.

"I'm not the same person I used to be before I went in. That's all I can tell you."

The first things Genego went over were the points in DeSantis' habeas petition.

A writ of habeas corpus, in English meaning "you have the body," is a petition filed by either a prisoner or his/her representative and is defined as "a judicial mandate requiring that a prisoner be brought before the court to determine whether the government has the right to continue detaining them," according to the About.com article "Definition of Habeas Corpus," by Martin Kelly. The Post-Conviction Justice Project (PCJP) Web site states, "A petition for writ of habeas corpus challenges the constitutionality of an inmate's imprisonment."

While in some aspects similar, DeSantis' and Gloria's issues in the writs were markedly different. In both, the lawyers felt Cleland had exhibited some egregious behavior and Masse's perjury applied to both of them, but Gloria's habeas writ needed to deal with issues specific to her case.

As Genego worked on all the points of the case, Gloria regularly chatted with Eskenazi, filling her in on specific details and answering any of their questions and also talked regularly with Genego's sister Barbara, who worked as his office manager and almost always answered the phone when she called. Gloria now had faith in the people she had around her: Joyce, Darryl, Bill, Lauren and Barbara. She was sure the results would be far different from her first trial.

Genego decided they would file for a writ of habeas corpus citing eight separate allegations. Each one, he believed, was strong enough on its merits to vacate her conviction and get her out of prison. They theorized that because of the habeas petition Masse would be impeached as a perjurer. Without Masse, the State had no case against her. If they granted Gloria the writ, she would go free.

It took Genego almost a year to amass all the information and file the petition in the California Supreme Court. The claims were:

1. **That Petitioner was Denied Due Process Because the Deputy District Attorney Knowingly Used False Evidence at Trial.** Genego cited that Masse's testimony was false (citing the letter that an agreement existed and that Masse lied), that his testimony was material and that the Prosecutor *knew* that Masse's testimony was false and material.

2. **The Prosecution's Failure to Disclose Exculpatory/ Impeachment Evidence Violated Petitioner's Constitutional Rights.** This claim dealt with the evidence that Cleland withheld from Thielen impeaching Masse's credibility, which included Masse's mental health medical records, evidence that Masse and the prosecutor had an agreement and evidence about Masse's previous false statements as an informant.

3. **Denial of Due Process Due to Doyle Error.** Under Doyle a prosecutor cannot impeach a defendant by her silence based on the assertion of her Miranda rights. Genego asserted that Cleland's accusatory questions that inferred Gloria's guilt in court, because she asked for a lawyer after they arrested her, violated her Doyle rights.

4. **Ineffective Assistance of Counsel Due to Deficient Investigation and Performance at Trial**. This claim asserted Thielen did not have the factors fully investigated. Thielen did not cite Masse's mental illness at trial, which was shown to affect his testimonial abilities, and he did not use DeSantis' testimony that Killian had no involvement in the crime and that it was Masse's wife, Joanne, who

went with Masse to the Davies' house. Thielen failed to object to the prosecution's Doyle error impeachment and failed to impeach other witnesses. The Doyle error's impact was strong, because Killian's testimony and credibility was crucial to contradict Masse. There was also, according to the claim, a host of other evidence Thielen didn't use to impeach other witnesses to weaken the prosecution's case.

5. **Ineffective Assistance of Counsel Due to Attorney's Actual Conflict of Interest.** The law firm Thielen and Thielen represented Masse in other criminal proceedings before representing Killian. This partnership imposed on Thielen a duty of confidentiality to Masse and directly conflicted with his duty to zealously represent Killian.

6. **Ineffective Assistance of Counsel on Appeal.** The petition argued that Julian Macias, who represented Stephen DeSantis, failed to bring a Doyle claim and provided the same inadequate counsel as Thielen.

7. **Denial of Sixth Amendment Right to Fair Trial Due to Cumulative Violations of Due Process Rights and Right to Effective and Conflict-Free Counsel.**

8. **Denial of Sixth Amendment Right to Fair Trial Due to Cumulative Violations of State and Federal Rights etc.** Finally, the argument was presented that the totality of the tainted proceedings is the most compelling reason that the habeas petition should be granted. The plethora and gravity of *all* the errors rendered the trial fundamentally unfair.

Joyce Ride and Lauren Eskenazi felt excited by the whole process. This writ to the California Supreme Court was a first for both of them and they felt sure they would win. There was just too much evidence and Masse had admitted he lied, but Bill Genego had his doubts, as did Gloria. The California Supreme Court rarely, if ever, overturned convictions or granted habeas writs, but it was a necessary step in the process. They needed to file with the California Supreme Court as a stepping-stone to get to the federal courts, which made their decisions based on the constitutionality of the trials. All court remedies in California needed to be exhausted before a federal court would hear a case.

Gloria and Bill both expected a simple postcard denial, which is what the court usually issued: a sheet of paper with one word, *Denied*; no reasons, no explanations. They looked forward to getting past this court and moving as quickly as they could to federal court.

In December, to everyone's shock, Gloria and Genego received an order for informal briefing from the California Supreme Court. Gloria knew that the Supreme Court was so conservative that it almost never heard a habeas petition and granted relief even less often. She hoped that perhaps her writ was so impressive and the constitutional violations so egregious that even this staid court was compelled to act. Was this some kind of Christmas gift? She thought about the chaplain at the Branch and her belief there would be a miracle for her.

Both sides filed their informal briefs. For months Gloria heard nothing. The wait was hard. She and Brenda walked the track every afternoon, Brenda counting the days until her parole and Gloria waiting for the ruling from the California Supreme Court. Every time Gloria became despondent, Brenda told her not to be so negative. Brenda had been particularly excited for Gloria when she learned of more evidence and desperately wanted justice for Gloria. She visited Gloria regularly at the law library and jokingly told Gloria to work on her own case.

The California Supreme Court took eleven months and then issued a postcard denial in September with no comments. Gloria was devastated; not by their denial, but by the fact that it felt as if time mattered to no one but her. She understood the court system, but it didn't make the time pass any easier. When she learned Bill needed to get a continuance, she cried and screamed alone in her cell. Yet she always tried to be gracious and understanding with others. Nevertheless, she felt life was so unfair. She'd been in prison so long and she hadn't done anything.

Then they filed in Eastern District Federal Court, where Genego and Gloria believed the fight for her freedom would truly begin.

Meanwhile, Gloria's fight for Brenda's freedom had moved forward. Since it began, Gloria and Brenda had done a great deal of work to further her cause to get her clemency. USC decided to publish a special edition of the *Southern California Law Review* about the issues of women in prison. They came to Gloria and Brenda and asked them both to write articles. While thrilled to be published in such a prestigious journal, Gloria couldn't believe the irony: typically, people were published in the law review while attending law school; she did it from prison.

She labored over her article for weeks, polishing each word, and then helped Brenda write hers. They wanted to do the best job possible, believing that their words in this journal would live on long after they were gone. The special edition on women in prison received publicity in the legal and political worlds in California. Eventually the California State Legislature held a special hearing on women with domestic violence cases at CIW, bringing even more focus on the issue.

Gloria helped write the testimony of many of the battered women who testified at the hearing. She also worked with the battered women's group Convicted Women Against Abuse (CWAA), which drafted and submitted a petition to Governor Pete Wilson requesting clemency for thirty-four women.

Wilson ignored the petitions for two years, but Gloria and Brenda didn't stop working. They continued to send letters and contact politicians, lawyers and the media. Gloria also worked to create the CIW/USC Post Conviction Justice Project (PCJP). According to its Web site, PCJP is an organization that:

> ...represents state prisoners incarcerated at the California Institution for Women serving life-term sentences for murder...For parole-eligible clients, [USC law students] visit the client in prison to prepare her to testify at her parole hearing; they collect information favoring a grant of parole and file a written submission; and they conduct the hearing...The Project also represents survivors of domestic abuse whose crimes stemmed from the abuse prior to the time when courts allowed expert testimony on intimate partner battering (formerly Battered Women's Syndrome).

Three months after Gloria met with Williams and Frampton, Governor Wilson responded to their petition, granting a compassionate release to an eighty-five-year-old battered woman named Frances Caccavale who had serious medical problems and finally granting clemency to Brenda Aris, who became the first battered woman in the state of California to be granted clemency. Her sentenced was reduced from fifteen years to life to twelve to life with a recommendation to the parole board that she be granted parole.

Initially the administration staff misread the fax and the next day sent both Brenda and Frances to R&R to parole. Frances was released, but someone eventually noticed that Brenda's clemency was a sentence reduction and a parole recommendation, not a release.

Brenda's entire family, including her three teenage daughters, was in the parking lot to pick her up and she was devastated when she learned she needed to stay in prison for at least another year. The associate warden offered her a visit with her family to explain the situation, but Brenda refused, saying, "You created this mess. You explain it!"

Gloria was so proud of her. This Brenda was so different from the one who came to prison years ago. And so was Gloria.

In April, Brenda was sent to the parole board and was granted parole with a one-year setoff date. The setoff date was the parole board's way of ensuring that they hadn't made a mistake and of keeping an eye on her for another year.

Gloria had new evidence. Brenda had a parole date. They promised to stay friends in their new lives on the outside.

| 19 |

Five Years of Waiting

Genego couldn't bring up any new issues in Gloria's habeas writ in the United States District Court, Eastern District of California, but didn't think he'd have to. He strongly believed there was more than enough evidence already for the judges to vacate her conviction. Federal courts are supposed to be cut and dried when it comes to reviewing habeas petitions that have been turned down by state courts; they need to be shown that the trial was constitutionally unfair. The Sixth Amendment to the United States Constitution states, "In all criminal prosecutions, the accused shall enjoy the right to a speedy and public trial, by an impartial jury of the State and district wherein the crime shall have been committed, which district shall have been previously ascertained by law, and to be informed of the nature and cause of the accusation; to be confronted with the witnesses against him; to have compulsory process for obtaining witnesses in his favor, and to have the Assistance of Counsel for his defense."

But the wait in federal courts is excruciating because of the huge caseload. What should take weeks takes months, if not years, and there is nothing to do but wait.

During the past three years, Joyce Ride had spent close to one hundred thousand dollars of her own money for investigators and lawyers and was sorely disappointed in the California Supreme Court, unable to understand how they could still keep Gloria behind bars after reviewing all the evidence. But Joyce pressed everyone involved to continue, because if she referred to herself at the beginning of the case as "annoyed by injustice," she now was mad as hell.

For five months after Genego filed in the federal courts, they heard nothing and then the court issued an Order to Show Cause why the writ should not be granted. Within weeks the attorney general's office filed their motion to deny the writ in the court of Judge Gregory Hollows, a recently appointed magistrate judge who had spent the bulk of his career as a federal prosecutor in Sacramento. Genego felt that Hollows had tended to side with the State's cases in his past decisions. For this case, he ordered an evidentiary hearing, which he scheduled for July, a little more than a year later. Genego and Killian felt it was Hollows' way of saying, "Let's see if you can prove these claims."

It had been five long years since Williams and Carlson found the new evidence and Genego and Gloria were pleased with this development. Finally someone was going to hear in person about the terrible things that had been done to her. The lies, suppressed evidence and secret deals were all going to become known. They could subpoena Gary Masse and whomever else they wanted. She was sure Judge Hollows would listen to the new testimony, read the case files and make the right decision, hoping that the wheels of justice would turn for her and set her free.

The clock was ticking and Genego had to put together a complete defense. The hearing was like a mini-trial, in front of a judge but without a jury, giving the judge complete power over the outcome. Genego had an opportunity to prove all the points of the writ in front of Hollows, showing that Masse lied, the prosecutor withheld evidence and Gloria didn't get a fair trial.

Gloria had given Genego fifteen thousand dollars from the trust of her aunt and Joyce had been paying for him for years. They needed money to hire an expert to testify on Masse's mental health and an investigator to find Gary Smith to testify that Bob Hord asked him to perform the crime and to pay for Genego's time, the days at the hearing, the interviews, the preparation and travel.

Bill was sure Gloria was innocent and Joyce had already spent so much money. Genego made a compassionate decision. The tough, intense defense lawyer stopped counting hours and he stopped billing Joyce Ride. The rest of the costs of Gloria's defense were on him. Injustice bothered him, too.

Genego looked through his list of possible witnesses for the evidentiary hearing. Virgil Fletcher was dead and Stephen DeSantis was ill and involved in his own case before the same federal court, albeit with a different judge. He'd bring in Gloria's former lawyer Ray Thielen and, if necessary, her appeal counsel, Julian Macias. He'd hire a medical expert to declare that Gary Masse had a mental deficiency during Gloria's trial and somehow locate Gary Smith. And he'd get Masse on the stand to admit he lied at Gloria's trial.

Genego wrote out a check to an investigator to find Smith, who had previously told Cleland and the police that Bob Hord had set up the robbery. Smith gave Gloria's defense a clear alternative scenario and his lack of appearance at her original trial was a mistake of counsel, Genego felt. But finding Smith wasn't going to be easy or cheap. Gary Smith was almost as common a name as John Smith.

When Gloria mused about the hearing, her thoughts swirled together in her mind: home, Sacramento, mom. She thought the California Department of Corrections would fly her to Sacramento and put her up in the new county jail downtown, close to the federal courthouse, only blocks from where her mother lived.

Every two weeks for thirteen years she had talked with her mother Helen, but her mother had never visited. Even when offered a free plane ride from Sacramento, Helen refused to set foot in CIW. Now this would be their chance to be together. She wondered if her mother's hair was still dark (Gloria's was already salt and pepper), and if she was still so tall, straight and statuesque as she nervously waited in line for the pay phone to call her and tell her the good news. She hoped her mother still smelled the same, that spicy-sweet perfume, and she bet her mother had kept her figure. She'd be proud that Gloria was thin and fit. Gloria made it a point to exercise daily and looked good, considering where she was. She couldn't wait to show her mother.

Gloria picked up the phone that evening more excited than she'd been in years and before her mother could even squeak out a hello, she babbled, "Mom, guess what? I'm going to be in Sacramento. Downtown, in the county jail. I'm going to find out the visiting hours as soon as possible and you can come see me."

Helen paused long and hard, more than a moment or two of silence.

"What do you mean?" she asked slowly.

"I'm coming home to Sacramento. You can see me. I just need to find out the times. I'll be right downtown."

"No," Helen said. Gloria fell back against the wall of the phone booth.

"Please, Mom, what do you mean no? I haven't seen you in thirteen years," Gloria pleaded, holding back tears.

"We'll see," Helen said. And that was it. Gloria knew better than to continue the conversation.

"Okay, be there soon. Love you," Gloria said, then hung up and staggered to her cell, hoping her mother would change her mind but knowing she wouldn't.

Meanwhile, after weeks of searching, Genego finally located Gary Smith in southern California and found out that the man who now owned a small trucking business had had a hard life over the past twenty years, spending most of his time in federal and state prisons until he found religion and went straight. Smith was thrilled when Genego's investigator found him. He felt sure Masse was involved, Hord set it up and Gloria had nothing to do with the robbery. Smith said he had gone to Cleland years before and told him all of this to try to cut a deal to stay out of prison for a few more months, because his wife was dying of terminal cancer. When the district attorney refused to help, Smith ran, got arrested in New Orleans and spent two years in a Louisiana prison and four more in a federal prison in Phoenix, then back to serve five more years in California.

Smith said he was happy to testify that Hord was the one who said he set up the Davies robbery. He was glad to go to Sacramento, Smith said, to tell the truth and to help Gloria, and he wanted to pay his own way. It was the right thing to do.

For the next six months Genego poured hours into preparing for Gloria's evidentiary hearing. He worked on the case a few hours and then took his beloved Jack Russell terrier out for a walk. He loved to take the small dog around Santa Monica to the beach near his office. Being out with the dog in the fresh beach air relaxed him and helped him think. The dog was the one link that kept him connected to his head and his heart.

Genego had a list of witnesses including Gary Smith, Thielen, Macias and someone who would testify about the mental state of Gary Masse. He reviewed transcripts, depositions and police reports and he was ready. There was just one piece of the puzzle remaining: He needed to talk to Gary Masse, who had been subpoenaed and was waiting for him in Folsom Prison.

On the Sunday afternoon before the hearing, Genego took a plane from Los Angeles to Sacramento, then made the hour-long drive to

Folsom Prison, wondering what Masse would be like. He'd been belligerent with the attorney general's office, refusing to speak with them at all, and Genego thought it might prove the same with him. Subpoenaing meant Masse had to show up, but Genego had no idea if he would talk or what he would say. Masse had told the attorney general he planned on taking the fifth.

Masse was unhappy at Folsom. It was cold, dank and dark, much different from Mule Creek, where the fifty-four-year-old inmate had been housed for most of his term. He was sick and tired of this case. It made him angry and resentful, because he did all the talking and was still rotting in prison. He wondered why it seemed everyone was going to get out but him. Always a "what's in it for me" kind of guy, Masse wondered how he could play the angles on this and certainly didn't trust the attorney general. The government had promised him no more than twelve years when he testified against DeSantis and Killian and almost twenty years later he was still in prison with no parole in sight. In Genego's strong opinion, Masse most likely wasn't going to talk for them. Masse would be interested in what he could get for himself, nothing more.

Masse was watching intently when the COs brought in Genego and a young woman. He looked like he didn't care and just sat grim and stone-faced.

Genego wondered how he was going to break Masse's silence as he neared the prisoner in the attorney room at Folsom. He was with another lawyer whom he hired to work with him on this case after Eskenazi left the firm for another job.

His years as a defense lawyer and student of human nature gave him an excellent sense of people, especially criminals. He knew asking Masse why he lied or about the case in particular would get him nowhere. *Maybe he won't talk about Gloria right off the bat*, Genego thought, *but I bet he'll talk about himself.*

He sat across from Masse, who looked mean, vicious and older and harder than his age.

"I ain't gonna say nothing," he immediately told Genego. "I didn't say nothing to the AG and I ain't gonna say nothing to you. I'm just gonna take the fifth."

Genego looked intently at him and nodded. To Genego, Masse's words conveyed toughness and ruthlessness. Obviously he was not filled with any remorse. Genego had to find a way to loosen Masse up, as it would be a disaster for them if he wouldn't talk at all.

"Look, Gary, you need to do what's good for you, but one thing I just don't get is why fifty percent? Why give some thirty-five-year-old female law student fifty percent of a heist?"

Gary looked at Genego. He was listening.

"Why would a smart guy like you give her fifty percent? That, at least, had to be a lie."

Slowly Gary nodded. Genego knew Masse was smart enough to realize that he wasn't an idiot who would give some lady 50 percent when he was only giving guys like Hord and Herbst 10 percent.

"Yeah, that was a lie. There were a lot of lies."

"Lots of lies, Gary?"

Gary nodded. Bill pushed, hoping he had cracked the criminal open a little.

"What were some of the lies, Gary?"

Surprisingly Masse began talking and he and Genego went back and forth, with Masse telling the lawyer, "She didn't have nothing to do with it. We just used her. She had nobody" and then changing his story around a few minutes later. Genego saw the criminal liked to talk and seemed to like the sound of his own voice a lot.

Genego knew he wasn't dealing with someone stable or trustworthy. This was a career criminal who still played games, so he pressed Masse, asking the lying convict if he planned on telling the judge the next day what he had just said: that Gloria was totally innocent. Masse, however, was cagey, always looking to play what was best for him. "I'm not saying that's what I'm going to say tomorrow. To say it would not be good for me."

Genego knew that, too. It wouldn't be good for Masse, because doing so would still implicate his wife Joanne as the woman who went to the door. Masse also knew it wouldn't look great to the parole board if he admitted having set up an innocent woman; they would never let him out of prison. So Genego had a problem. How could he get Masse to tell the judge he lied at Gloria's trial, knowing that the thug still wanted to play some games and could not be trusted to tell the truth? It was a problem Genego had to solve, because he needed Masse to admit he knowingly lied on the stand during Gloria's trial about citing her as the mastermind, about his deal with the prosecution and about Gloria calling him up after the murder for her share of the loot. If he could get Masse to admit these particular lies, the court would have to overturn the conviction based on false evidence and perjured testimony.

Genego nodded, then stood up and took a long last look at Gary Masse. Then he and his colleague left.

Genego had a good idea as to what his approach was going to be. He was going to let Masse talk as much as he wanted. Let him tell his story again and again until he was feeling at ease and amenable to questions. Genego knew that the dialog with Masse would be his only opportunity to save Gloria's life. But he also knew he had time to employ his strategy. Since there was no time limit to keeping Masse on the stand, he felt confident. The one thing he had was time.

Gloria never made it to the downtown Sacramento jail, but it didn't matter: Her mother had refused to visit. The weekend before the hearing, authorities moved her to the Valley State Prison for Women at Chowchilla and decided they would transport her the two hours to court each day. Since her location changed, her flight plans did as well and on the Sunday Genego spent in Folsom, Gloria rode through central California for nine hours, chained in the back of a van, the only saving grace the stops for fast food. She was amazed how delicious a junk-food burger and fries could taste.

Valley State Prison is the antithesis of CIW in that it looks, smells and breathes like a men's prison: no grass, no trees, razor wire every-where. Her transportation officers dropped her off at Receiving and Release, unchained her and left. Within the hour she was strip-searched, given a muumuu and a fish kit, put in a cell by herself and told to go to bed.

Luckily for her she fell asleep quickly, for at 3:00 A.M. the COs racked her cell door, yelling, "Get up! You are going to court."

Gloria did her hair and makeup as best she could and put on her State-issued navy blue pants and pink flowered blouse. She walked out of the cell, saw a CO drinking a cup of coffee and stared at him. He looked at her, smiled, walked over to the coffee pot, filled a cup and gave it to her. Moments later he walked her into the cool night air to the medical unit where a car was waiting.

"I'd tuck the shirt in if I were you," the CO said. "You don't want to get it all wrinkled from the belly chains." He cuffed her wrists loosely to the chain so that she could eat the sack lunch they had brought her in lieu of breakfast.

This was only the second time in years that she had been driven anywhere and, in the dawn light, drifted off into a reverie imagining the hearing working out the way that she hoped it could. Her fantasy scenario visualized the judge so horrified by the evidence that he ordered her immediate release. She knew it was impossible, but it was fun to dream about.

As they neared Sacramento, Gloria got more excited and began looking out the window. She'd never expected to come back in a squad car—really she never expected to come back at all—but against all odds she was back in Sacramento. They turned the corner and she saw the new federal courthouse, thinking that this home of justice was a beautiful building. As soon as they entered the courthouse she knew she was home. The inside temperature was sixty-eight degrees, like every public facility in Sacramento. Gloria hadn't been in air conditioning since she went to prison and she loved the feel of the cool, stone building.

The CO straightened the collar on Gloria's blouse and led her into the courtroom to where Bill and his colleague were waiting.

Then they heard, "All rise. The Court for the Eastern District of California is in session. The Honorable Gregory Hollows, United States magistrate judge, is presiding."

Hollows was everything Gloria thought a magistrate judge should look like: tall and majestic with salt and pepper hair and a beard to match.

Genego asked Hollows if the court could remove Gloria's handcuffs and chains so she'd be able to write and help with her case. Hollows agreed and the CO uncuffed her and removed the chain around her waist. Gloria was glad to be more comfortable.

The first witness Genego brought out was a forensic psychiatrist and Harvard lawyer, there to establish that Gary Masse, "during the time periods covered by medical records…suffered from a mental or emotional deficiency that would have affected his ability or motivation to fictionalize or misrepresent."

The expert testified, "If one reviewed the medical records, as I have, it appears that Mr. Masse was diagnosed as having some type of serious mental disorder…The most common of those serious diagnoses is some kind of schizophrenia…additionally, the records contain many entries about problems with memory and at one point Mr. Masse endeavored to hang himself. He was also a very substantial substance abuser."

Gloria thought he did great.

The next witness Genego called was Ray Thielen. With Thielen, Genego had the job of proving his claim that Cleland had withheld evidence and showing that the evidence that Thielen did have was not effectively used.

Genego began his questioning by asking Gloria's trial lawyer if he knew about the letter Cleland wrote asking to strike the special circumstances for Masse, to which Thielen replied he did not.

Genego then asked if it would have assisted him in cross-examining Masse. "Definitely," Thielen responded.

"What would you have done if you'd known about the letter from Masse that said he 'lied his ass off' and that there was a verbal agreement that Masse would only serve twelve years?"

"If I would have known about it I would have moved for a new trial. I would have used the entire letter as a basis for a new trial."

"Did you know of the special treatment Gary Masse was receiving and that he was mentally ill?"

"I definitely didn't know any of this and it would have been helpful both in cross-examining and in argument before the jury."

"Did you have a physician review any medical records or [evaluate] Mr. Masse?"

"I did not," Thielen admitted.

"Do you remember requesting any records?"

"I recall not doing that."

"Did you have a tactical reason for not pursuing the issue of Mr. Masse's medical records?"

"No."

"Do you believe that you should have pursued the issue of trying to get Masse's medical records to find out if there was more information that would have enabled you to assess his credibility with the assistance of an expert?"

"Yes."

Genego asked Thielen if there was a tactical reason he did not bring an expert to testify about Grace Davies' physical and mental issues to exculpate Gloria and implicate Joanne. Thielen again answered no.

"And do you remember any tactical reason that you had at the time for either not interviewing or not attempting to call Mr. Smith as a witness on behalf of Ms. Killian?"

"No."

Genego continued questioning the effective use of evidence at Gloria's trial. He asked, since Cleland named Neva Snyder as the link between Killian and Masse, why didn't Thielen bring up Neva Snyder's testimony in the DeSantis trial?

Genego pressed Thielen. "Was there a tactical reason you didn't call Snyder as a witness in Killian's trial?"

"I can't think of any reason why I wouldn't have called her. I recall they were doing daily transcripts of the DeSantis case. If I had read it then yes, I would have or should have called Ms. Snyder as a witness."

His point about Snyder made, Genego returned to DeSantis and Thielen stated he should have known that DeSantis claimed not to know Gloria and called DeSantis as a witness.

When it came time for cross-examination, Thielen held firm.

Tom Brown was the next witness called. As always, the casually dressed detective looked relaxed and his demeanor was calm. Brown calmly asserted that when he got the "lied my ass off" letter from Masse, he went to see Masse, who told him "that he had been truthful in court and this was something he said specifically to get our attention to get me to go down to see him." Brown admitted that he took Masse on visits with his family and to public restaurants to have meals and did not disclose that information in any of the reports.

But the next day, Tuesday, July 13, was to be the big day, the day they brought in Gary Masse. Gloria slept fitfully that night, as did Genego, wondering what this man would say.

Masse arrived a half hour late for court and strolled up to the stand looking clear-eyed and calm. He took a seat and Gloria stared at him. In all the times she'd seen him, at all the preliminary hearings and at her trial, he never once looked at her or met her gaze. This time he looked directly at her; he stared blankly, but he met her gaze.

Genego walked up to Masse. The first thing Genego wanted to do was to make Masse feel at ease so he would talk. He had time and he had a plan. Genego began asking Masse about the poor state of his mental health when Masse turned himself in.

"I was pretty messed up mentally," Masse said. "I was pretty confused and medicated at the time."

Masse told the court it was Lieutenant Biondi who introduced Gloria's name to him. Genego then got Masse to admit that Tom Brown personally told him he would not do more than twelve years in prison and that he could "write his own ticket" as long as he did his part: "That statement—'write your own ticket'—was used in, you know, you give us what we want without screwing it up, you know, Killian and DeSantis and you can basically write your own ticket. But they didn't come out and say the word *lie*, but I have to do what I have to do to get the job done."

Masse stated that what he said about lying in the letter was true.

"Did you tell Mr. Brown that the reason you had said that in a letter is because you wanted to make sure he would come and visit you?"

"I wanted to get his attention."

"Does that mean what you told him in the letter about lying your ass off was untrue?"

"No."

"It was true?"

"It was true."

"Was it also true, even though you wanted to get his attention by saying it and putting it in writing, that you understood there was an agreement, a verbal agreement, of no more than twelve years?"

"Yes."

Slowly but surely Masse was telling Genego what the lawyer felt the court needed to hear. But it was taking time and Judge Hollows started losing patience. He began interrupting Genego, asking Masse questions himself. While an evidentiary hearing is not a trial court, having a judge interrupt and ask numerous questions during the interview of a witness isn't normal. Genego didn't like it, but he abided by the court and he waited.

"Let me ask you this, Mr. Masse," Judge Hollows began. "Look at this letter, line ten. I'll read some portions of it: 'I have been upfront and honest as I could be. I gave you DeSantis and Killian. I did my part all the way 'til the end.' Was that true? Were you upfront and honest as could be with respect to DeSantis and Killian?"

"Yeah, all the way up to—what I did though—I couldn't go no more," Masse answered.

"It says, 'I even lied my ass off on the stand for you people.' Now what did you mean by 'I even lied my ass off'? What lies did you tell?"

"What lies did I tell? Uh, I told—when I was questioned on the stand, there were certain things I had to lie about, because I couldn't tell them the truth. I was told not to say anything."

"I want you to remember every one of those," the judge requested.

"Tom Brown—I told them I have a hard time remembering things. I believe they asked me if I had been back to the scene of the crime or anything they don't know about and I had to lie. I had to tell them no."

"Anything else you can remember?"

"Was I on medications. I lied and told them no."

"Did you lie about the facts of the case? Did you ever do that?"

"Well, I had...Miss Killian...I could only go so far with that. I could only go so far. I couldn't tell the truth, because there would have been no more deals. I wouldn't have come through for them."

Genego was sure this was not the right tack to take with Masse. Genego tactically objected. But Judge Hollows continued his questioning.

"I'm going to subject him to the questions of the attorneys later on. You can make objections or motions to strike, but let him finish. I want you to tell what was true about Miss Killian's involvement and what was untrue about it as far as you can remember. Tell me about her involvement or lack of involvement."

Masse then went through a long and confusing explanation of what happened, often contradicting himself:

"We used Gloria on a couple of occasions to get into the house, but it never worked out, so we kept going back. We were going around there too much and we put Gloria out of the picture, but Gloria... she wasn't the master planner of the whole thing. They just used her. They needed a third party. They needed a third party to make it look like it was her thing so it didn't come back to the guy who really set the whole thing up.

"So Gloria, she's still there. She doesn't even know she's out of the show. She's not even in the picture. I kept it as much as I can and even Tom Brown, I told him I can't give her up. I'm not going to give them people up and he knew and all I had to do was to give him her. I had to carry that on my shoulders for all those years. All she got, thirty-something to life for attempted robbery. It turned out to be the big master planner. She didn't plan shit. She didn't have my people. She didn't have no people. All she had was herself. Nobody gave a shit about the evidence at all. They wanted her. They wanted her and I had to give them her and after I gave them her, it didn't mean nothing to them."

"Was your wife involved?" Judge Hollows wanted to know.

"Yes, my wife was involved, too. She went out there with me and she was going to do it. There have been times where me and her was going to do it ourselves, but we never ended up doing it."

"Did your wife go up to the door or ring the bell?"

"No."

"Did Miss Killian ever go up to the door or ring the bell?"

"Yes, on one occasion I believe."

"All right." The judge turned to Bill. "Mr. Genego, any questions?"

Genego was stunned. He strongly felt the judge's rushing in thwarted Genego's own plan to get the real story slowly from Masse and that Masse was lying about Gloria's involvement yet again. He had to make a decision and he had to make it fast. He could try to get Masse to take back what he said about Gloria's initial involvement, but that could end in an angry battle with the career criminal that wouldn't get them anywhere and could cost him dearly.

Genego decided to ignore Masse's lying statements and establish that Masse lied at Gloria's trial. If he admitted to lying at the trial, her conviction would have been based on perjured testimony. Genego redirected his questioning to get at the points he needed to make to assert that Masse lied at the trial. He believed in the letter of the law. He knew Gloria was innocent and was never involved in the robbery, but that was not the point of the hearing. Branding Masse, the prosecution's make-or-break witness, as a liar, a perjurer, made her trial constitutionally unfair. He set up a line of questioning to make those points.

"Your answer of 'No, there weren't no bargains made.' That was not true, was it, that testimony you gave?"

"No."

"You were asked the following questions," Genego said, reading from Killian's trial transcript. "'Did you have a verbal agreement that you would get twelve years if you cooperated with the prosecution?' And your answer is, 'I don't believe so.' That testimony was not truthful, was it?"

"No."

"You said," Genego continued reading, "'That's what I felt my part should be. They didn't say if you testify we are going to see everything we can do to get you twelve years.' That testimony was untruthful, right?"

"Right."

"And you were asked if you had any idea who her people were, right?"

"Yes."

"Did Miss Killian have people?"

"No."

"So your testimony that you were fearful of Killian's people was not truthful, was it?"

"In a sense, yes."

"It wasn't truthful, right?" Genego pressed.

"No, not on her... If I implicated the people that were involved in it, I would have problems. My family would have problems."

"Your testimony denying other people were involved was untrue, right?"

"Yes, untrue."

"In fact, you did not tell the whole truth with respect to Miss Killian."

"It would have to be yes," Masse admitted.

Satisfied he'd done what he needed to do, Genego said he had no further questions and the cross-examination went to Michael Weinberger, the smart, well-dressed attorney from the attorney general's office. Weinberger tried to discredit Masse's stance about being promised the reduced twelve-year deal for his perjured testimony, but Masse held firm. "They told me if I could pull this off without screwing it up I can write my own ticket. I heard that so many times it wasn't funny."

In redirect, Genego returned to showing that Masse had never had any conversations with Gloria, but it was hard to shake the nagging sensation that Hollows had taken the questioning off course.

"Mr. Masse, as you sit here right now, can you tell us any conversations you had after you went to the door with Miss Killian and before the robbery occurred?"

"No."

Genego did not realize it then, but this seemingly innocuous line of questions must have sounded to Hollows like Genego agreeing to the fact that Killian had talked to Masse at some point in time, something Genego didn't believe at all. It would cause him the deepest pain and sadness he'd ever experience in any of his cases.

Meanwhile, Gloria was pleased and amazed as she listened to Masse, finally admitting that he lied about almost everything, though she knew he'd never completely clear her. She learned after writing so many parole appeals and helping women prepare for board hearings that no parole board in the country would release a man who set up an innocent woman. Masse was still trying to game the system. She knew it wouldn't matter; he had admitted to lying on the stand about her.

It was time to break for lunch and as the lawyers left, Gloria was marched back to her holding cell. It may have been a brand new courthouse, but the cell was no different from the dozens of others she'd seen over the years: plain white walls, a long, hard wooden bench and a toilet with a water fountain attached at the top. Feeling like a dog stuck in a kennel while everyone else went out to a nice lunch, she laid back on the bench and looked up at the camera trained on the cell thinking, *Will this nightmare ever end?*

For the afternoon session, the attorney general's office brought in Kit Cleland. Gloria had noticed him and felt he was making joking remarks to Hollows earlier when they came back from lunch, which made her very nervous. But it was not that strange—both were lawmen who made Sacramento, a pretty small town, their home.

Weinberger asked his witness a number of questions that supported the AG's position that there was no wrongdoing on the prosecutor's part.

But Genego got Cleland to talk about how he handled discovery and why he didn't hand over Masse's letter to any of the lawyers.

"And did you make this discoverable to the defense?" Genego asked Cleland.

"That time all proceedings against the several defendants were concluded in the trial court, so no, I did not."

"That was the reason you had for not turning it over?"

"I didn't know who to give it to."

"Did you know that DeSantis, having been convicted of special circumstances, murder with a death penalty, would have counsel be appointed to him on a mandatory appeal from the Supreme Court?"

"I still didn't know who to give it to. I don't think he had a lawyer then."

"What about Mr. Thielen? Did you think about giving it to him on behalf of Miss Killian?"

"No."

"So you just kept it."

"Yes, I kept it."

Genego strongly felt that Cleland had done the wrong thing and withheld evidence.

Once he finished questioning Cleland, Genego called his final witness, Gary Lee Smith, who repeated his story that it was Bob Hord who solicited him for the Davies robbery and then made the point that he told that exact story to Kit Cleland, a pivotal piece of information that had never been revealed before in Gloria's case.

Gloria was thrilled. Masse admitted he lied during her trial and she believed Genego had established that she had not had a fair trial, which was the criteria for granting the writ. She felt they had won.

Genego felt differently. While he thought he had a good chance, he knew that when Hollows interrupted his direct examination of Gary Masse with his own questions, it altered Genego's original plans. He felt that Hollows was retrying Gloria's case rather than establishing the criteria for the writ. This hearing wasn't supposed to be about her alleged guilt or innocence; it was about whether she got a fair trial.

"Now the testimony from Mr. Masse this morning was interesting," Judge Hollows said as the hearing came to a close. "If I were to characterize it, it was more or less that Miss Killian was guilty or was convicted of a crime she thought she was involved in and really it's her state of mind that is important for conspiracy. Was she convicted on conspiracy?"

"She was convicted on conspiracy," Weinberger replied.

"That's what I thought," Hollows continued. "And there were alleged overt acts, so it doesn't make a difference if people in their own minds exed her off the list of involvement. She still formed the conspiracy and hadn't confirmatively abandoned it, at least from the testimony Masse gave—and I hate to say this about Mr. Masse: I thought he was trying to tell the truth today. But you need to tell me, Mr. Genego, where his testimony gets you, because I don't think it left you with any great arguments except with respect as to some of the things he told you that weren't the complete truth and whether in a habeas action the prosecutor knew this. I don't think so. He never asked him."

Hollows' comments at the end of the hearing didn't help Genego feel better, but he felt sure that they had the law on their side and felt confident he'd proven their contentions and established that Gloria's trial was unfair.

All they could do now was wait for Hollows' decision.

| 20 |

Free at Last

Since the opening of the CIW/USC Law Project, the board of prison terms had been busy investigating cases of women with domestic violence claims and Gloria's legal and coaching skills were regularly put to the test. Maria Suarez's claim had been substantiated in full and Gloria needed to prepare her next board hearing while she worked with Glenda Virgil, who had killed her abusive boyfriend, on her habeas petition. While there had been more settlements and lawsuits in the medical department, there always seemed to be a crisis brewing. Crises were just what Gloria needed to keep her mind off waiting for the Eastern District decision. Laughter helped too.

Many of the pregnant inmates had been getting disciplinary write-ups and were punished for having urine tests that returned positive for alcohol. Pregnant offenders were lining up in the law library swearing to Gloria that they weren't drinking. Gloria discussed the odd situation one day at lunch with an inmate who was in prison for civil disobedience and who had an idea why this might be happening. She found research that stated all pregnant women would test positive for alcohol due to the mild state of ketosis caused by pregnancy. Gloria wrote an appeal to change the testing procedures and won.

Staff members were also lining up for Gloria's services. A male staff member had been wrongly accused of stealing food and supplies from the Family Visiting Unit. He wanted Gloria's help but was so nervous that his supervisors would see him getting advice from an inmate that he insisted that Gloria meet him behind the Education Building where no one would see them talking. She told him how to handle his first interviews with the institutional investigator and soon all charges against him were dropped.

One bright happening in the months of waiting for Judge Hollows' decision came at Christmas. After years of fighting for the right to sing Christmas carols, the women at CIW were finally afforded the privilege to sing two days a year. Several days before Christmas, Gloria and a group of women started to practice and soon a lieutenant and one of the chaplains agreed to be part of the caroling crew. For two evenings the women and the two staff members strolled through the entire prison: to Ad Seg, to the mental health unit, to the Reception Center and finally to each housing unit, bringing Christmas cheer to one of the unhappiest places. Gloria loved Christmas caroling, because it brought the spirit of Christmas to everyone. People told her she had a beautiful voice, but she always wondered where it came from. *Perhaps*, she thought, *the country-singer father I never knew.*

On Christmas day, Gloria experienced pure joy watching the women's eyes well with tears as they sang along. For a few minutes, inmates and staff were all just human beings together, celebrating the joy of the season. For months afterward, women came to her in the law library to tell her they had seen her singing in the Reception Center or Ad Seg and that she made them cry or reminded them of their childhood. Many times after the caroling was over, Gloria longed for the life she lost and the Christmases at home with the family she sorely missed. But she never let the staff see her cry.

It was the coming of the millennium and Gloria hoped that the New Year signified not only a new century, but also a new beginning and a new life. She wouldn't let herself think anything but that her conviction would be reversed and she'd finally be free from the hell that was prison.

On the first weekend after the New Year, Gloria telephoned her mother, but to her surprise got no answer. The next Monday, Gloria was called into Program Services.

The lieutenant, a motherly woman, asked Gloria to sit down. The lieutenant she seemed upset.

"Gloria," the lieutenant said, "your mother passed away over the weekend."

Gloria sat quietly thinking about the last time she saw her mother, at the Branch so many years before.

"Is there someone I can get to help you?"

"Yes," Gloria managed to say. "Please get Della, my roommate."

Della came, held Gloria's hand and walked her to see her counselor and get permission for extra phone privileges in order to take care of the legalities, as Gloria was Helen's closest living relative. After Gloria made the necessary arrangements, she took to her bed, stricken with grief. She cried for what she lost and what she never really had: a warm, caring and supportive mother. Three days later she pulled herself together and went back to work, because her mother had raised her to know that whatever happened, life had to go on. Her daily life didn't change with the passing of her mother, but Helen's death made Gloria acutely aware of how much prison had cost her. She pondered how much she had truly lost and how little family she had left. Her Aunt Louella was living in a nursing home suffering from Parkinson's disease and her Uncle Arvid was in his eighties.

For the next six weeks Gloria threw herself back into work and was just beginning to find emotional stability when she got a call to pick up some legal mail at Program Services. Arriving there, her stomach tightened and she grasped the large manila envelope which was waiting for her.

She walked back to the cell, afraid to open the heavy envelope which could bring the promise of freedom. She held it in her shaking hand. She touched it, smelled it and sat on the bed for minutes just looking at it.

Finally she tore open the top and pulled out the papers. It was a thick document, sixty-three pages long, far longer than she'd expected. Quickly she scanned the first page and her heart sank. The judge had denied the writ. She sat in a stunned silence, unable to move, unable to cry.

Eventually she pushed herself to read the decision and couldn't believe what she was reading. The judge seemed to agree that Masse lied repeatedly and that exculpatory evidence was suppressed. Unbelievably, it appeared to her the judge's remarks seemed to indicate that her own lawyer said she was guilty. That couldn't be so! She read the entire document again slowly. Hollows started off noting how rare it was to find a credible claim of actual innocence, went on to state every fact in her favor, noting how Masse committed perjury, but then denied the writ claiming that he felt her attorney had indicated that she was guilty. She knew that was wrong; she had been at the hearing and couldn't imagine what the judge was talking about. She was shocked, but a big part of her, sadly, was not surprised, because she knew too well that the justice system could fail. It had failed her so many times before.

She got up and she ran next door to her friend Glenda. Gloria explained what had happened and then they both sat there stunned. Glenda had been in prison as long as Gloria had and recently won her appeal in the same federal court that had just denied Gloria's writ. Gloria was thrilled that Glenda had won, but it made it even harder to accept her loss. She couldn't understand how Glenda, who killed someone, albeit in self-defense, was going to get out and she was going to remain in prison knowing she never did anything wrong. She hated herself for those jealous thoughts, because she felt Glenda deserved to get out, but when would she have a chance? Why was she punished?

She wanted to talk to Genego and find out what her lawyer thought had happened. She needed to talk to him to try to make sense of all of this, but she had no phone privileges scheduled. She asked Glenda to help her find someone to trade phone time with. It was really important she get to talk with Genego.

In fact, the lawyer, who had also received the documents, was going through many of the same emotions his client was feeling. Never in all his years as an attorney had the tough-minded barrister cried. He knew there were difficulties in the defense game, but he had faith in the system. He turned page after page, the sick feeling growing in the pit of his stomach. Even glancing at his dog, curled up, sleeping in her bed near his desk didn't make him smile. In all his years, through countless judicial decisions, he never read or felt anything like this. He swallowed the lump in his throat as he read:

> Petitioner's counsel initially brought out the substance of petitioner's true involvement in the Davies robbery.
>
> Genego: At some point in time, in your mind, Mr. Masse, did you consider that Ms. Killian was no longer a participant in the crime that you and Mr. DeSantis planned?
>
> Masse: Yeah. Me and DeSantis, we stopped using her. She wasn't involved anymore. She probably thought she was, but we stopped using her.

Bill Genego felt strongly the judge had made a grave error. He felt the judge hadn't understood that Genego had made a strategic decision and then was making a tactical move to question Masse only about his lies on the stand at Gloria's trial and avoid a fighting match with the thug about who did what and when. He couldn't believe the judge mistook the way he questioned Masse as if Genego believed in Gloria's guilt. If Genego had asked Masse straight out if Gloria was involved, Masse probably would have not said anything or lied and said she was involved all the way. He was incredulous at the interpretation the judge had made.

Not only that, but also Hollows was of the opinion that "The evidentiary hearing testimony itself does not exonerate petitioner. Nor does it put the facts that were presented at trial in such a false light that petitioner was convicted on the basis of perjured testimony...Petitioner is not actually innocent of the crimes for which she was convicted."

Genego knew that once the judge had concluded Gloria's guilt, there was no way he was going to allow the writ. Genego knew legally he had done his job getting Masse to admit he lied at her trial and was a perjurer. That he could lie again now was par for the course.

What gave Genego some solace was that Hollows now understood and had put on the record that Masse was a perjurer and a liar and had lied at Gloria's trial, citing, "The court has found that Masse perjured himself at the state trial in several respects, including the 'whole truth' about petitioner's involvement in the crime and Masse's own belief that he had a 12-year deal with the prosecution." But Genego just couldn't understand why Hollows decided to believe Masse about Gloria's "initial involvement" and base his decision on that.

Genego believed they would have a strong basis to overturn this decision in the Ninth Circuit, but what would he say to Gloria? He felt this disappointing decision was his fault.

His sister Barbara, who had been crying since reading the decision, walked into his inner office. "I have Gloria on the phone."

Bill picked up the phone, feeling choked up. "I'm so, so sorry," he said and as he listened to Gloria's wounded gulps, he knew what he needed to do to right this situation.

"I'm going to make a motion to withdraw as your counsel. That way we can explain to the judge what I was doing tactically and show him and the Ninth Circuit that I believe in your innocence and show how Hollows misunderstood my line of questioning."

He listened to Gloria say she understood but still wanted him to be her lawyer. When, through her tears, she said he was the best lawyer she'd ever seen, he finally smiled.

Walking into the visiting area at CIW, Joyce Ride was profoundly sad, yet she too felt firmly that they would overturn this decision in the Ninth Circuit Court of Appeals. She sat down across from her friend and told her that she was thinking of bringing Gloria to her house. After Gloria's mother passed away, Joyce began considering offering Gloria a room in her home to live in when Gloria was released. The widow found it lonely in her large three-bedroom house in Pasadena, her only roommate a springer spaniel.

Genego filed the motion to withdraw as counsel, which stated that if the Court believed Genego thought Gloria was guilty, he shouldn't be her lawyer:

> Upon my reading of the findings and recommendations, it appeared to me that the Court inferred from my examination of witness Gary Masse at the evidentiary hearing that I endorse as true or at least I do not dispute that Ms. Killian was initially involved in the crimes of which she was convicted. I did not and do not accept as true Masse's testimony at the evidentiary hearing that Ms. Killian was involved initially or participated at

any time in the crimes of which she was convicted.
Nor did I intend to convey or suggest by my examination of Masse at the evidentiary hearing that I
accepted as true or did not dispute his testimony
that incriminated Miss Killian. I did not examine
Masse in a manner that challenged or attacked that
part of his testimony, because I thought it would be
ineffectual and result in Masse simply repeating and
affirming the points on which I challenged him.

Hollows denied the motion but added that Genego, in submitting
this motion, was a credit to the Bar Association.

Genego now had a clear document showing his motives and tactics
that would be read by the Ninth Circuit. Gloria was thrilled, because
it meant he could keep fighting with her to clear her name. The Ninth
Circuit was their last chance. If they lost in the Ninth Circuit, the only
step left was the United States Supreme Court, which was unlikely to
hear a case like this.

While the Ninth Circuit Court has the power to reverse the decisions of the Eastern District Federal Court, it doesn't do so very often.
Generally, it reverses less than 10 percent of lower court decisions and in
habeas cases the reversal rate is far less. In the previous decade the Ninth
Circuit had reversed one of 274 cases. Gloria had a shot, but it was a
long shot. A 274-to-one long shot.

Genego worked long and hard refining the petition, adding issues
and points from the evidentiary hearing. For weeks he pored over documents and wrote briefs, feeling responsible for the denial in the Eastern
District. Gaining Gloria's freedom rested heavily on his shoulders. For
Genego, this case had become personal.

In his opening brief he cited five issues the court needed to look at
to appeal the Eastern District's decision and allow Gloria's habeas writ:

1. **The pervasive perjury of the prosecution's "make-or-break witness" requires petitioner's conviction vacated.** Given the district court's finding that the prosecution's "make-or-break witness" against the petitioner committed perjury in testifying falsely as to participant's role and participation in the crime, did the district court err in denying relief?

2. **Petitioner was denied due process by the prosecution's failure to disclose exculpatory evidence.** Whether petitioner was denied due process by the prosecution's non-disclosure of exculpatory evidence (the Masse "I lied my ass" letter among others).

3. **The prosecution's reliance on petitioner's assertion of her Miranda rights violated due process.** Whether the prosecutor's use of petitioner's invocation of her right to remain silent violated petitioner's federal constitutional rights.

4. **Petitioner was denied her right to effective assistance of counsel at trial.** Whether the petitioner was denied her federal constitutional right to the effective assistance of counsel at trial.

5. **Petitioner was denied her right to a fair trial by the cumulative effect of the errors.** Whether petitioner was denied her federal constitutional right to a fair trial by the cumulative effect of the errors.

Genego handed in the appeal and waited anxiously for the date that he'd have to appear in front of the Ninth Circuit to argue the case.

The Ninth Circuit Court of Appeals states its mission on its Web site as "to provide an impartial forum for the just and prompt resolution of cases through the uniform and coherent application of the Constitution and the laws of the United States of America." Its federal jurisdiction covers the states of Montana, Idaho, Washington, Oregon, California, Nevada, Hawaii, Alaska and Arizona and it is one of the busiest courts in the United States, with twenty-nine authorized judges in the jurisdiction. The court only hears oral arguments by an attorney and does not hold evidentiary hearings, relying exclusively on the facts found in lower courts. And it only gives each lawyer around fifteen minutes for his or her oral argument. Fifteen minutes.

When Genego was aboard his flight to San Francisco, his stomach twisted in knots. He'd been in front of the Ninth Circuit before and it wasn't something he relished. He had spent the past few weeks preparing for his fifteen minutes, because he knew he held Gloria's freedom in his hands. He was comforted that the letter of the law was on his side.

His nerves were on edge, but that, in his opinion, was a good sign. He always felt that if one stopped feeling nervous in these situations then one should stop doing the job.

At that time, the Ninth Circuit was housed in a small post-World War II courthouse that, to Genego, looked more like a post office.

Slowly Genego walked up the stairs and into the courtroom. Three judges, two men and a woman, looked down from the bench at him. Pat Whalen was there to represent the attorney general's office.

The court was called to order and Genego was up first. Genego told the court he felt Hollows made a huge error by agreeing that Masse lied at Gloria's trial yet wrongly using Masse's testimony at the evidentiary hearing to convict her. Genego stressed the point to the three judges that Masse admitted he lied about substantial matters at Gloria's trial and that since he was the make-or-break witness, she must be given a new trial. He argued about the Doyle error, citing Cleland's violation of Gloria's rights when he impeached her for invoking her Miranda rights.

The judges listened for few minutes then interrupted with what Genego thought were encouraging questions, enabling him to illuminate even more salient points to help Gloria's case. After the final few moments, after Genego had made all his objections, he took a deep breath.

Pat Whalen defended the State's position, but Genego was pleased that the judges seemed harder on him, making penetrating queries that, although Genego felt Whalen answered well, showed they were looking deeply at the arguments. It was now up to these judges to see what Genego saw so clearly from the first time he read the case: Gloria was innocent and her trial unfair.

It had been five long years since the evidence came out and Gloria had spent over fifteen years in prison.

Afterward, Bill Genego sent Gloria a tape recording of the hearing, which she listened to in her counselor's office, and it sounded like music to her ears. She thought Genego was brilliant and that the three judges asked insightful questions, which gave her even more hope. Her positive feelings were not without reason. She had read every single Ninth Circuit decision that came down in the years leading up to her case and she felt she knew how the court thought. Still, she was very cautious, because she'd made the mistake of feeling encouraged too many times before.

Albeit hopeful, waiting for this decision was the hardest time she ever did. She rocketed back and forth emotionally, one minute believing she would get out, the next wanting to commit suicide. The idea of losing and of spending the rest of her life in prison was something she could no longer tolerate. What kept her from following through on her dark thoughts was the fact that Joyce Ride, Bill Genego and others had given up so much to save her. She couldn't do that to them. She also knew her eighty-four-year-old Uncle Arvid, who had supported her throughout her ordeal by sending her one hundred dollars a month from the first day she was in prison, would be absolutely devastated if she died. Gloria was all he had left in the world.

Her final blow during the long wait for the court's decision was her removal from her position at the law library, her only source of positivity for the past sixteen years. Many clerks throughout the California Department of Corrections (CDC) had held their jobs for years and, like Gloria, practically ran whole departments. When it was discovered at a men's prison that an inmate was stealing from the department he worked in for years, CDC headquarters initiated a policy that inmates could only hold their jobs for two years. Gloria had to go.

Though she was upset, Gloria got another, easier job in a graphic arts class where she played with color wheels, turned in a few assignments, made jewelry and watched a movie every Friday afternoon. It was a big change from the heavy duties and emotional problems she dealt with at the law library. Eventually she learned to enjoy these activities and to stop pushing herself so hard.

A year had passed since Genego's brilliant appearance in the Ninth Circuit and still there was no word. It was two years since the Eastern District Court's denial of her writ and seven years since Scott Williams came to see her with the new evidence that set her appeals and her hope in motion. As was always the case, no one could tell her how much longer she would have to wait to find out her fate.

It was a cool March day at CIW. The air was typically thick with the stench of chemicals and fertilizer when Gloria walked out of the cafeteria, having just finished her coffee and cereal, and headed to the WAC shack. It was a tiny, one-room wooden building in the center of the yard that served as the office for the Women's Advisory Council, the liaison between the administration and the inmates. Gloria was on the WAC executive body that met with the administration to work out inmates' issues that couldn't be resolved at a lower level. She was at the WAC shack to talk to the chairperson about a medical issue involving one of the women. Suddenly an inmate she barely knew called out to the small shack.

"Is Gloria still here? Has she been released yet? My boss wants to know."

Gloria stuck her head out the window, confused.

"I'm right here. What are you talking about?"

"It's in the paper; it's in the paper! You won your case! The CO showed it to me."

"Are you sure?" Gloria asked and felt a tingle run down her spine.

"Yes, yes!" the inmate nodded.

"Go see if she will let you bring me the paper so I can see it," requested Gloria, not willing to believe anything unless she saw it on paper. She sat down on a chair in the tiny building, her mind racing. She couldn't go to her housing unit and call Bill, because the unit was already locked down for cleaning and she knew that her housing officer wouldn't let her back in. She just had to wait and, thanks to more practice than anyone could ever want, she had learned how quite well.

Gloria looked out the tiny window of the WAC shack. Suddenly it seemed as if all the doors in the prison had opened up. Staff came rushing out of every building, running in every direction shouting, "Gloria! Gloria!"

"I read it in the newspaper! You won!" yelled the sponsor of the Long Termers' Organization as she drove up in one of the electric golf carts that the staff used. At the same time other staff and inmates were also screaming, "You won! You won!" as they passed the tiny shack window.

Gloria began to get excited, afraid to believe what might be true. *It must be true,* she thought to herself, but not one person had a copy of the newspaper so she couldn't be sure. She didn't think all these people could be wrong, but she wasn't going to start screaming for joy until she heard it from her lawyer.

It took three hours for her unit to open and Gloria nearly tore the door off the hinges getting inside. The next problem was that she had signed up for an evening phone call. She tried to negotiate a swap with the woman whose phone time it currently was, but the woman wouldn't budge. Gloria turned to the woman in the next slot and begged her to trade places with her. The woman agreed and Gloria got the phone. With shaking hands she dialed Genego's number and before his sister Barbara could say hello, Gloria shrieked, "Is it true?"

"It certainly is," Barbara said. "Let me get Bill for you."

Genego was calm and professional, but inside he felt like cheering. He had felt sick inside ever since the Hollows decision and now both he and Gloria were vindicated. With a huge grin on his face, he listened to Gloria babble on with joy and reflected that it was these times that reminded him he loved his job. He told Gloria the grounds of the decision and said he'd send her a copy in case the court didn't and also the article from the *Los Angeles Times*.

While an animated and joyful Gloria was on the phone with Genego, a crowd began to form around the small glass phone booth as word of her release spread. Right after she hung up with Genego, she managed to sneak a quick call to Joyce, who said excitedly that she would be there to visit that evening.

Gloria stepped out of the phone booth and was mobbed by inmates and staff, hugging and congratulating her. She grabbed Glenda and raced across the yard to tell Della the good news. Her office was out of bounds to inmates who didn't have a pass, but Gloria tore into the building, ran around the corner of the office and yelled for Della to come outside.

Gloria, Della and Glenda ran to the center of the lawn and jumped up and down hugging each other in sheer joy. She felt vindicated. In this sad and lonely place, for one moment she felt totally free. Gloria and Glenda were headed back across the yard when a CO Gloria had always been fond of came out of another housing unit and told her to come inside in the gruff, formal way she usually addressed inmates. Once hidden from view, she took Gloria by the wrist and pulled her toward the back of the unit.

"Is it really true?" the CO asked eagerly, a crack in her usually professional demeanor.

"Yes," Gloria answered happily.

With tears in her eyes the CO gave Gloria a huge, long hug and told her how happy she was for her.

The rest of Gloria's day was frenzied, filled with people calling her unit on the office phone or coming by to find out if the news of her win was true. Most of the staff and the inmates thought she'd be leaving prison the next day, but Gloria knew better.

As soon as count cleared that evening, Gloria was called for her visit. Sitting in the visitors' room was Joyce Ride, who had made the two-hour drive that night herself, smiling all the while. Gloria ran to her friend and benefactor and they hugged, cried and laughed. Soon the news flashed around the room and other visitors joined the celebration. It was a truly joyful evening, with the bulk of the room buzzing and high on Gloria's great news.

Joyce and Gloria didn't make plans that evening; they just enjoyed the taste of victory and what they thought was the end of a long and hard-fought battle. It was pure bliss!

On Gloria's way back to her unit after her visit with Joyce, she saw a group of lifers seated at one of the cement picnic tables. These were women she hadn't seen yet that day who had come over to her unit to wait for her to return from her visit. One of them yelled, "There she is" and everybody started cheering. She ran over to the table and was encircled by hugs and kisses. Even inmates she wasn't friendly with were jubilant. To Gloria it seemed like the whole institution was celebrating.

Gloria received her copy of the written decision by the end of the week. When she picked the papers up and began to read, she got just as excited as when she first heard the news.

The Ninth Circuit decision was short and clear-cut:

> We must decide whether the use of perjured testimony,
> the withholding of evidence that would help show the
> falsity of the testimony, and the reliance on the perjury by
> the prosecutor in final argument, alone or in combination
> justifies habeas relief...

I. The Perjury of the Prosecution's Main Witness

Following the evidentiary hearing held before the
magistrate judge, one cannot reasonably deny that Gary
Masse gave perjured testimony at Killian's trial. Perhaps
most importantly, Masse conceded that he lied at Killian's
trial about not having a verbal agreement of leniency in
resentencing in exchange for testifying against Killian...
In short, Masse's testimony was the product of someone
with incentives to lie for himself and his wife's sake...
Because Masse perjured himself several times and because
he was the "make-or-break" witness for the state, there is
a reasonable probability that, without all the perjury, the
result of the proceeding would have been different.

II. Failure to Disclose Impeachment Evidence

Three undisclosed letters are signally important here...
The government responds that none of the undisclosed evidence relates to the core facts establishing Killian's guilt...
If the "make-or-break" Masse was thoroughly discredited,
then the evidence was plainly insufficient to convict
Killian. Alternatively, if one looks at the "core facts establishing Killian's guilt," the chief evidence of those "core
facts" derives, again, from the now thoroughly discredited
Gary Masse.

III. Prosecutorial Commentary on Privileged Conduct

...if a person is told she can exercise her right to be silent whenever she wants without penalty, she should not be badgered by a prosecutor eight times, as she was here, about whether she has "something to hide" by exercising that right.

IV. Cumulative Error

Even if the failure to disclose impeachment evidence, Masse's perjury, and the prosecutor's comments on privileged conduct were not each sufficient to justify habeas relief, we note that if there ever was a case for application of cumulative error principles, this is it. The collective presence of these errors is devastating to one's confidence in the reliability of this verdict and therefore requires, at the very least, a new trial.

The district court's denial of Killian's habeas petition is reversed, and we remand to the district court with instructions to grant the writ unless the state grants Killian a new trial within a reasonable time.

The realization of its meaning hit her again. People now knew she didn't commit the crime for which she had been convicted and she wasn't going to have to stay in prison anymore. Having the truth out in public for everyone to see felt good. Really good. Both Gloria and Genego didn't see how there were grounds for a trial, because Gloria was innocent.

The following Sunday morning, Gloria's cell door flew open at 6:05 and standing in front of her was one of her housing officers, "Killian, why didn't you tell me you were innocent?"

Gloria, still groggy and barely awake, rolled over and stared at him. "Would you have believed me?"

When Kit Cleland got the March notice from the Ninth Circuit, the decision made it clear that the State had to retry Gloria or let her go. With Masse impeached as a witness the prosecution had no case, but Gloria could be kept in prison for at least a couple of months more if Cleland notified the court he was trying to locate witnesses for a new trial. That is exactly what he did, submitting a motion to keep her in prison for the next sixty days, pending a new trial, and then renewed it for another sixty days.

While Cleland did everything in his power to keep Gloria in prison, the State Bar served him a notice that they were investigating his possible prosecutorial misconduct based on the Ninth Circuit Court decision in Gloria Killian's case.

The smart prosecutor turned to Jesse Rivera, a partner in Moreno and Rivera, a local Sacramento law firm. Cleland had fought hard to keep Gloria in prison and he was going to work even harder to clear his name. Cleland had a near perfect thirty-plus-year record and he intended to keep it unblemished.

Gloria had known she wouldn't get out the same week of the decision, but she figured she'd be free in no more than thirty days. There was so much going on, including interviews and press coverage. The *Daily Journal*, a legal newspaper, interviewed Gloria by phone and published a long article discussing Gloria's case and her legal work for others while in prison along with pictures of Gloria and Genego. The *Daily Journal* also interviewed Cleland, who criticized the Ninth Circuit and reiterated that, to him, Gloria was absolutely guilty. Award-winning columnist Steve Lopez interviewed Joyce Ride and wrote a column on Gloria's release for the *Los Angeles Times*. It seemed to Gloria that after years of proclaiming her innocence and being ignored, the whole world suddenly cared about what was going on.

Her housing officer and a prison guard union steward now frequently pulled her into the office for pleasant chats about prison, prison guards and the finer points of politics.

The attorney general's office had filed a motion for an *en banc* hearing, meaning that every judge on the Ninth Circuit had to review the case to determine whether the court should hear it. It was a massive case and, of course, that took time, but not one single judge voted to hear the case. The attorney general then filed a petition for writ of certiorari in the United States Supreme Court. But Genego and Gloria knew there was no way the Supreme Court would even hear the case. They felt the bottom line behind all the legal maneuvers was that Kit Cleland didn't want to let Gloria go free.

In prison vernacular, inmates who were close to going home were usually referred to as "short and shitty," reflective of the prisoners' behavior. In her first few years in prison, Gloria could never understand how an inmate could develop a bad attitude when she was close to going home. It seemed to her that an inmate would be so happy to get out that nothing would bother her. But as Gloria waited for her release, she found short and shitty is real. Everything about prison that she had withstood for years began to drive her crazy: the meanness of some of the staff, the petty squabbles, the stupid little rules. She wanted to scream and punch the walls, couldn't sleep and was so restless she couldn't focus. One month, two months, three months passed. Her decision had come down in March and it was already summer.

In early August, Genego filed a motion with the Ninth Circuit to hasten Gloria's release and the district court was ordered to set the terms. Joyce flew to Sacramento for the hearing, because she had made arrangements for Gloria to live with her and Gloria was to be released in her custody. The federal government required bail until all the state appeals were finished and they set Gloria's federal bail at two hundred thousand dollars, yet allowed her to be released before it was posted. When Joyce got back from Sacramento, she knew it was a matter of days.

Like everything in prison, any joy was mixed with sadness. With Gloria just days away from freedom, an inmate and Gloria's dear friend, Marge Tanner, passed away, sending the prisoners and staff into shock and disarray. That night Gloria stayed in her bunk and cried. Not one to rest on her laurels, even on her last day, Gloria marched into the office of the chief deputy warden, who was fairly new to CIW. Gloria told the warden that she felt poor medical care and the prison authorities were ultimately responsible for all the recent deaths and they had a moral obligation to help the inmates.

At 3:00 P.M. on August 8, Gloria's housing officer told her that Receiving and Release wanted her at 5:00 P.M. This was it! She called Joyce but couldn't reach her. She called Bill, who told her Joyce was already on her way to the prison. Gloria was getting out. But in typical prison fashion, they locked her back inside—it was time for the count.

Joyce drove onto the CIW grounds, wondering how the living arrangement with Gloria would work out. Since Gloria had no family and no means of support, Joyce, who had become her good friend, had earlier offered to share her home and Gloria had accepted. Joyce had brought a favorite song to play on the ride home: a classic rendition of "Don't Fence Me In." She thought Gloria might like that.

While Gloria waited for count to be over, she quickly packed her few remaining possessions; she'd already given away her television, appliances and clothes to other inmates who had very little. She packed some paperwork and a few sentimental possessions and hid her prison ID, privilege cards and a couple of pieces of jewelry that weren't on her property list in her sports bra, knowing she wasn't going to be strip-searched.

Once the count cleared, the cell doors popped and the unit was released for dinner, but no one wanted to eat. Instead, the whole unit gathered around Gloria's cell and poured into the hall, waiting with Gloria for the call from Receiving and Release. Gloria's eyes were filled with tears as she hugged the women good-bye.

A CO yelled from the cop shop, "Killian, R&R wants you now!" and the whole unit exploded in screaming and clapping. She looked at some women on the hall, lifers whom she knew would never get out, and they seemed to be cheering the loudest. She walked out of the building with the unit of women tagging behind her. They followed Gloria to other units as she said goodbye to more women and picked up more followers. A huge crowd circled toward R&R. Gloria felt a little like the pied piper.

As she led the procession to her freedom, an officer pulled alongside in a golf cart.

"Get in, Killian," he said. "I'll drive you over."

"No, thanks. I'll stay with my friends," she said.

"Come on, you need to leave in style."

Gloria agreed and got into the cart with the procession falling in behind them. When she got to the gate that divided the yard from R&R, the tower officer yelled down from his high perch, "All you people aren't going over there."

"We know," Gloria called back to him. "They just walked me to the gate." This was one prison tradition she was happy to uphold. Gloria got out of the cart and tearfully hugged the dozens of women good-bye again. Suddenly the crowd heard the CO's voice boom from the doorway: "Killian, get over here."

Gloria gave Glenda one last hug and walked through the gate into R&R. She gave the CO her tiny box of property to search and the watch commander came to release her personally. Gloria was touched that both the CO and watch commander had chosen this assignment to say good-bye.

"Let's go," the commander said and they walked to the sally port; the same sally port Gloria drove through almost seventeen years before.

Gloria saw Joyce sitting on a bench outside the gate waiting for her. As she handed the paperwork to the gate officer who was to open the gate, the officer stopped her. "Wait a minute. This isn't right." The commander looked at the paperwork. "I can't release you."

Gloria looked at Joyce, who had a horrified expression plastered on her face.

"Don't worry," Gloria yelled out. "This is 'CI Wonderful' and the paperwork is always wrong. We'll be right back."

Sure enough, it was a minor error that got cleared up quickly and in minutes they had the correct paperwork in hand. The gate officer processed her out. Gloria walked out of CIW and into a big hug from the usually reserved Joyce Ride.

"Let's get out of here," Gloria said. As she turned around, she was facing the visiting building, which was packed full of inmates, their families and their visitors. Everyone was staring at Joyce and Gloria. Then the inmates stood up and began waving and shouting good-bye. Even the sergeant stood in the breezeway outside her office waving good-bye.

Gloria had never felt such an outpouring of emotion in her entire life and it brought more tears to her eyes. She waved and blew kisses to everyone as she and Joyce walked to Joyce's car.

The car smelled good and felt cozy and comfortable. It had been many years since she'd been in a vehicle without wearing shackles and chains.

"Would you like to take a victory lap around the parking lot?" Joyce asked her, smiling.

"Hell, no!" Gloria responded. "Let's get out of here."

As Joyce drove down the road away from CIW, quietly letting Gloria take in her first breaths of freedom, Gloria saw everything around her with completely new eyes: the roads, the cows, the trees, the cars. On the freeway it seemed to her as if every car was going a million miles an hour. Everything felt alive.

After about an hour Joyce asked Gloria if she was hungry. It was 7:00 P.M. and having eaten dinner at 5 o'clock almost every day for sixteen years, Gloria was starving. They stopped at an Italian restaurant in Duarte, a small town midway between Pasadena and CIW. The café had an outdoor patio with a fountain and Gloria had her first meal and glass of red wine instead of prison fare.

Around 8 P.M. they arrived at Joyce's home in Pasadena and her spaniel met them at the door. Gloria hadn't touched a dog in decades and she thought of Brian's dog who had tried to protect her from the police. She held the dog for a moment then followed Joyce to her new room, but she felt there was no way she was going to sleep that night: everything was strange, the room was too quiet, the bed was too comfortable. But Gloria didn't mind a restless night. She relished every moment. She was finally free.

| 21 |

Full Circle

On her first day of freedom Gloria woke up to find a pool of curled up fax papers that had flown out of Joyce's ancient fax machine into the hallway all night long. The media had gotten hold of Gloria's story and it seemed everyone wanted to talk to her, but she had more important things on her mind, specifically going to federal court in Sacramento Monday morning for her bail hearing. After the ordeal she had with the prosecution trying to increase her bail the first time she was released twenty years before, she was taking no chances. She put the media requests on hold and took a plane with Joyce to Sacramento.

Being back in her hometown brought a deluge of mixed emotions; it was the first time in nearly eighteen years she was home and free. There was a sense of relief, ease and comfort in the familiar sounds and smells until she reentered Judge Hollows' courtroom, where she was overcome by flashbacks of sitting cuffed and shackled.

The state had set up her probation in Sacramento, even though she was to live in Pasadena with Joyce. Ostensibly, they wanted to introduce her to her probation officer, but Gloria felt the real reason was to let her know in no uncertain terms that she had thirty days to post the bail money or she'd be back inside. It was highly unusual for the federal government to release anyone without posting bail, especially with appeals pending, and Cleland had made it clear to the courts he'd go all the way to the Supreme Court to put her back in jail. Even though she was free, Gloria was feeling tremendous pressure.

The same night they took a plane back to Los Angeles, she and Joyce made a plan.

Their first stop was to see a bail bondsman whom Bill Genego had recommended. The bondsman's office was in an expensive-looking building on Santa Monica Boulevard and Gloria and Joyce walked in to find a slender, well-dressed man watching a small portable TV in a wood-paneled room. He didn't get up from his seat when the two petite, grey-haired women marched confidently into his office.

"Are you in the right place?" he asked as they walked up to the counter.

"We are if you're a bail bondsman," Joyce said calmly.

"Okay," he slowly said, "which one of you is Thelma and which one of you is Louise?"

The tension eased, Gloria got right down to business.

"I've just been in prison for almost seventeen years and I need a bail bond," Gloria said as the man looked at her.

"Can you help us?" Joyce inquired. "We're going to have to raise the money ourselves, so do the best you can for us. She was wrongfully convicted, you know." Joyce then launched into her "do the right thing" speech.

In the many years he was in business, the bondsman had never before seen two women as committed to fighting for freedom as Joyce and Gloria. He cut them a deal. "Forget the twenty grand; give me fifteen in cash and I'll write the bond."

"That's sweet of you," Gloria told him. "But I have no idea how I'm going to get that either." They left the office happy to have gotten a break but still facing an uphill battle to raise fifteen thousand dollars in less than a month.

At Joyce Ride's church, the Women's Issues Committee which Ride had once chaired had been actively involved in fighting for Gloria's release. On a personal mission, the church elder gathered the group around her and, together with the acting rector, organized fundraising events on Gloria's behalf. Night after night and day after day, Gloria talked to church group after church group and hundreds of fair-minded men and women donated what they could to her bail fund. A church woman, who had worked with Gloria on the Christmas project while she was imprisoned, came to Joyce's house and handed Gloria a check for five thousand dollars. Another woman Joyce knew held an afternoon party and Gloria left with handfuls of checks. With about a week until the deadline, Gloria had her fifteen thousand dollars, a host of new friends and renewed faith in the goodness of people. Since so many people now believed her and believed in her, she knew it was time to get to work.

During her early years in prison Gloria had sworn that if she got out she would help the women she left behind and dreamed of founding her own organization. The only problem was she had no idea how to do it. Networking wasn't exactly part of the curriculum at CIW.

Once free, however, people came from all over to help her. A social worker she'd met in prison offered to assist her but told her the first thing she needed to do was to take care of herself a little, like dealing with the effects of prison-induced post-traumatic stress disorder. Gloria thought she was doing just fine.

"Oh, really?" the social worker said. "Are you sleeping?"

"Not a wink."

"Do you startle?"

"If someone comes up behind me, I almost faint."

"And what about your nerves?"

Gloria realized the social worker was right. "Yikes."

She understood that she would need therapy so she could heal but still felt that had to come later. What she needed most was a driver's license, which proved almost as difficult to acquire as her release. In her first few weeks of freedom, Gloria spent almost as many hours at the department of motor vehicles as she did at Joyce's house. The problem was that the DMV refused to accept her prison ID as proper identification. No matter what she said or did, she couldn't prove to them that she actually existed. After an extensive search, Gloria found her birth certificate and that enabled her to secure a driver's license. However, the name on the license was Gloria Goodwin, a name she hadn't used in decades.

The social worker also took Gloria to her first meeting of the Action Committee for Women in Prison (ACWIP), an offshoot of the northern California-based Criminal Justice Consortium. The group met in the garage of Susan Burton, a tough, smart African-American woman who had founded A New Way of Life, an organization which provides homes for women who are recently released from prison in an effort "to help other women break the cycle of incarceration, homelessness, addiction and despair," according to the organization's Web site. Burton had purchased a small home in South Central Los Angeles and used it to give a second chance to women who had no place to go after they were released. During Gloria's time in prison, Susan Burton had been in and out of the system herself, so Gloria was surprised and pleased to see her as a vibrant, healthy woman who had turned her life around.

Gloria's social worker friend also helped Gloria get a part-time job with the California Criminal Justice Consortium working on Proposition 36, which sought to put drug offenders in treatment programs rather than incarcerating them. While she enjoyed the work, drug treatment wasn't really where her heart was.

She wanted to work with the ACWIP and her sisters in prison, so Gloria spent all her free time trying to organize a committee to raise money for them, speaking at the USC Law Clinic and the National Lawyers Guild Convention. She talked about battered women and the issues of the wrongfully convicted to any group she could find.

It was hard yet rewarding work and Gloria thrived on it. In her first few months out, ACWIP received letters from numerous inmates at the Los Angeles County jail, commonly known as the Twin Towers, talking about mistreatment and horrific conditions. ACWIP was granted permission to go into the Twin Towers and Gloria was excited, because she knew she could talk to the women inside and they would relate to her and open up. As they were about to walk inside, a lieutenant stopped Gloria.

"You can't go inside. You need to wait here," the lieutenant told her.

"Why?" she asked, finding it slightly ironic that she wasn't allowed to go into a jail.

"We believe you were released on a technicality, so you can't enter the jail."

She found it incredibly frustrating, but there was no exception. Her colleagues toured the jail while Gloria sat in the office. Undaunted, she helped them write articles that were presented in Washington, DC, at the National Women's Conference and in Pasadena at the National Convention of the Commissions on the Status of Women.

Six months after her release, Gloria, filled with energy and spunk, was appointed chair of ACWIP at Susan Burton's request. Burton's life was now dedicated to providing direct services to women leaving prison, whereas ACWIP was a committee that did more advocacy and policy work. Each woman fit into her own special niche and they agreed this was the best arrangement. Shortly thereafter, the Southern California Criminal Justice Consortium closed its doors, leaving Gloria without a job and ACWIP without its parent organization. Gloria and Joyce agreed it was important to keep the work going and decided to do something about it.

Gloria spoke with the directors of the Consortium, whom she knew from her prison days, and they agreed to allow her to use the ACWIP name and turn it into an independent, non-profit organization. ACWIP had gotten some good publicity lately and there was name recognition for both Gloria and ACWIP. There was no pay and no money in the organization, but she planned to run it with money she made giving speeches, from lecturing and from private fundraising. Joyce helped by letting Gloria continue to live at her home rent-free, an arrangement that had worked out well so far.

With the full weight of the organization resting on her shoulders, Gloria found she had a lot of work to do. One of the first things she focused on was securing the freedom of Maria Suarez. Suarez, her dear friend at CIW, had spent twenty-two years in prison, convicted as an accessory in the murder of a man who bought her as a sex slave when she was just sixteen years old. Suarez had been paroled but not into the arms of her family. Instead, she was sent straight to federal detention. Although Maria had come to the United States legally, her visa had long since expired and her murder conviction targeted her for deportation. Here was a woman sold, beaten and raped, wrongfully convicted and now about to be deported from the country she called home. Gloria and Maria's niece, Patricia, worked frantically to alert the media and get massive publicity about Maria's case. Because she had been kidnapped and held as a sex slave, Maria was found to be qualified as a victim of trafficking. Several lawyers volunteered their services for Maria. To pay them, Gloria and Patricia ran their errands, did legal research, organized protests and held fundraisers. One of the lawyers sent Gloria to the Federal Detention Center to interview Maria and get all of the facts written up correctly. As the two women spoke, they marveled at how their lives had changed.

Within a few months, thanks in large part to the efforts of Gloria, Patricia and the team of lawyers, Maria was released from federal detention and granted a T visa, allowing her to remain in the United States. It was a monumental victory, not just for Maria and for Gloria, but also for all battered women, especially those sold into trafficking.

The next year the American Civil Liberties Union (ACLU) sent Gloria and several other exonerees to lobby the Senate Judiciary Committee in Washington, DC, where they were fighting against the Streamlined Procedures Act. The act was a bill that would largely strip the federal courts of jurisdiction to hear writs of habeas corpus, which meant that had it existed when Gloria and the other exonerees were in prison, it would have been impossible for them to have gotten out. The ACLU wanted the group to speak in front of the senators to explain why they shouldn't pass this bill.

On the flight to the nation's capital, Gloria reflected on how much her life had changed. Less than three years before she was sitting in a cell at CIW and in a few hours she was going to speak to a group of United States senators.

She walked the marble halls of Congress in awe, noting the names she'd read about in newspapers on the doors, and was finally led into the hearing room of the Senate Judiciary Committee. Gloria was moved immediately by the sense of history that echoed in the room. Momentous events had occurred in these rooms for decades and now she was there too, standing with Senators Joe Biden, Diane Feinstein and Patrick Leahy. She felt exhilarated as she listened to the committee take testimony from Barry Scheck of the Innocence Project and others who often referred to the exonerees in the room.

Afterwards, Gloria met with Senator Feinstein and the two women quickly found common ground. The senator had served on the parole board at CIW and she and Gloria discussed the many changes that had occurred in the parole process over the years.

Senator Feinstein, recognizing that Gloria and others would never have been able to get her conviction reversed if the proposed act had been in effect, became a staunch opponent of the Streamlined Procedures Act. She made sure to tell Gloria's and others' stories on the floor of Congress, putting Gloria's name and her story forever in the Congressional Record. The bill was defeated in the Senate, a moment of real pride for Gloria and the other exonerees who had endured such injustice and told their stories in the hopes of helping do just that. It was also the first time that Gloria had met and worked with other exonerees and it gave her a sense of family. They had all been to hell and they had not only survived, but now they also had triumphed.

In November, the same Streamlined Procedures Act came up in the House of Representatives and Congressman William Delahunt of Massachusetts requested that Gloria return to Washington, DC, to appear before the House Judiciary Committee. He discussed her case at length during the hearing and the same awful piece of legislation was defeated there as well.

While attending a Young Lawyer's event as a noted speaker, Gloria met Mike Farrell. Besides being a popular star of the television show *M*A*S*H*, Farrell also heads Death Penalty Focus, a group that advocates the abolition of the death penalty. He invited Gloria to speak at an awards dinner for the organization in Beverly Hills where she told her story and how she felt when she was imprisoned in the Branch, innocent and with the possibility of the death penalty hanging over her head. This event brought yet another focus to her advocacy work and led to a long collaboration with Farrell.

Within months after Gloria's release from prison, fifty-nine-year-old Kit Cleland retired from his prosecutorial career. The State Bar Association opened an investigation of possible prosecutorial misconduct in the case against Gloria Killian.

For two years, Cleland filed motion after motion against the State Bar's investigation of his conduct in the Killian case, maintaining that her case had not yet been exhausted and was still under appeal. Finally, in December 2005, the State Bar advised Cleland's lawyer that since no

further appeals were pending, it was moving forward with its investigation of Cleland.

It was an unusual move by the Bar Association to keep pressing
against the former prosecutor, since Cleland had recently retired from
the DA's office, but they felt very strongly that what Cleland had done
in the Killian case was egregious.

Twenty years after Gloria was sentenced and more than twenty-
five years after the murder of Ed Davies, the California State Bar served
Kit Cleland with disciplinary charges for his prosecutorial conduct in
the Gloria Killian case.

Using the Ninth Circuit's opinion as a blueprint, the State Bar cited
some of the same issues it had used to set Gloria free. The State Bar charged
that Cleland illegally failed to disclose two letters in which he allegedly
sought leniency for Masse based on his cooperation in the prosecution of
Killian and a third letter, in which Masse told Cleland he "lied [his] ass off
on the stand" to get Killian's conviction. They also charged Cleland made
repeated improper commentaries on Killian's right to remain silent.

The lawyers at the State Bar, supervising trial counsel Donald
Steedman, veteran trial lawyer Sherrie McLetchie and deputy trial
counsel Wonder Liang were confident they had a strong case against
Cleland and put together a pretrial statement in which they listed the
charges and recommended punishment.

Cleland was charged with five separate counts of misconduct:
Failure to Comply with Laws; Moral Turpitude—Suppression of
Evidence; Suppressing Evidence Contrary to Legal Obligation; Moral
Turpitude—Misrepresentation; Employing Means Inconsistent with
Truth/Seeking to Mislead Judge.

In the Bar Association's count one, "Failure to Comply with Laws,"
Cleland was cited for not disclosing the exculpatory evidence and
making improper commentary on Gloria's right to remain silent. In
count two, "Moral Turpitude," the claim was that he had intentionally

suppressed the "lied my ass off" letter and one other letter. In count three, the bar charged he willfully violated the rules of professional conduct by failing to reveal the letters. In count four, the bar charged he violated business and professional codes by lying to the jury by stating "we have nothing to do with how much time Gary Masse serves." At the time he made the statement, the State Bar charged that Cleland knew it was false and misleading. Finally, in count five, the bar charged that he willfully violated the business code by seeking to mislead the judge. The bar charged that by misrepresenting the prosecution's impact on Masse's sentence, Cleland employed means inconsistent with the truth and sought to mislead a judicial officer.

McLetchie, a seasoned pro who had been a Bar Association lawyer for years, had done a great deal of research on the case and the savvy, blonde attorney was ready to take the retired prosecutor head-on. In her pretrial statement, according to the *California Bar Journal* article "Ex-DA faces allegations of withholding evidence," McLetchie said the bar sought "a lengthy suspension for Cleland" and "pointed out that disbarment is still an option for the Supreme Court, which has the final say in attorney discipline cases."

Steedman, McLetchie's boss, was also adamant that they were doing the right thing by bringing Cleland to trial, even though they only brought a very small percentage of the State Bar's prosecutions against public sector lawyers or prosecutors. He believed very strongly that cases like the one they had against Cleland, based on their own assessment of the evidence, not just the decision of the Ninth Circuit court, were significant, because they concerned important principles of justice.

Cleland kept fighting hard to get the charges dropped, citing that it happened long ago and that the State Bar took too long to press charges, but Steedman felt strongly that the time it took was not unprecedented, especially since the alleged misconduct wasn't discovered for a long time. He believed the decision to prosecute Cleland would serve as a warning to other lawyers.

Livid about the decision to prosecute him, Cleland voiced his outrage in the newspaper article "Ex-prosecutor faces trial—Bar court to hear misconduct claims in case of '81 murder" by Denny Walsh in the *Sacramento Bee*, which then became an out-of-court battleground between the two factions.

"What they're doing will have a chilling effect on prosecutors if they think they are going to be micromanaged by the State Bar. We need vigorous prosecutors who are not afraid to exercise their independent judgment," Cleland told the newspaper and he insisted that, according to the article, "nothing in the letters would have affected the defense and they didn't need to be disclosed." The article continued:

> ...Cleland compared the bar's attorneys to a character in Lewis Carroll's classic "Alice's Adventures in Wonderland."
>
> "It's like talking to the Queen of Hearts," he said. "No matter what you say, their response is 'Off with his head.'"

Meanwhile Gloria, far away from the machinations in Sacramento, moved forward with her life and her life's mission. Gloria's work advocating for the rights of women in prison and of wrongfully convicted inmates and for the abolition of the death penalty took her all over the country and the world. She became a featured speaker at the National Lawyers Guild, the California Legislature, Death Penalty Focus, the University of California, Los Angeles, the Innocence Network and the Northern California Innocence Project. She was invited to Paris to be a featured speaker with Ensemble Contre La Peine de Morte (an anti-death penalty non-governmental organization).

But she made sure to be in Sacramento to watch Cleland's trial. A date was set, April 1, 2008—April Fools' Day.

As she waited outside the San Francisco courtroom where Cleland's trial was to take place, she looked around and realized once again that she was a free woman living her own life. Suddenly it didn't matter what happened to Cleland at the trial; just the fact that he was brought to trial on *her* case was enough for Gloria. The world would know not only that she was innocent but also what happened to put her there.

Soon the courtroom began to fill and people started to circle Gloria like a celebrity. Women she knew from the Northern California Innocence Project arrived, bringing with them a group of interested lawyers and students. Friends with the American Civil Liberties Union (ACLU) ran up to hug her. As she broke from one hug, Gloria turned around and saw Kit Cleland. His back was to her, but she knew exactly who it was.

Cleland turned around and glanced at Gloria. In the nanosecond of recognition his face went from calm to one Gloria felt radiated contempt, disgust and anger.

For a moment Gloria got the old sick feeling in the pit of her stomach, but this time looked him straight in the eyes. This time it was her turn. This time *he* was the one on trial.

Gloria listened, filled with anger, to Cleland's testimony, but she maintained her composure and ultimately she felt good inside. In her opinion, this trial, no matter the outcome, was an ignominious end for the prosecutor.

Kit Cleland defended himself strongly and when directly confronted with the contents of the "lied my ass off" letter, Cleland said, "Well, I compared the new information, the content of it, what, how significant it was, and compared it in connection with and contrasted it with the evidence that was presented during the trial. And it did not in any way—ever give me a brief scintilla of doubt about the correctness of the conviction."

Gloria shook her head. Was Cleland saying, unbelievably, that Masse stating he lied his ass off on the stand had nothing to do with the correctness of Gloria's conviction?

Later Cleland went on: "So I kind of just got to the point where efforts along those lines of trying to find a way to disclose it just—I was just stymied and, I guess, gave up. I figured that it would all come out in the wash anyway because of the automatic appeal to the California Supreme Court and that's what happened."

The trial continued for another day in April and another day, two months later in June. This time Gloria didn't go. It was Cleland's problem, not hers.

Gloria felt strongly that there were many people in prison who needed help, men and women who were wrongly convicted and needed a voice. Too many people were dying in a country that still sent men and woman to death. Sometimes, as Gloria knew all too well, these were innocent men and women.

Gloria's life now was about her work and she had just begun to fight. There were fierce battles on her horizon. There were laws to change, lives to save and issues of injustice to confront every day. She was busy.

In addition to all of her other endeavors, she started a radio show on the Internet that streamed live every week around the world. She also started the March for the Wrongfully Convicted in California and testified before the California legislature on women in prison, medical care and various other issues, winning activism awards from Death Penalty Focus and Soroptimists International as well as helping to change laws, speaking out for incarcerated women and freeing innocent people.

With all her compelling and important endeavors, what gave her the biggest thrill was being a regular speaker to women at CIW. Gloria visited her friend Glenda every week at CIW, spoke at the Long Termers Organization meetings, attended WAC banquets and introduced programs such as Choice Theory and Talking Circles to the prison. She was doing and continues to do just what she set out to accomplish the moment she was freed: fighting to change the lives of the wrongfully convicted and of the women she left behind.

Epilogue

In November 2008, Judge Pat McElroy found Cleland guilty "by clear and convincing evidence" of two of the charges: failing to disclose exculpatory evidence to the defense and improperly commenting on a defendant's invocation of her right to remain silent. The court noted that an admonition was an appropriate disposition of the matter. No prosecutor in Sacramento in the preceding fifty years had ever received an admonition in this way.

Gary Masse is incarcerated at the Mule Creek State Prison in Ione, California. He has been in prison for over thirty years.

Virgil Fletcher, Stephen DeSantis, Dale Herbst and Grace Davies are all deceased.

Bill Genego's criminal defense and post-conviction work has saved the lives of numerous men and women in the state of California.

Gloria Killian still lives with Joyce Ride and chairs the Action Committee for Women in Prison (ACWIP) full time. She lectures around the world on wrongful convictions, the death penalty and the plight of women in prison.

Acknowledgements

GLORIA KILLIAN

This book would not have been possible without the continued love and support of my friends, lawyers, and supporters, especially Larry who is always there for me no matter what happens. A special thank you goes to my co-author, Sandy, for putting up with all my craziness and never losing faith in me.

SANDRA KOBRIN

Getting this story told has been a long and arduous process. While there are so many wrongfully convicted stories there is only one Gloria Killian and I thank her for her friendship, opening her heart and telling me her amazing story.

I'd like to thank Bill Genego for his help, guidance, patience and for keeping his numerous files years after the case had been closed. Without that documentation and his counsel, the book never could have been written.

A thank you to agent Paul Levine who was able to sell this book in days.

Thank you to Amy Friedman, a talented writer and teacher whose friendship and support kept me going through the entire process, and to the women in my writer's group, Hope Edelman, Christine Schwab, and Deborah Lott, who were there for me.

A special thank you to my three children, Justin, Andrew, and Mia Wolfson who have been supportive and caring despite having a very distracted mom.

But the biggest thanks needs to go to my husband Jason Levin. A brilliant writer and editor, he was my strength from day one. Without his invaluable help, willingness to listen, editorial skills, love and patience, there would be no book. You can have your wife back now.